T.REXTASY

The Spirit Of Marc Bolan

T.REXTASY
The Spirit Of Marc Bolan

Danielz

WP
WYMER
PUBLISHING
Bedford, England

First published in Great Britain in 2012
by Wymer Publishing
Bedford, England
www.wymerpublishing.co.uk
Tel: 01234 326691

ISBN 978-1-908724-03-8

Edited by Jeremy Francis-Broom.

Every effort has been made to trace the copyright holders of the
photographs in this book but some were unreachable. We would
be grateful if the photographers concerned would contact us.

Typesetting, layout and design by Wymer UK.
Printed and bound by CMP, Poole, Dorset.

A catalogue record for this book is available from the British Library.

Front cover design by Duncan Muir.
Front cover photograph © T.Rextasy
All photos © Danielz except where noted.

CONTENTS

I would like to dedicate this book to the following:

Marc Bolan
Mickey Finn
Steve Currie
Steve Peregrine Took
June Feld
Dino Dines
Tony Howard
Chelita Secunda
Jack Willans
Gordon Willans
Doreen Thomas
Nikki Sudden
John Peel
Family members that have now passed on and fans of
Marc Bolan, T.Rex, & T.Rextasy who are no longer with us.

Hats off to...

This also gives me the opportunity to say 'thanks' to other musicians who
have inspired me over the years:

Jimi Hendrix
Bob Dylan
Rory Gallagher
Ritchie Blackmore & Deep Purple
John Lennon
Jimmy Page & Led Zeppelin
Ozzy Osbourne & Black Sabbath
David Bowie
Rod Stewart & The Faces
The Sex Pistols
David Gilmour & Pink Floyd

Foreword

Meeting Danielz face-to-face almost made my tear ducts go into overdrive. He looked so much like Marc Bolan I thought I had seen a ghost. This was in 1997, when my daughter Lara had become a T.Rex fan when she discovered their music on my CD shelves, at six. Soon afterwards she also came face-to-face with Danielz in New York, and for her it was just like meeting Marc, she couldn't stop smiling and staring at his curls.

Danielz and I hit the stage for the first time at the Fez Club in New York, playing at a Marc Bolan tribute. When I messed up a chord at rehearsal it was Danielz who was quick to correct me and I found his knowledge of Bolan's music to be near perfect. There was only one thing I knew that he didn't - the A chord in 'Get It On' is A minor, not major (virtually all guitarists think it is the latter). He did not accept this on the spot, instead I later had to play him the master tape of 'Get It On' and isolate Marc's rhythm guitar track before he believed me! Since then I have had a long friendship with Danielz.

I have been onstage with him and other members of T.Rextasy on several occasions, all of which were delightful and moving experiences. I have been in two T.Rex performances as a musician, one as a substitute for an under-the-weather Mickey Finn on *Top Of The Pops* (from a distance we looked alike - I was wearing a yellow motorcycle jacket), and another time on stage in Copenhagen playing a second bass alongside Steve Currie in an encore. I have a clear memory of watching Marc from the side, jumping around enthusiastically with his corkscrew hair bouncing away - and all of that flooded back to me when I was onstage playing a few songs with T.Rextasy, watching Danielz going through his own interpretation of Marc's songs.

Yes, T.Rextasy gives me goosebumps. They are all great musicians and their interpretations of Marc Bolan's songs are powerful and emotional. In 1997, tribute bands were an uncomfortable concept for me. Something was always wrong, either the musicianship was below par, or the members looked nothing like the originals, nor had they any large degree of the charisma of the stars they portrayed. But Danielz raised the bar for me. I think they are the best tribute band in the touring world. If you missed T.Rex live when you were growing up then T.Rextasy is the closest you'll ever get to that experience - really close, even down to the stage clothes and ceramic decal on the white *Stratocaster*!

Tony Visconti
New York City, 2012

Foreword

After moving to Los Angeles after my father Marc passed away, the music of T.Rex was a major connection to my father. From my mother's record collection, as well as the gifts my father's parents would bring from England, brought me closer to him in so many ways. The older I got, the more I appreciated the unique sound and the musical contribution that T.Rex made in Europe as well as America. I can still remember the moment when Def Leppard and Guns N' Roses featured a clip of the band jamming out 'Get It On', and Slash wearing 'The Slider' album cover on his t-shirt. Living in the land of the stars and Hollywood I figured everyone's parents were famous rock stars, but I had a lot more to learn.

In 2007, I had just graduated from Loyola Marymount University where I became very close with Mark Volman from The Turtles, and a featured background vocalist on some of the early T.Rex work. Who would have ever thought that we would end up in the same class so many years later after he worked with my father? But life works in magical ways. After making such a great connection with Mark, I started to look forward to returning to London for my father's anniversary, and truly discovering my legacy. I didn't know what to expect but my main purpose was to represent my family and embrace the fans on such an important date in history. The time had come for me to experience the "T.Rextasy" from the years that passed.

Right off the plane it was all things T.Rex. From the first event I knew this was going to be a great chance to celebrate the music and help fill the hole that I had from losing my father. I embraced each moment with open arms and I started to meet many fascinating people with different stories about how important T.Rex was to their lives. From fans to business associates, there are many sides to the story. I do remember one thing in particular, at several of the events I kept seeing similar people and some seemed to stick out more than others. Once the sudden rush from the events faded, I became closer with the Bolan family and we shared a new connection. When I first met Danielz I was very curious with his involvement in the T.Rex scene. I was still getting used to the fans and the sudden attention, and I was starting to get comfortable with my new friends. A small group of family and friends gathered for my birthday at Planet Hollywood, and Danielz and I had a chance to get to know each other, and I learned more about the impact T.Rex had on his life and his music. By the end of the night I was invited to make an appearance at a T.Rextasy show in Cambridge.

At this point, my experience with tribute bands was very fresh. On the way to the show, I had a chance to talk with each member and see how much love they had for the music, and the night looked promising. I was just starting my music career and my stage experience was very limited. Danielz and I came up with the idea that I would make a guest vocal appearance on the song 'Dreamy Lady'. I was scared because of how important these songs were to me, and the crowd of fans. Sometimes you just take one for the team. All I remember that night is seeing the passion and precision that T.Rextasy delivered to the music of T.Rex, and how happy the crowd was to share the experience. This was the first time I heard those songs performed live, and it changed my whole feeling towards the music. What was truly special was seeing the new generation of fans, from mothers to sons, the music made its mark in the people's hearts. It was a very special night and I thank Danielz and the band for sharing that with me. Not too many bands stick together, but for T.Rextasy, this journey has kept growing, and they truly help keep my father's music in the minds of thousands.

Rolan Bolan Feld
Los Angeles, 2012

Foreword

More than any of the musicians and singers I've loved and admired, none has inspired and affected me, and changed my life more than Marc Bolan. From the first time I saw him perform, glitter on his cheeks on *Top Of The Pops*, he exuded a magic, he was a Star.

In 2007, 30 years after his death I was invited to take part in a celebration of his music and life, and it was there I met Danielz and his band T.Rextasy: The World's foremost and greatest Marc Bolan and T.Rex tribute band. It was a strange thrill and for a time when up on the stage performing with Danielz, I felt as though I could have been performing with the great man himself. I believed it because Danielz had such a belief in himself, in the music, and like Marc he was a Star. Everything about him told you he was: The corkscrew hair, the small frame, the spangled stage outfits, the *Gibson Les Paul* guitar and the stage movements, the shake of his hair, the arm thrust skyward after the chords to 'Children Of The Revolution' or Metal Guru, it wasn't an impersonation, he became Marc Bolan himself in spirit and musicianship. His love of Marc Bolan's music shone through and gave the songs so known and loved of Marc's, extra power and resonance. On that stage he brought him to life and through him like a medium, the music, showmanship and Marc's legacy lived on. Tony Visconti conducting strings behind him and Gloria Jones in the wings. The illusion was complete.

For many too young to have seen Marc or T.Rex it gave them an experience of what it must have been like, to those who had been lucky enough to have seen Marc himself it was memories made fresh. An emotional experience to relive, the heady excitement of a Marc Bolan and T.Rex show. I've been lucky enough to have seen Marc and T.Rex twice and stood so close I could smell his perfume and for a while up on that stage I believed I was back in 1972 living a dream. It is one of my favourite performing memories.

Thank you Danielz from this Marc, carry on keeping Marc Bolan, his music and his magic alive, and for keeping a bit of Marc in their hearts.

Marc Almond
London, 2012

Preface

This book is something that I have been meaning to write for sometime. Although it's taken me a good while to sit down and start the process off, I think that twenty years of being in one band has given me the push and incentive that I needed, to begin what you are about to read. I have included many photos, memorabilia, advertising posters, flyers, and pictures of interest that I have accumulated along the way on this amazing journey, and I hope that this will add to your enjoyment when you peruse the pages that follow.

This has been an enjoyable book to write. It is not a 'warts-and-all', or an infringement of anyone's personal details, nor does it include character assassination, or fabricated story telling. What this is, is a totally honest account of my time with a band that I have thoroughly enjoyed being a part of; everything that I have remembered over the past twenty years, and from various pieces of documentation I have kept for reference. I have had many run-ins with various people along the way, but this is all part of the process of pushing one's way forward. There is nothing vindictive, nor are there personal attacks, and if anyone does feel hurt by anything I have included, then I'm sorry, but I have just been honest and truthful to myself. This is also not supposed to be a book of literary merit, but more of a one-to-one, almost as if I'm telling the story face-to-face.

Like in any band, there have been plenty of ups and downs, lots of arguments and disagreements, but it always settled down and made way for a better future in the end. There is a saying in the music business 'what goes on the road, stays on the road', and thankfully, although I have lived this life mainly clean and mostly healthily, I know that various members of the band or crew have strayed from that path. I am certainly not going to incriminate anyone, mainly because this is a book about my life in T.Rextasy, not about individual members, and I think that would be unfair to them.

Considering what I set out to do, I have covered every ambition for T.Rextasy, something that I am very proud of. When I look back on the career path I have walked, I am quite astounded myself. I always wanted to play Wembley Arena, tour Japan, obtain a worthwhile recording deal, and tour the UK and abroad in good venues. Also to appear on the bill with the likes of Marc's contemporaries such as Slade, Sweet, Ian Hunter, Gary Glitter, Suzi Quatro, Roy Wood, Steve Harley & Cockney Rebel, Uriah Heep, The Glitter Band, Alvin Stardust, and The Bay City Rollers. Better still, playing alongside members of T.Rex, such as Mickey Finn, and Bill Legend, and pulling in members to join my band, such as Dino Dines. Not to mention attaining very special guests up on stage with us, such as Tony Visconti, Gloria Jones, Rolan Bolan, Andy Ellison, and Howie Casey (who played sax for T.Rex, Paul McCartney, and Mott The Hoople).

I suppose what I never expected was to gig or play with other original stars, such as Miller Anderson from T.Rex, Marc Almond from Soft Cell, Clem Burke from Blondie, Linda Lewis, Alvin Stardust, Dr Robert from the Blow Monkeys, Ray Dorset from Mungo Jerry, and The Damned. I also never expected to receive the recognition or credibility to the extent of receiving accolades, or endorsements from Marc Bolan's catalogue managements, such as *Wizard [Bahamas] Ltd.*, *Westminster Music*, or *Spirit Music Ltd.* It has also been a pleasure to have had some of Marc's own family, such as his brother Harry Feld, wife June Feld (Bolan), partner Gloria Jones and son, Rolan Bolan, and the fan clubs around the world, giving their blessing and approval too, as well as so many of Marc's own band-mates.

Being in T.Rextasy has given me the opportunity to meet and be in touch with people that I guess I would never have had the opportunity to do. Such as meeting David Bowie, or recording at Abbey Road with one of Japan's biggest superstars, Tomoyasu Hotei; meeting up with drummer Cozy Powell, and Peter Green from Fleetwood Mac; receiving mail from the likes of Sylvain Sylvain from The New York Dolls, or even acting in the DVD 'Ride On', not to mention 'Bolanic' photo sessions in magazines like 'Bang!' and 'Arena'.

I have always strived to obtain credibility as a musician and a songwriter and to some extent and ironically, being in a tribute band has only helped me achieve that. I was able to obtain a single deal in the UK and

Japan, a three album deal with *Madman Records* in the UK, and a two album deal in Japan (one on *Columbia Records*, and the other on *Quattro Records*). For the single deal in the UK, I was actually able to negotiate an original song for the A-side, and I was able to include two original songs on each album release, thereby issuing self-penned numbers side-by-side with Marc's songs. To add to the album deal, *Madman*, together with *Quattro Records*, actually put up the money for us to record a one-off video - which so happened to be for my original track, 'Baby Factory', something that remains very unusual for a tribute band to do.

I like to think that somewhere along the way we achieved a status that has reached a little beyond the boundaries of just plain 'tribute'. Something I know that people such as Dave Hill and Don Powell from Slade, Dino Dines and Miller Anderson from T.Rex, and some reviewers from the likes of *The Times*, and *The Independent* have mentioned previously, along with other musicians and press. And that is something that is justly pleasing.

I do hope that you enjoy reading about 'my life in Marc's shadow' as much as I have enjoyed writing and recalling some of what has happened over the past two decades. I still sometimes have to pinch myself to think that all this happened to me because of being a fan of Marc Bolan, and wanting to play his music to people and fans that would appreciate it. Who would've thought that it would turn into a full-time professional career and would run and run and run... certainly not me!

Marc Bolan of T.Rex (30th September 1947 - 16th September 1977). At 5 feet 7 inches tall, he sang "*I know I'm small, but I enjoy living anyway*" on a track called 'Spaceball Ricochet', from the 1972 T.Rex album 'The Slider'. Not tall for a man, and indeed, I ended up exactly the same height as Marc when I entered adult-hood too - this was ironic in years to come when it helped me no end, entering the world of T.Rextasy.

Marc was a hero and a total inspiration in my growing up listening to music, not to say a future lifestyle. As a teenager, I wanted to learn to play guitar along with those iconic T.Rex albums of the 1970s. If it wasn't for Marc, I may not have even bothered to learn to play!

1

1

Growing Up With T.Rex

I can't actually remember the very first time I heard that distinctive voice of Marc Bolan. But I do recall dancing to 'Hot Love' at a school disco sometime in 1971. A group of us all singing and moving simultaneously to the 'la la' coda, gradually forming a circle together as we used to do in those days. But at that time, it was football, not music, that ruled my life and nothing got in the way of my football. Whether it was watching it on television, playing the game at school, or at home at weekends, football really did rule a lot of my very early teenage life. I was very much into sports and if football wasn't on the criteria at school, then I would've been competitive at basketball, or table tennis. That competitive streak would, I guess, never go away. When the more academic lessons were in place, I took a strong interest in English Language and English Literature - something I threw myself into more and more as I got older, and reading especially was something that increased.

I was the oldest son. My Dad, Jack (he was christened John, but everyone called him Jack), was from the north of England and grew up around County Durham. He joined the Army at an early age in the 1950s, which took him to the Far East, when countries and islands such as Hong Kong were still considered British Colonies. My Dad met my mum, Lourdes, while serving out on the island of Hong Kong. They got married and had me shortly before they were transferred back to England. Mum was born out of a combination of foreign blood, which included Spanish and Irish. After a couple of years, we were posted to Cyprus, where my brother Graham was born, before returning to England again, where my youngest brother Gordon was born. After a while we were, once again, transferred to the Far East, where we spent a couple of years in a high-rise flat, contained with many other British Army families, within an Army base surrounded by fields. We then moved to a tiny island which was also occupied by the British Army situated in-between Hong Kong and Kowloon called Stonecutters Island. I used to have to catch a small boat to school in the mornings, along with a few other 'army kids' who also lived around the small land mass. We all had to be careful when we were walking around the streets, as there were many snakes - a throwback to when the Japanese had occupied the island years before and had bred snakes for both medicinal and edible purposes.

After living on the snake infested island, it was a culture shock when we moved to West Germany just as the 1970s began, first to Osnabrück, then onto Münster, then to Soest, where my sister Rita was born. It was nice to have a sister in a house full of brothers, and it must have felt a little more evened for mum too.

It was while living in Münster that music, slowly but surely, began to take over my life. It was one afternoon in the winter of 1971, the radio was on some English speaking channel, and a song came on that was to change my life way beyond anything that I could have imagined. Out of the speakers a voice hit me that was so unusual, and a tune that immediately soaked into my head so much so that I just couldn't seem to dispel it from my mind - I didn't associate it at the time with the same band that I had heard in the disco just a few months earlier. The song was 'Jeepster', a stomping slice of pure seventies rock 'n' roll. It literally shook the foundations of how I had previously lived as a child, and turned me into a teenage Glamster immediately. My clothing slowly developed in style, as did my taste in hobbies. Music, and especially Marc and T.Rex, was about to change my life forever.

About a year later, either for a birthday or Christmas present, I can't remember which, my parents bought me a bright red *Framus* electric guitar, (a brand that Jan Akkerman used in Focus) and a small practice amplifier on which I eventually learnt to play songs from the album's 'Electric Warrior', and then 'The Slider', in a somewhat staggered but enjoyable fashion. A mirror in the bedroom was my biggest audience in those days. Watching my reflection turned me into a wannabe rock star, along with the millions of other children around the world. I had been on and on to my parents about buying me a guitar, and now I had one I desperately wanted to learn how to play those fantastic songs. I wasn't really bothered at the time about learning songs by other bands, I only wanted to play and learn the songs of T.Rex.

My friends were more into bands like Jethro Tull and some of the more progressive groups of the period. I lost count of the arguments I used to have with people joking about the way Marc looked and posed about. The most annoying criticism was when they used to knock his guitar playing. Some of them just didn't 'get it' and thought that unless one played a ten-minute solo on each track, they were not worth listening to.

As the years passed my obsession with music sometimes still fought with my love of football, but music always won through in the end. My musical tastes then, as now, were mostly locked into rock as opposed to pop music. Rory Gallagher, Black Sabbath, Deep Purple, Led Zeppelin, Pink Floyd, Status Quo, Uriah Heep, David Bowie, Alice Cooper, and Mott The Hoople, mixed with a sprinkling of Rod Stewart and The Faces, Sweet, Slade, and Wizzard, not to mention a giant spoonful of Bob Dylan, began to dominate my album and singles collection. However, it was Marc Bolan and T.Rex that always remained at the pinnacle of my most treasured pieces of vinyl art.

Over time, I did get to see many of my favourite bands and artists in concert but it was on 1st February 1972, coincidently on my Dad's birthday, that I went along to my very first proper rock gig. It was the impressive Münsterlandhalle venue, in Münster to see T.Rex. No one I knew was really that bothered about going to see Bolan and his band, as most of my friends were still heavily into either football or other bands, so I ended up going to the concert alone. I didn't mind though as I felt as if I was with a family of thousands of like-minded people. Outside the venue I remember a couple of guys selling illegal posters of T.Rex. The posters were spread out on the ground, and excited fans were scrambling to purchase anything that had Marc's face on it. I managed to get one with a close-up of Marc and Mickey Finn, which ended up pride of place, on my bedroom wall with all the other Bolan pictures and posters that were slowly covering every inch of space.

Before entering the venue, there were posters advertising the evening's performance. These posters were nowhere to be sold as far as I could see. They appeared to be for promotion only, which I felt was a great shame as the image used was adapted from the inner sleeve artwork from 'Electric Warrior'. It had Marc on one side and Mickey on the other - but had been coloured in and used to amazing effect. I would have loved to have purchased one of those, but as they were not for sale I ripped one down from a nearby wall. It wouldn't come off easily and the ends and sides ripped a little. However, I managed to peel it off in full, and years later I still have that ripped poster in my collection.

The support band was Status Quo, who had recently released its album 'Dog Of Two Head'. The Quo were excellent and I became a fan immediately and remained a big fan right up until Alan Lancaster (the original bass player) and John Coghlan (the original drummer) decided to take their leave a few years later. When they lost their original rhythm section I felt that they lost some of their no-nonsense heads-down rock 'n' roll of which they were so good at. However, this was 1972, and my god, they were fantastic. Three guys all with heads down banging out the dirtiest, loud, and gritty rock music one could ever imagine. As soon as I could, I purchased the 'Dog Of Two Head' album, which sat proudly alongside my slowly growing record collection.

When it was time for T.Rex to hit the stage I became instantly ill from excitement and began to get stomach cramps, which annoyingly stayed for the duration of the show. But I was glad I made the effort, as I wouldn't have missed it for the world. The energy and the volume was the first thing that hit me when Marc, Mickey, Steve, and Bill walked onto the stage. The screaming from the fans alone before the band kicked in was enough to send me deaf!

As I didn't know how to act or behave at a rock concert, I was taken aback when suddenly the crowd surged forward leaving me standing in the middle of the venue, stunned but excited. I watched the band, but didn't take my eyes off Marc. I couldn't believe that I was in the same room as him, watching him perform those songs that I had only heard on my record player. The gig went by so fast. To this day, if I am totally honest, I can't really remember the songs that were played.* I was practically in a trance, hypnotised by the whole event. It wasn't until years later when bootleg tapes began to emerge, that certain aspects of the evening and the concert came back to me.

The next time I saw T.Rex was on what was deemed *The Slider Tour.* This was on 16th February 1973 at the Grugahalle in Essen. This time I

---

* The performance included: Cadilac, Jeepster, Baby Strange, Spaceball Ricochet (acoustic), Girl (acoustic), Cosmic Dancer (acoustic), Hot Love & Get It On.

went with two friends. The three of us had all skived off from school so that we could make the gig. We got there really early and heard the band sound checking and rehearsing. I guess if I had any sense I would've tried to get backstage, but in those days I was just happy to have the opportunity to attend the concert, so we just listened intently from in front of the closed doors. I remember us all getting excited hearing the band rehearsing 'Chariot Choogle' (from 'The Slider') and various other songs that they had planned for the evening's performance. The advertising posters for this show were black and white and showed Bolan with his *Fender Stratocaster*. Again, I wanted one and did the usual trick of ripping one from the wall as a souvenir. Sadly this one didn't quite come off so easily and was a little worse for wear.

The excitement was just as intense as when I saw the band the previous year, but thankfully without the stomach pains. I can't recall who the support band was, but when T.Rex came on, the place erupted. Marc's guitar was obviously out of tune to him when he came on stage and he had to immediately tune up. The performance was a little heavier than I expected from when I had last seen them in Münster. Marc did a lot more lead guitar and played songs from the latest album, 'The Slider'. It was amazing to hear tracks like 'Buick Mackane' and 'Chariot Choogle'. The only regret I had was that because the soloing took up such a lot of time in each song, it meant that the band only ended up playing about eight songs for the whole gig.*

I didn't see T.Rex again until I returned to England. Although they did play a few dates in 1974 and 1975, my first fix of live T.Rex in the UK arrived in 1976 on the *Futuristic Dragon Tour* on 18th February at The Lyceum Theatre in London. By this time the band had changed personnel and seemed to have become more of a pop act as opposed to the rock band I had seen a few years earlier. Marc no longer had Bill Legend on drums and it was only a matter of time before bass player Steve Currie would depart. Marc had recruited his girlfriend Gloria Jones on backing vocals and clavinet, Dino Dines on keyboards, and Davey Lutton on drums.

To me personally, T.Rex had changed from that moment. The harder, rockier edge had gone, and a more relaxed and fun element to the

---

* The performance included: Chariot Choogle, Baby Strange, Metal Guru, Telegram Sam, Buick Mackane, Jeepster, Hot Love & Get It On.

proceedings had taken over. Mind you, I did like the large smoke breathing dragon situated behind the drum riser. It was the first time I had seen the band play with a prop as a backdrop, and it did make the stage setting look pretty cool. It was great seeing Marc playing an acoustic solo spot, although I was disappointed that he had forgotten the words to some of his most famous songs, mainly due to the fact that he appeared quite drunk.* The band did seem a little under-rehearsed and song endings were sloppy, but it still didn't matter to us - the fans - it was just seeing Marc on that stage that was important. I actually went to the gig with a die-hard Deep Purple fan who thought the standard of the show and timing was below par. Admittedly, Marc wasn't at his best, but the feeling of the evening was that of total love for that guy standing centre-stage, and I for one, was happy just to be one of the many who felt the same way.

Certain songs like 'Jeepster', '20th Century Boy' and 'Get It On' had lost something in the live transition, and they took on a totally different feel, as if someone else had re-arranged them and dissected the structure of their original composition. I wondered at the time what the future held in store. I must admit, I did prefer 'T.Rex rock band' as opposed to 'T.Rex pop/funk/soul band', although I never faltered in my loyalty to Marc and stayed with him in whatever direction he decided to take.

I was paid back handsomely when just over a year later Marc would come back with an almost glossy relation to that of his earlier days of 'Electric Warrior'. Marc formed yet another hybrid version of the band he would still call T.Rex. This line-up retained the keyboards of the very amiable Dino Dines, and also employed the services of Miller Anderson on rhythm guitar, the top session bassist Herbie Flowers**, and Tony Newman on drums. It was interesting to note that Marc had employed both Herbie and Tony - two of the musicians of whom David Bowie had used on his epic 'Diamond Dogs' album a couple of years earlier. It was rumoured at the time that Marc and Bowie had discussed using them on their recordings, and it came to fruition for all to see when their names were also credited on 'Dandy In The Underworld'. As well as Herbie and Tony, Miller was a well-established and respected guitarist who had carved himself a career in the

---

* The full set list for this show was: 20th Century Boy, Jeepster, Funky London Childhood, New York City, Solid Gold Easy Action, Children Of The Revolution, Teenage Dream, Telegram Sam, Debora, One Inch Rock, Life's A Gas, Dreamy Lady, London Boys, Hot Love & Get It On.

** Flowers had played and come up with the very memorable bass line on Lou Reed's 'Walk On The Wildside'.

music business since the 1960s, while earning heavyweight friends such as Ritchie Blackmore and Ian Hunter.

The only show in London in 1977 took place at The Rainbow Theatre, in Finsbury Park, on Friday 18th March. It was a day that I would look back on with both sadness and thankfulness. I didn't know at the time that this would be the very last time I would ever see Marc live on stage. As I arrived for this concert on the upper floor of a double-decker bus, I looked down from the window to see not only Marc Bolan fans, but also a great deal of punk rockers who had come to see the support band, The Damned. They had been deliberately chosen by Marc to support because he had seen Captain Sensible (their bass player) wearing a Marc Bolan t-shirt! Marc was a great supporter of punk rock as it reminded him of his younger days when he was with John's Children.* Inside the Rainbow Theatre one could feel a tension in the air with the two factions of the audience. Some of the punks tried to put on an air of threat, but most were there for just a great rock 'n' roll experience.

I did my usual thing and tore off a large round 'Dandy In The Underworld' promotional poster, which remained in great condition as this time it had only been stapled to a board, rather than heavily glued, like the posters I managed to get from earlier gigs. I also pocketed a few A5 TV adverts for The Damned, who were later booked to appear on the ITV programme *Supersonic.*

The Damned put on a great show, and lead guitarist Brian James was outstanding. Their audience went crazy and I wondered how they were going to respond to T.Rex. Times had changed and it was the beginning of a different era. However, when Marc strutted onto the stage with the 'new' T.Rex it was like he had never been away! The theatre went absolutely ballistic. It was fantastic to see even the punks going crazy. Marc had won them over even before playing a note. "Welcome to the church of Bolan" he commented with his usual Bolanic grin. I felt that even Marc was exceptionally touched and pleased with this support. He had taken a risk in employing The Damned as a support band, but as he welcomed the 'punk' scene with open arms, in doing so, he had in turn become known as the 'Godfather of Punk'. It made me proud to be a Bolan fan and I was so happy

---

* This anarchic/mod band had upstaged The Who with its antics as the support act in Germany in April 1967. The performance included Bolan whipping his guitar with a chain, and they were removed from the tour.

to have seen his progression through the years, his downward period, and then his rise up to great respectability again.

What an amazing show we all had that night. Marc was so proud of his new T.Rex that he had rehearsed well and included many songs from the 'Dandy In The Underworld' album.* This was the first time I had seen Marc play a *Gibson Les Paul Standard* that was not the famous semi-opaque orange guitar. I wondered what had happened to it, as that instrument was almost synonymous with Marc as much as anything else. It wasn't until later that I learnt that it had actually been stolen.**

Marc's guitar playing, with his new cherry red *Gibson Les Paul Standard* was truly brilliant. He was clean, or at least appeared to be, and really concentrated on his craft and showed it off to perfection. The new songs such as 'Hang Ups', 'Visions Of Domino', 'The Soul Of My Suit', and 'Dandy In The Underworld' were performed with gusto and panache. Marc was really in his element and appeared to enjoy the whole experience along with the throng of fans that now also included some of the initially sceptical punk rockers. To some, Marc was back, but for me, he had never been away, just at times perhaps taking a stroll off the rock 'n' roll track.

Each time I saw Marc was a special and unique experience. He had such an aura that captivated all those around him. The fans were happy just to have him speak to them, or play a few bars on an acoustic guitar. It didn't matter as long as he was there, in that room with us all. Of course, one never thought that Marc would leave us. I mean - he was a special human being. I very nearly didn't go to the Rainbow concert, but a few months later I was so glad that I did. When Marc was taken from us all by a freak road accident in Barnes, West London on 16th September of that same year, it took me, just like thousands of fans, a long, long time to adjust and accept that he was no longer around.

However, to this day it shows the strength of the Bolan legend that thousands of fans still exist. And even a strong hold of younger fans that were much too young to have ever known the power that Marc held in his grasp over most of the Western World, and of course parts of Asia too.

---

* The full set list for this gig was: Jeepster, Visions Of Domino, New York City, The Soul Of My Suit, Groove A Little, Telegram Sam, Hang Ups, Debora, I Love To Boogie, Teen Riot Structure, Dandy In The Underworld, Hot Love & Get It On.

** The guitar was stolen in 1977 while the roadie was loading gear in to the van, outside the rehearsal studios near Waterloo, never to be seen again.

A very young John Willans in football kit. Years away from becoming 'Danielz'.

My concert ticket for T.Rex at the Münsterlandhalle, Münster, Germany in 1972. It was annoying that the ticket had been under-printed with Jethro Tull who had nothing to do with this show!

GRUGA-HALLE ESSEN

T. REX

21

Einheitspreis

DM 13,–

incl. 5,5 % MWSt.
u. Vorverk.-Geb.

Innenraum
unbestuhlt

Freitag
16. 2. 73
20.00 Uhr

Veranstalter: Mama Concert - AMGE
Veranstaltung Nr. 21

Keine Haftung für Personen- und Sachsch.
Beim Verlassen der Halle verliert die Karte
Gültigkeit. Kartenrückgabe ausgeschlossen.

Haubold, Eschwege

7700

DEREK BLOCK presents

T. REX

plus Support Group

LENNIE MACDONALD BAND

on WEDNESDAY 18th FEBRUARY 1976

LYCEUM The Strand, London W.C.2

Doors Open 7.30 p.m.

Tickets £2.00

No. 0679

RAINBOW THEATRE
FINSBURY PARK

Harvey Goldsmith Entertainments present

MARC BOLAN and T. REX

at 8 p.m.

Friday **MARCH 18**

STALLS

Including VAT £2.25

D 46

TO BE RETAINED   For conditions of sale see over

18

My other T.Rex
concert tickets

11

2

Wilderness Of The Mind

It took a long while before I had the initiative and courage to try and enter that mysterious world of the music business. But as I grew older and slowly improved my ability on the guitar, I began writing my own material. In 1979 I ended up recording a song entitled 'Ancient & Square' coupled with a song written by a friend at the time, Paul Sinclair, called 'Oscar Automobile'. We called ourselves Weird Strings - taken from a note that Bolan had hand-written on a quarter-inch tape box, referring to the backing string section on the song 'Celebrate Summer'. Both songs were recorded and self-produced, and even though the production was pretty dreadful, we managed to enter the top 50 in *Record Mirror's* indie-chart. Paul was producing a Bolan fanzine at the time called *Cosmic Dancer* but ended it's publication when he decided that he wanted to pursue a career in music and writing. In fact Paul was the author of an early soft back Marc Bolan biography entitled *Electric Warrior - The Marc Bolan Story*, which was issued by *Omnibus* in 1982.

I later recorded a follow-up single on my own under the guise of Weird Strings II. It was a double 'A' side with tracks entitled 'Criminal Cage' and 'Millionaire'. I had some photos taken in a local graveyard in Crayford, Kent, where I was living at the time, which made up the black and white picture sleeve. Again, both songs were dubiously self-produced and released on the Kent based *Ace Records* in 1980. Naïvely, I decided to take a copy along to Radio One in London and was lucky enough to meet John Peel, the renowned famous DJ who had championed Tyrannosaurus Rex years before.

I turned up unannounced and asked the security guy at the desk if he could "Call Mr Peel and tell him that Danielz is waiting at the front entrance for him." Unbelievably he did, and after waiting for a few anxious minutes, John came down and said, "hello". After a short conversation I gave him the single. He said "I'll only play the record if I like it or I think it has something." That night to my surprise, he played 'Criminal Cage' on his radio show. He didn't say too much about it, only, "it says Weird Strings two on the label, and that was Criminal Cage", as if he was slightly confused as to where Weird Strings one had got to!

Like so many music fans, I am indebted to Peel for all the years of his quiet anarchic fashion of radio shows from *The Perfumed Garden* to *The John Peel Show*. I never met him again even though I listened to his shows off and on until he passed away on 25th October 2004 at only 65 years of age. His biography *Margrave Of The Marshes* portrayed his life even more interestingly than I thought it was, and more than ever today we need someone like John Peel to come along and shake up the industry, although I feel that John was definitely a one-off.

Around this period I was asked to play guitar for an album that Paul Sinclair was recording under the banner of Midnight Rags. He had now decided to call himself Paul Roland and had clinched an album deal with *Ace Records* before signing with the indie-label *Cherry Red Records*. I went with him into a studio in Kent and recorded a few guitar tracks that were eventually used and released on an album entitled 'The Werewolf Of London'. There is a 10 x 8 black and white promotional photo of the band around somewhere with my hair slicked-back, all in PVC black trousers and white *Fender Stratocaster* slung over my shoulder!

Paul also recorded a single entitled 'Hot George' - a Bolan track that was originally included on the posthumous album 'Billy Super Duper' and before that on various bootleg cassette tapes, that had been in circulation after Marc had died. Paul called this short-lived group Beau Brummel and recruited Knox from the punk band The Vibrators to play some additional guitar, Andy Ellison from Radio Stars and Bolan's first band John's Children, to guest on backing vocals, and myself to play guitar. Although my guitar tracks were used for the recording, I was a little despondent that I was only thanked on the single sleeve credits but not listed for my contribution as a musician. One can guess that Paul and I kind of drifted apart after that, but still remained on good terms.

After being disillusioned with my contributions being ignored, I decided to return to the studio again, recording some of my original material just for my own pleasure, using musicians that I had worked with on the "Werewolf" album. Tracks with titles such as 'Observations', 'Total Disguise', and 'Atomic Pride' made it to sixteen-track tape and mixed down to quarter-inch but the project didn't really get any further than that. As many budding musicians did at the time, I made up cassette demo tapes and sent them to all the usual record companies but with no joy. I didn't really bother at the time sending my recorded songs to independent labels as my material mainly catered for the commercial major-label listening market, but without good management, getting through those doors proved impossible.

Most companies didn't even bother to reply - although I have no doubt that my tape was one of a thousand that the A&R guys must have received every day of every week. I had a full-time job working in an office for the Civil Service, so having only weekends to do what I really wanted to do was sometimes quite difficult. As I worked in the West End of London, commuting everyday from Kent, I would sometimes try to get to spend a little time in the King's Road, or Carnaby Street, just for the vibe. I was even offered a job in a great little record shop called *Rock Dreams*, but the pay was so lousy that I just couldn't accept it. A short time later, I realised that I had made the right decision because sadly the shop closed down.

The early 1980s was the beginning of the rock 'n' roll memorabilia boom and in 1983 *Sotheby's* held its first proper rock 'n' roll auction. It was rammed as music fans covered every inch of spare space inside the auction rooms. I was there as I'd heard that there would be some Marc Bolan items available. This was probably the most exciting auction of Bolan memorabilia there has ever been (and I've attended many rock 'n' roll auctions since then). There were well-known outfits and hand written lyrics to Marc's well-known songs, some of his guitars, and so many other items - it was unbelievable.

I managed to obtain a lot of five pairs of trousers that included the blue lamé dungarees that Marc had worn on *Top Of The Pops* for his performance of 'Metal Guru', a crimson pair of satin dungarees that he had worn in the USA, a pair of green satin trousers with 'MARC' in sequins around the waistband, and two pairs of glitter trousers, one of which he had worn on the *MARC* shows in 1977. To try and pull back some of the money I had borrowed to buy these items, I eventually sold the two pairs of glitter trousers to another fan. I had originally wanted to purchase the set of handwritten lyrics to 'Metal Guru' as that had been my favourite T.Rex track of all time. Sadly I was up against the *Hard Rock Café* with their never-ending pot of cash, so I didn't have a hope in hell of getting them. A few months later, I went into the *Hard Rock Café* in Park Lane, London and sat down next to a few pieces of rock 'n' roll memorabilia, one of which was the framed lyrics to 'Metal Guru'... if only I had a screwdriver and a lot more bottle...

A year later in 1984, while attending another rock 'n' roll auction at *Sotheby's*, I was approached by *The Times* as they thought I looked a little different and stood out from the crowd. They asked if they could take a few snapshots of me playing a piano of Elton John's that had been put into the auction. The next day a large black and white photo appeared in their second September edition. I was really happy with it, as you could see that I was wearing a Marc Bolan 'Slider' t-shirt!

I would attend many other auctions over the years, and even one in 1990 where Marc's famous 1976 red dragon jacket appeared for sale. It was obviously out of my price range but I did manage to persuade the guy in charge to let me slip it on for a couple of minutes to have two photographs of me wearing it!

Musically, the 1980s were very productive. At *Alaska Studios* based underneath the arches of Waterloo Station, I recorded an original track 'I Wouldn't Lie', inspired by a phrase I liked from the Bolan track 'Nameless Wildness'. Plus a version of Bolan's 'Cadilac' with The Vibrators' guitarist Knox, Colvin Mayers from the progressive band, The Sound, and The Vibrators' bassist, Pat Collier in the production seat. This version of 'Cadilac' ended up being included on a compilation vinyl album entitled 'An Exalted Companion to T.Rex Nights' on the Marc Bolan related *Barracuda Blue* label, an independent company run by Marc Arscott, an ardent fan who has always been dedicated to keeping Marc's legend alive.

I decided to send a few of my recordings to *Rock City Studios* in Shepperton, a studio that had connections with the likes of Gary Numan, and David Coverdale from Whitesnake. I was surprised when a few weeks later I was offered and received a recording deal with Brian Adams, the producer and part owner of *Rock City* (not of course to be confused with the Canadian superstar of the same name!) I ended up recording numerous songs with some excellent professional musicians such as Ced Sharpley (Gary Numan's drummer), Blackfoot Sue (who had a hit in the 1970s with 'Standing In The Road'), Paul King (songwriter, guitarist, and jug player from

Mungo Jerry), and Lindsay Bridgewater (keyboard player with the Ozzy Osbourne Band).

The studio at Shepperton was great and very hi-tech for the time. I remember that they had a room in which they had set up ambient microphones to record the drums. When Ced Sharpley began recording the drums for a couple of my compositions, 'Observation' and 'Voice From A Silent Heart', the volume in that room was unbearable. He was the loudest drummer I had ever heard and come to think of it, I don't think I have heard a drummer as loud as him since then.

On one occasion Billy Bremner, guitarist for the Dave Edmunds Band who'd, had a hit in 1970 with 'I Hear You Knocking', was waiting for his allocated time in the studio while I was just finishing my session. I wanted to finish the mix as it was very nearly completed. I was already running thirty minutes over and Billy was getting very irate, ranting and raving about "who was I to keep him waiting" and the usual musician's temperament. About forty-five minutes later I walked out expecting a confrontation with Billy, but he was as calm as anything and just asked me if it all went well and how the recording was going!

On another occasion I was at the tail end of mixing a recording of 'I Wouldn't Lie'. Jimmy Pursey, vocalist with punk band Sham 69, who was also signed with *Rock City* at the time, walked into the mixing session uninvited. As he stood behind us he said, "what this song needs is a rock 'n' roll piano." Neither the engineer nor I turned around to respond, and in that, he turned around and walked out! I never saw him again.

One of the songs I recorded with the Farmer brothers, who were better known as Blackfoot Sue, was an original number I had written called 'Baby Factory'. We had a lot fun recording it, as the brothers were great at sounding like female backing singers, so I had them sing the chorus behind my lead vocal. Paul King, one of the founder members of Mungo Jerry engineered the session. After we had recorded the song he told me that he had a track that was ideal for me. It was called 'Children Of Darkness' and was to be the B-side of 'Baby Factory'.

I liked 'Children Of Darkness' and recorded it in the same way that we did 'Baby Factory', in that the Farmer brothers played as my backing band. After the final mixes of both songs, the package was presented to the management but it was suddenly decided by the powers that be that the Baby Factory' lyrics were too rude for a *Rock City* release; 'I wanna be in your baby factory, I wanna play in your baby factory' didn't seem to me very risqué. At least not compared to the then recent Frankie Goes To Hollywood song, 'Relax'. I disagreed intensely, so much so that our partnership slowly crumbled away and I walked out from the deal with mutual agreement and again with no release or contract.

So it was once more I was musically in a black hole with just a batch of recordings under my arms with no outlet. Then a few months later, I saw an advert in the music press advertising for a "Charismatic lead vocalist for melodic rock band." I'd had enough of scouting around trying to find a record company that would believe in my material instead of coming up with excuses about unacceptable lyrics etc. So I was pleased when after auditioning for a group of East End guys, I suddenly found myself fronting a great rock band, which we later called Tarazara.

Throughout the early 1980s we were, in our own minds, taking the country by storm. We built up a decent following and played various venues around London such as The Marquee in Wardour Street. We recorded live radio sessions for shows such as Tommy Vance's Radio One *Friday Rock Show,* and gigged up and down the country in just about every black-walled rock venue that would have us. Ritchie Blackmore from Deep Purple/Rainbow even came to see us play at Dingwalls in Camden, London, much to the reviewer's delight from *Sounds* who mentioned it in his review column the following week.*

It was with Tarazara that I had my first encounter with Brian Connolly from Sweet. We were playing support to Brian's newly formed version of the band at The Marquee. The room was small, but filled with die-hard Sweet fans. No one at that time really knew who we were, but after that one night we were able to obtain our very own headline dates at The Marquee from then on. I never spoke to Brian who kept pretty much out of our way most of the time, but it would be only a few years later that our paths would cross again, by which time I was in a totally different band.

We were also billed with Gary Glitter at The Wolverhampton Civic. Once again, we went down well, even though the audience didn't know one single song in our repertoire. Afterwards we spent quite a bit of time with Gary and had pictures taken together. It was fate that yet again, our paths

---

*This was published in the 6th July 1985 edition, but refers to Blackmore's appearance as "pre-Knebworth". The Knebworth Fayre was the first UK show by the reformed Deep Purple, and took place on 22nd June 1985.

would cross a few years later.

As a unit, we were all for one and one for all and through our early period we really thought that we were going places. For instance, we were invited to go onto the latest rock TV programme on Channel Four called *ECT*. This show was broadcast after the season of *The Tube* had finished its run. It was actually broadcast live on 17th May 1985, not recorded, so that everyone had literally a run-through, before going on air. It was quite nerve-racking to say the least, but we performed two of our original numbers, 'Fantasy', and 'Behind The Mask' very well. We were happy to be included on the bill with the guitarist Snowy White, who had recently been a member of Thin Lizzy and had just had a hit with the guitar led ballad 'Bird Of Paradise'. It was to be our first and last television appearance, but never the less a great experience.

The music magazine *Kerrang* took us under its wing and we were heavily featured whenever possible, even getting whole page interviews and colour photo promotion. We were lucky enough to have some of our studio sessions produced by ex-Iron Maiden guitarist Dennis Stratton and ended up with some fine, polished recordings. We recorded nothing but original songs with titles such as 'Wake Up', 'All Too Late', 'Fantasy', 'Behind The Mask', 'Master Of The Deadly Kiss', and 'Sweet Suicide'. We were on the verge of signing with *FM Records* in The Midlands when we were suddenly offered a tentative deal from *Atlantic Records*. We of course turned down the *FM Records* deal and decided to run with *Atlantic*, only for that to fall at the last hurdle - something that I suppose so many musicians have come to experience over the years.

Around this time we were invited to perform a live set at the impressive *Earls Court Guitar Extravaganza Show* in London but we became quite disheartened by the *Atlantic Records* situation, and eventually decided to split and go our separate ways. The Tarazara legacy doesn't quite end here though, as you will see later on in this story of how an album's worth of our recordings were finally released officially in 2010.

Only a few weeks passed until I was quickly picked up by manager Adrian Millar who signed me as a songwriter. This was around the tail end of 1985 and I quickly began writing and recording songs like there was no tomorrow. Adrian would buy me guitars and we would book a studio with a group of musicians and just record. I would spend my days writing songs and at night we would go out to restaurants or meet up with fellow musicians that he had known over the years. Adrian had managed a band called The Baby's that had some real success in the USA. Their lead vocalist was John Waite.* Around this period I was, I suppose, blinded by the money I was being handed in cash from Adrian. He was a pretty wealthy guy and I wanted for nothing, be it handmade clothes, guitars, hair styled, I had my bills paid, and I was on a retainer too which meant that I always had a wad of cash thrust into my hands if and when I needed it for anything.

Adrian was also a formidable character. He'd had quite an 'eventful' life and was the kind of guy that would keep thousands of pounds under his bed in a suitcase. He always dealt in cash and a handshake was binding, or you may suffer the consequences. He was a large Jewish guy who had a strange basin type haircut. He always had it cut at the same hairdressers in Bayswater, London, and had it coloured a very, very dark purple, almost black. One day I met him as arranged. It was winter and although it was only about 5.30pm it was dusk. I tapped him on his shoulder and he turned around with a flick-knife ready opened. He told me not to shock him again like that as he said that he never knew who was around who may want to "have a go."

I had a good relationship with Adrian as we both liked music and going to restaurants. He kept his 'underground' life to himself and never got me involved or even spoke to me about it, although I knew that dodgy dealings were always on the cards with him. He knew some powerful people but not necessarily in the places I wished to frequent. Money was never an issue and it seems neither were cars. We were travelling down to West London from Holloway, where I lived at the time, and suddenly the power steering in his Jaguar XJS just packed in. He drove it into a corner, called someone to pick it up and sort it out. For the rest of the day he spent a fortune on the two of us travelling around London in Taxis.

I did have an enjoyable time recording in some good quality studios. I also did some recording with Steve Mann, who later became a guitarist in Andy Scott's Sweet, and had also worked with the Michael Schenker band (MSG). We recorded my compositions such as 'Woman In The Gallery', and I Don't Need A Reason'. I also came across Martin Dobson, who had played saxophone on many tracks by The Eurythmics and at that time was quite a

---

*After The Baby's, Waite went solo and had a hit with 'Missing You' in 1984. It reached number nine in the UK and number one on the US Billboard chart.

sought after session musician. So when I was booked in to record a triplet of songs at *The Simon Henderson Studios* in Berkshire, I asked Martin to come along and play saxophone on all three tracks: 'Personal Touch', 'Some Romantic Night' and 'Where Were You'. They became available years later as downloads

I was still getting frustrated though as nothing seemed to be actually happening. I was recording all of these songs, going into photo sessions, but every time I asked Adrian about progress, he just said that "everyone loves you but we still haven't found the right deal." I ended up with the impression that although Adrian and I got on really well, he was never really trying that hard to get a deal for me. I felt that the recordings and the pop-star treatment was just a game to him and he just enjoyed the two of us going out to places and to be honest I think he just liked my company.

However, this was not what I wanted. I was still eager to find my way in the music business and so one day I told him that I was quitting and going back to 'normal life' - this wasn't exactly the truth of course, but I knew that I should lie low for a while until the dust had settled and Adrian was out of my life for good. He took back all of the guitars he had bought, but left me with all my handmade clothing and good wishes for the future. Sadly, I was told only a few years ago, that Adrian had died from heart failure. I'm not sure if it was drug related, but I was always certain that he did now and then succumb to substances.

Before the 1980s drew to a close, I was offered a deal with *Barracuda Blue*. The label's boss Marc Arscott was compiling an album of Bolan cover versions to be released under the title of 'An Exalted Companion to T.Rex Nights' (a lyric extracted from 'Dandy In The Underworld'). He had heard my recorded version of 'Cadilac' and wanted the track on the album. The song was eventually included on the vinyl-only LP, along with tracks from Miller Anderson, and Boz Boorer (Polecats and later Morrissey's guitarist) amongst other artists. The compilation came out in 1988 with a black and white photo of Bolan on the cover with an informative inner sleeve pull-out with details about all the artists included on the album. As a follow up, a 'cassette-only' compilation of original and cover version songs by Bolan related musicians and fans was released in 1992 called 'The Point & The Rays'. It included my original version of 'Baby Factory', and the Tarazara recording of 'Fantasy'. Other artists such as Andy Ellison, and Nikki Sudden (Swell Maps) also contributed to the release.

In 1990, along with my girlfriend Caron Thomas, I began writing and compiling a book that was dedicated to Marc, his writings, his music, his lifestyle, and performance. We managed to clinch a deal with *Xanadu Publishing*, who had issued books on Bob Dylan and John Lennon, so we felt that we would be in good credible company. We called it *Wilderness Of The Mind*, after a title Bolan had come up with for one of his books that never saw the light of day.

We included many of Caron's personal photographs and also sheets of original writings, poetry, and hand written jottings and ideas from Marc that we had in our collection. We also included interviews with Bolan associates that, at the time, had never been interviewed to any extent. People such as Mike Mansfield, the producer of the outrageous and formidable TV music show *Supersonic*, Andy Ellison, and one of Marc's very early manager's Mike Pruskin, who managed Marc from 1965 - 1966.

We also decided that we needed a foreword by someone well-known, so we got in touch with the inimitable Morrissey. Caron had known him before he had even formed The Smiths in the 1980s while he was still known by his full name, Steven Patrick Morrissey. We arranged to meet him backstage at a North London gig and spent time talking over what the book would be about. Morrissey was and still is a fan of Marc Bolan and after discussing the concept he decided that he liked the idea and ended up writing a lengthy piece on two sheets of A4, in his unique, spikey handwriting which was later transcribed.

We also got in touch with Tony Howard, who managed Bolan from 1972 until the day he died. Tony was at first quite wary of getting involved so he asked to meet up with us first. We invited him to our flat in Holloway and he accepted. It was dusk when he arrived and I went down stairs to greet him. At first glance he was shocked at my appearance as he said that I reminded him of Marc. We sat and talked for an hour or so and he said that he would be very happy to write a foreword, as he believed that we were both genuine people who obviously had a great admiration for Marc. Tony had also remembered Caron from when he used to see her at T.Rex gigs and I'm sure that helped sway his decision. In the end, we agreed with our publishers that as we had two very important and influential people who had agreed to write forewords, that we should use them both!

Wilderness Of The Mind was eventually published in 1992 as a limited edition of 1,000 hardback coffee table style books of which we had to hand-sign every copy, retaining numbers 1 and 2 for our own collection. It was then issued in an A4 sized soft cover with a different cover photograph, again in a coffee table style design. The book did extremely well receiving excellent reviews from the monthly music magazines and press alike, and was critically acclaimed by fans. Sadly, *Xanadu* went into liquidation a few years later so there was never the opportunity for a reprint, which is why today, copies are sometimes seen on the various auction sites for quite extreme prices.

A few years later and out of the blue, a Japanese company *Quattro Publishing* who, without our knowledge, but had been tipped off by the Japanese Fan Club, found out about the book and got in touch. They offered us a deal to release an updated version translated into Japanese. It was the first ever UK book about Marc Bolan to be translated and was published in 1999. The book looked lovely in the typical soft-backed A5 sized publication, which is how many standard music books are issued in Japan. They added some colour photographs and additional information, along with a lovely fold-over cover and wrap-around obi* which all added to its unique look. This is actually still available and still ticks over quite nicely in the Far East.

With all the 'nearly' happenings, and the 'almost' deals, I was, like so many others before me - disenchanted with the music industry and their open-holed promises. I decided that I would take a break from it until the time arrived to do something that I would enjoy and not bother too much if it came to nothing. The epiphany arrived in 1992 in a pub in London's West End where Bolan fans met for socialising every so often. I was there with Caron and a few friends when I had the strangest and ridiculous idea to form a band dedicated to my lifetime idol Marc Bolan. Little did I know that this one burst of an initiative, would at last propel me into a professional musician's life that I had always wanted…

---

*An obi is a sash for traditional Japanese dress, worn for martial arts or as part of kimono outfits. Japanese books and records reflect this with a paper band wrapped around the product, normally with the product details written on it.

Left: In the late seventies with Keith Pears, a mutual Bolan fan and friend. Keith and I had gone to see T.Rex together at The Gruga-Halle in Essen in 1973 when we both lived in Soest in Germany.

Below: Wearing my black satin bomber jacket on 16th September at Golders Green Crematorium in the late seventies for Marc's commemorative anniversary. The jacket had 'Marc Bolan & T.Rex' printed in gold lettering on the back.

With Paul Roland (Sinclair) in *Ace Recording Studios*, Kent. I'm wearing a Sex Pistols Destroy t-shirt and playing my red *Framus* guitar. We called ourselves Weird Strings for one self-financed double A-side single in 1979.

Left: A very short lived band of mine - Paladin Heat, 1979. The name was taken from the lyrics from Bolan's 'Liquid Gang'.

Above: A concert ticket for the only gig we played, supporting Matinee Idols, whose lead singer was involved with the embryonic stages of T.Rextasy!

Left: The only single released by Weird Strings in 1979.

Below: The cover of my second self-financed single, 'Criminal Cage'. I gave the record the band name of Weird Strings II. The photo on the cover was from the 1980 Crayford graveyard session.

Left: A dubious photo session taken in 1980 in a graveyard in Crayford, Kent for the 'Criminal Cage' single. This was probably the last time in my life that I had shortish hair.

Right: A snapshot from another short lived band. I called this 23 Tales, for this one-off gig at Shepperton Studios in the early eighties, while signed to *Rock City* in Shepperton. I'm wearing a pair of pink trousers that Bolan wore on his *MARC* shows in 1977. They were slightly too big for me at the time.

Tarazara memorabilia: Stage pass for our TV appearance on the live rock show *ECT*, on Channel Four; a Dingwalls gig listing; a list of tour dates from *Kerrang!*; my top three albums in Kerrang!'s 'Star Choice' selection (I chose 'Electric Warrior', 'For Those About To Rock' by AC/DC, and Led Zeppelin's 'Presence').

Three solo
promotional shots.
(Mike Lever)

TARAZARA

Above: Tarazara promotional photograph.
Left to right: Jeff Williams (guitar), Damian Manestar (Keyboards), yours truly (vocals), Simon Henderson (drums), Mike Lever (bass).

Left: Two Marc Bolan flexi-discs that my friend Paul Thomas and I issued in a little self-financed venture in the eighties. They included the tracks 'Electric Boogie' (from a 1971 T.Rex session), an acoustic version of 'Left Hand Luke', a recited poem, and Marc & Mickey Finn on the 'Flo & Eddie Radio Show'.

Right: Wearing a 1976 Bolan stage jacket. The jacket was sold by *Christie's* in London. I was kindly given permission to wear it for a couple of photos.

Morrissey and I backstage. Moz, Caron, and I met up to talk about him writing a Foreword for our forthcoming Bolan book *Wilderness Of The Mind* - London 1991

Wilderness Of The Mind - Marc Bolan, written by Caron and I and published by *Xanadu Publications UK* in 1992. Below: hardback edition.

paperback edition

Japanese edition

3
The Birth Of T.Rextasy!

The embryo of the band began with guys and people that I knew: Mike Bezzi, a friend and guitarist, and a keyboard player called Vince Lyte. We were all Bolan fans and dug the idea that we should form a band playing songs that were purely either written or recorded by Marc. I already had in my mind the band name that I wanted to use - T.REXTASY - a brilliant turn of phrase that had originally been conjured up and used as a front page headline in *Melody Maker* in 1972 in conjunction with a live review by Michael Watts.

We held auditions in rehearsal studios in North London and recruited a bass player by the name of Tim, who wanted to be known as Tiger Tim after a lyric from Bolan's 'The Street And Babe Shadow' from 'Tanx'. We never got to know his surname! And a drummer Nigel Silk who had recorded with the legendary producer Joe Meek in the 1960s. Tim was already a fan of T.Rex, so there was no problem with him learning the basics. Nigel however didn't know any T.Rex songs, so we ended up rehearsing week in week out until we felt we were ready to go out and play.

Our debut appearance took place on Friday 18th September 1992 in a tiny pub in London's East End called The Dove. The stage was a small, no a tiny, raised platform in the corner. It was so small in fact that part of the neck of Tim's bass guitar was thrust outside an open window to get us all on it! Our timing for staging the gig was pretty good as there had been a Bolan party a couple of nights before in London commemorating the 15th anniversary of Marc's death, so we attracted many of the people who had attended that gathering. We were in high spirits to find that Bill Legend had come to see us play, too.

Caron had designed a couple of A5 flyers, so we had them

photocopied on the sly at work. There was no Internet then, so it was promoted by either word of mouth or handing out the flyers where and when we could. The pub packed out slowly but surely and we were all obviously nervous, as nothing had really been done like this before. Would Bolan fans accept a band trying to play a T.Rex show? It was early days and I wore my old clothes from the Tarazara period and everyone else wore clothing that we all thought was appropriate in keeping to a Glam style.

I didn't have a Bolan-style guitar then, just an average *Gibson* and a normal combo-amplifier. We played the usual hits, with some B-sides and album tracks such as 'Raw Ramp', 'Baby Strange', and if I remember correctly 'Jupiter Liar' amongst our one hour set. We went down well enough to attract the attention of an agent who had also been watching that night. One must remember that in 1992 there wasn't the wealth or scene of tribute bands that is present today.

The gigs were slow in coming at first. We played a few of the smaller rock clubs in and around the vicinity of the M25, but not too much happened in the first few months. The one place that we played a few times was The Swan in Fulham, West London. This was enough to tick over and keep it all together. In fact, it was a great kick-start as we slowly made our way up the ladder, obtaining decent cash fees along the way. It enabled us to buy better equipment and in turn become a little more authentic in our look and sound. The respected weekly *Melody Maker* gave us a favourable review stating that we were, "Utterly dandy and cosmic. I applaud like a multitude. Looks and sounds to spellbinding effect and devoutly sincere. They bring a glow to my zip-gun heart."

Because we were, I suppose, a novelty in those days, being only one of a small handful of bands that would eventually be known in the scene as a tribute, we were lucky enough to be invited to appear on the popular television programme *This Morning with Richard and Judy*, which was, at the time, still being recorded at the Liverpool Docks for ITV. We were approached at short notice and Tim had gone away on holiday so I got in touch with a bass player I knew called Bob. He had not only played bass in some of my past ventures in the 1980s, but was also in the embryonic stages of T.Rextasy before bowing out prior to any gigs taking place.

ITV arranged for a coach to pick us up and take us to the studios. Unbelievably the coach broke down on the way and we all had to wait for it to be repaired before completing the journey. When we finally reached the studios we spent the usual time hanging around for what seemed like hours before our chance came around to perform a live version of 'Hot Love'. By this time I was getting some lovely Bolanic clothing made by a genuine fan and seamstress called Helen Bennett. She had made me a replica of Marc's purple velvet smock-top, a lovely garment that he wore at various shows and occasions, one of the most famous being on the London Weekend Television programme *Music In The Round.* I had decided to wear my version of that top for this show. It looked great on the screen monitors, so I knew it would come across pretty authentically. The recording took a few stops and starts to get the correct camera angles but it all went quite smoothly.

I was asked to stay until the following day for a live interview and also asked if I would wear exactly the same clothes I performed in for continuity. They would then link up the two and people would assume that we were all in the studio on the same day when in fact the song had been recorded the previous afternoon. It was then that I realised that some of these programmes that pertained to be totally live, were not actually live at all! The band was driven back home, and Caron and I were given a lovely hotel room and extras for the evening, all on the ITV tab.

I woke up early the next morning, for the early start, not forgetting to make sure that I put on exactly the same stage gear and make up that I had worn the previous day. I ended up doing the interview with Richard & Judy's stand-ins as they themselves were on holiday at the time. Before I was ushered in I had a chat to the television weather presenter Sian Lloyd who was also due to be interviewed on the show. The interviewers didn't seem to know too much about Marc Bolan or T.Rex and hadn't been passed much information to the background of T.Rextasy either. However, it was our very first slice of television exposure and I had a ball of a time.

Work was still a little slow in coming, but we managed to get other gigs, mostly around the London region. We played at venues such as the St John's Tavern in Archway, North London. The PA was unremarkable and the sound pretty awful, but we accepted just about anything we could get at the time as I was still trying and pushing for as much exposure as possible. I was then and some say I am still, ambitious, pushy, egocentric and sometimes a little too aggressive. I didn't want anything to get in my way of achieving some kind of reasonable success under the guise of T.Rextasy. A friend of mine, Paul Thomas, an animator and artist, began designing flyers for our shows and we used his images of Marc for years to come in many advertisements and forthcoming events.

Already though, even before the summer of 1993 had started, cracks were beginning to show within the unit and it appeared that Mike, our rhythm player, didn't feel that he could give the band the dedication and time that was required. Or at least the time that I insisted on, to lift our profile to obtain more and more gigs. So even though Mike was a friend, I had to dismiss him from the group. We ended up playing our next show, a double header with The Counterfeit Stones at Essex University, without him. It wasn't ideal as I had to play both rhythm and lead guitar, but the gig went well, with Vince covering on keyboards when I went into a solo. This concert was our first gig promoted by John Hessenthaler, a professional promoter and someone that would employ T.Rextasy for a great deal of our career.

A short time later we were offered another gig with the well-known agent and promoter from the 1960s, Hal Carter, who had worked with many popular bands and chart groups, such as The Kinks. Suddenly we found ourselves being offered a show at The Derngate Theatre in Northampton with Brian Connolly's Sweet and Les Gray's Mud. On the day of the concert we all sat around waiting for Vince to turn up but he didn't show. I rang him up only to be told that he wasn't coming, as he basically felt annoyed for the way I had dismissed Mike from the band. Even though it was something that he had agreed needed to be done for the band to move on.

From that moment on I realised I had to get musicians with a professional attitude and not get involved with those who wanted to play just for a hobby. We had, a couple of weeks earlier auditioned guitarists to replace Mike on rhythm. One guy who stood out from everyone was Neil Bufton, who decided that he wanted to be professionally known as Neil Cross. He looked like a rock star, played guitar like a pro, and was, importantly to me, a very big fan of T.Rex. At this time he had hair that reached halfway down to his waist and looked every bit a rock guitarist.

Initially I had previously been recommended another contender by a fan called Belinda who told me that she had met a guy called Jimmy, who was interested in joining the band and although she did not have his telephone number, another guy she had met called Neil would have it. When I phoned Neil, I was stunned to find out that not only had he been a big fan of T.Rex since the early seventies, but he was also an accomplished guitar player as well. After chatting to him for a while about Bolan, we both forgot about the reason I had phoned him in the first place, and he asked if he could come down for a play, so I invited him along for an audition. After Neil had played with us for a couple of hours in the rehearsal rooms in London's *Holloway 313 Studios* we immediately knew that he would fit in nicely. He had previously been in Sister Midnight, an outrageous Glam rock band in the 1980s and since then had done various session work and song writing. He was interested in joining T.Rextasy but at the time we hadn't quite made our decision.

Because we had been let down by Vince, I decided to call on Neil. Thankfully at the time he was living in Islington and I was living in Holloway, so it was only a matter of a ten-minute drive to his basement flat. I knocked on his door and he was surprised to see me standing there offering him a gig at The Derngate Theatre with Sweet and Mud! He agreed straight away although slightly bewildered, and after quickly packing some stage clothes, guitar and amplifier, we all made our way up to Northampton.

After setting up our equipment it was our turn to soundcheck and so a nightmare began. On practically his first strum, Neil broke a string and a few minutes later his amp completely packed in! Thankfully, after an embarrassing half-hour or so we got it all together and the remainder of our soundcheck went ahead without any further complications. A couple of hours later we were told that The Sweet weren't going to turn up, and we were asked if we could play for a little longer than our contracted and allocated forty-five minute spot. Thankfully, because we had rehearsed and played with Neil in the studio, and the fact that Neil had been playing Bolan songs all his life anyway, it wasn't a problem. The gig went down very well and afterwards we all agreed that Neil was the guy who should be in the band. We offered the position to him there and then and he accepted - he's been in the band ever since!

A short time later we played our first show in Germany. This was on the 5th June 1993 in Marburg. We drove all the way from London to the venue in a hired minibus. The journey's only main event was when Neil was physically sick outside his window while we were travelling through Germany. Along with my brother Gordon, who was our roadie at the time, they had drunk a whole bottle of *Jim Beam* between them, but it was Neil that the drink returned on. When we finally got to our destination, one side of the vehicle wasn't a pretty sight with a combination of drink and vomit trailing from Neil's window to the rear end of the bus. He had the not-so-pleasant task of hosing it down before our return. All in a day's rock 'n' roll.

We finally got around to soundchecking later in the afternoon and while going through some of the songs we noticed an evil looking guy in a wheel chair who kept staring at us. When we all got down off the stage he started shouting and ranting in German and frantically trying to run us over. He didn't seem to like the fact that we had come from the UK to his town. We all thought he was some kind of Nazi, but we just kept out of his way and made sure we stayed together.

Bookings were finally starting to come in and we were beginning to get some decent gigs, along with some strange and incompatible invites. For instance we were offered a gig at London's Astoria Theatre to play support to the hair-raising punk band King Kurt. We had to perform on a sheet of polythene as we were told that King Kurt's fans tended to throw eggs and raw meat at them during their performance. As the crowd gathered outside the security banned them from bringing in such foodstuffs. We suddenly heard a commotion and looked out from the dressing room window onto Charing Cross Road. There was a loud cheer, and a roar. King Kurt fans had begun pelting shop windows and passers by with their stock of raw meat, eggs and flour! A group of Hari-Krishna chanters came by just at the wrong time and that was it - they were suddenly drenched and covered with raw meat, eggs and flour!

In the dressing room, I said for a joke that we weren't being paid for the evening's performance. No one took any notice of course, except for Tim, who grabbed his bass and walked out. Our roadie Gavin chased after him and got him back before he managed to get on the tube train! I was livid. Up to this point Tim had never bothered to learn the bass lines on the records preferring to come up with his own, he also never bought an amplifier as he preferred to put his bass through the PA system. None of the band or engineers who worked for us liked him doing that. It was time for change and we all agreed that this was the last straw. We decided we would audition for a replacement in the coming weeks. Thankfully, our show went without a hitch and we watched the manic King Kurt from the wings while they tied their fans to the 'Wheel of Misfortune' while pumping them with alcohol through a pipe and watching them throw up when they could take no more. I must say that although it was carnage, there was no trouble inside the venue and everyone left in high spirits!

We held auditions for our next bass player in our usual rehearsal studios in Holloway. Just like when we were auditioning for drummers, it amazes me how many people actually think they are competent enough to join a band, when in fact they are still only bedroom players. We settled for Paul Rogers, who was once again, a fan of T.Rex and also of 1970s punk bands. His playing was very much in the style of Steve Currie and played his bass lines in that fashion. Paul lived in Crayford, Kent, which was quite handy as our roadie Gordon, lived close by so it helped a great deal regarding travel logistics.

The line-up of Danielz, Neil Cross, Paul Rogers, and Nigel Silk is what many people consider to be the real beginning of T.Rextasy proper. We were dedicated to the band and we wanted to be as successful as possible, and to get as much work as we could - our aims were focussed as much as a professional outfit could be, except of course that we were still at this time only semi-professional! It was around this period that we also hired a backing vocalist called Lisa DaVinci.

It was in August 1993 that we published the first T.Rextasy Newsletter. It was four pages long with news and details of forthcoming shows. As the years rolled by the newsletters had to morph into a newsletter/gig list and down to one double sheet, purely and simply because of the amount of work that was incoming, and the sheer amount of people that were joining the list - we just didn't have the time to do four pages anymore. The fan base grew so rapidly that before we knew it, we actually had some kind of fan club of our own.

This was still of course a little before the Internet, website, and email generation, so every now and then we did a *Newsletter Special*, where there would sometimes be four or more pages included and even photographs if something different or unique had happened. Such as our very first trip to Scotland where we were seen by Lenny Zakatek, the lead singer of the hit group Gonzales. They'd had a massive dance hit with the Gloria Jones song 'I Haven't Stopped Dancing Yet'. Lenny was managing a Japanese guy called Hotei. Lenny, Hotei, and a few of the members of a Japanese group called The Yellow Magic Orchestra (YMO) were in the audience and afterwards tried to get backstage to see me.

As it had been a regular policy not to let anyone backstage that I didn't know, I initially I told the bouncers on the stage door not to let them in. Luckily, Caron recognised Lenny and came in to tell me. Caron had known him from the seventies when she first met the band when they were backing

Gloria Jones on the Bob Marley tour. They all filed into the dressing room with Japanese accents and enthusiasm. I was introduced to Hotei and the YMO. Lenny told me that Hotei was a massive superstar in Japan who could sell out venues such as the famous Budokan and many of the giant baseball stadiums in the Far East. I witnessed this personally at a later date.

Lenny had bought tickets for Hotei as a special birthday present to see us play, as most of his life he had been a big fan of both Marc Bolan and David Bowie but never had the chance to see T.Rex in concert. He was so enthused and excited that Lenny couldn't translate what he was saying fast enough - Hotei couldn't speak much English, but he said that he would love me to record something with him, when it was appropriate. I didn't think anything of it at the time, but I did like him and I was so grateful for his comments about the concert.

I was still trying to promote the band as much as I could and I was fortunate enough to obtain some good radio interviews. One of the best was on 14th August 1993 on the GLR Radio London *Liz Kershaw Show*, where I did a substantial interview and live acoustic versions of 'Children Of The Revolution', and 'Spaceball Ricochet'. I was very happy when I was asked back, but this time with the band, on Friday 3rd September, to perform another live session, which included 'I Love To Boogie', 'Get It On', and 'Electric Boogie'.

Later that day I was invited to the opening of a Marc Bolan Exhibition in Hackney, in London's East End. Caron and I were asked if we would contribute. We lent them the famous blue tapestry-lapelled jacket and Marc's blue lame dungarees with 'T.Rex' in sequins on the bib. Harry Feld, Marc's brother, supplied the brown leather top hat that Marc had worn in the film *Born To Boogie*. I was asked to wear the hat while standing next to both Harry and the Mayor of Hackney for a photo session, of which many of the shots later appeared in local North London newspapers.

A few weeks later I did yet another interview for GLR Radio but this time on the *James Whale Show*. Again I was able to have substantial airtime for an interview and perform live acoustic versions of 'Cadilac' and 'Telegram Sam'. We also managed to get on the Channel Four arts programme *Naked City* on Friday 20th August where they showed a live clip of the band in concert and a brief interview with me. There was a growing interest in what T.Rextasy had to offer. I was even asked to appear as a special guest in the audience of *Hot Stuff*, the West End seventies music show. I mixed and chatted with Barry Blue, Nina Myskow, Sonia, Alvin Stardust, and Linda Lewis. Sky News also did a short interview with me, which was broadcast later that evening on Wednesday 18th August 1993.

I was always interested in the more unusual bookings and two of them happened towards the end of the year. The first one was an open-air concert in October where we supported the soul singer Ruby Turner who headlined the event in the grounds of Hackney Marshes. The day was actually to promote the demolition of two eyesore tower blocks! Both T.Rextasy and Ruby played for about an hour each before the real 'headliner', the blowing up of the tower blocks took place. As the towers came down, the council hadn't had the forethought as to the amount of debris that the collapse would generate, so as the grime, dirt and dust hurtled towards everyone, hundreds of people started to run and scatter from the huge clouds of smoke that hung in the sky and began to penetrate into their throats and eyes. Mercifully, no one was hurt or scarred by the event, at least as far as I know!

Just over two weeks later, we were asked to perform a selection of songs for *Nintendo*, a company known worldwide for making computer games. This was an 'invite only' for the company, so we were surprised to see members of The Cult, Aztec Camera, and some of the cast of the BBC soap opera *Eastenders* in the audience. The drink flowed freely and so did the caviar, which we all tucked into without having to be asked twice. I had the notion that it was all starting to happen for us and one could feel the excitement in the air. It was hard to believe that my dream was becoming a reality and that this was just the beginning.

The earliest and short lived version of T.Rextasy.
Left to right: Tim (bass), me (lead guitar/lead vocals),
Nigel (drums), Mike (rhythm guitar). Vince (keyboards)
out of shot. This was my very first gig under the guise
of T.Rextasy - The Dove, Hackney, London - 18th
September 1992.

An early photo
session with
snake topped
cane in hand -
1993.

T.REXTASY - the one and only true
tribute band to the 1970's ultimate superstar
Marc Bolan - will be launched on Friday 18
September at 'THE DOVE', HACKNEY, EAST LONDON
(tel 071-275-7617 for further details).

Vocalist, Danielz, promises not only to be
playing some of the expected hits but also
a few of the many gems hidden away on T.Rex
albums and 'B' sides such as 'Raw Ramp', 'Baby
Strange', 'Till Dawn' and 'Jupiter Liar'. Baby
Don't miss out on the fun of this unique experience. 'T.REXTASY' - "Electric boogie, boogie
on...!!".

* THE DOVE, BROADWAY MARKET (OFF MARE ST),
HACKNEY E8 *

Rare A5 flyer for the debut
T.Rextasy gig at The Dove - September 1992.

A shot from an early gig at The Swan in
Fulham, London - 1992/3.

Left: My first ever live TV appearance as
T.Rextasy. We are playing the track 'Hot
Love' live in the *This Morning* ITV
Liverpool studios, which was broadcast the
following day. We used a stand-in bass
player called 'Boo' as our bass player had
gone on holiday! - 1993.

Right: Live at the legendary
Marquee Club in London.
Circa 1993.

Poster of T.Rextasy's first gig with
some of Bolan's contemporaries. The
line-up included Brian Connolly's
Sweet, and Les Gray's Mud.

One of the first of our many trips to Germany. We would later only travel to Europe by
air, but at this early stage we were not in a position to do so.
Left to right: Gavin Ingels (roadie/driver), Neil Cross, Judi Lidstone (friend), Ann Silk
(our drummer's wife), Graham Willans (roadie), Caron and I - 1993.

With Roy Wood (Wizzard) at the *Lark In The Park* festival in Hackney, London.

Left: Checking out my record collection at home in Holloway, London - 1990s

Below: In between Harry Feld (Marc's brother on the left) and the Mayor of Hackney (right) for a photo session promoting a Marc Bolan exhibition called *20th Century Boy*. I am wearing Marc's famous leather *Alice In Wonderland* hat - he had worn the hat for the cover sleeve of 'The Slider', and in the Mad-Hatter's Tea Party sequence in the feature film *Born To Boogie*.

4

On The Road To Wembley

It didn't take long before more agents and promoters began checking us out. It was while playing in the Sir George Robey pub, opposite the Rainbow Theatre in London, that on recommendation from a couple of Gary Glitter fans, Claire and Siobhan, Gary and his manager Jeff Hanlon had come along to see the band, in the expectation of a support slot to his mammoth Christmas arena concerts in December. I was tipped off that Gary might well be attending, so when I walked into the venue, I pretended not to notice him drinking at the bar. I walked straight past them and into the dressing room to get ready. We kicked into the set as usual and tried not to make eye contact with either of the Glitter guys, and just concentrated on the job in hand. After only a few songs, Gary and his manager left. But not before telling our roadie that we had clinched the tour support if we could sort out a reasonable deal, and for me to ring his manager to discuss everything and to sort out contracts.

Obtaining this deal was a major achievement. It meant going from playing pubs to playing 10 - 12,000 seated arenas in one swoop, and most importantly getting the name of T.Rextasy to thousands of people. We ended up playing in nearly every major arena in Britain, from Cardiff to Exeter, Aberdeen to Glasgow, Birmingham to London and more. But there was one venue that meant so much to me, and that was Wembley Arena. This was the most amazing venue and an ambition that I never thought I would achieve.

By the time we had reached Wembley after playing various monster venues on the tour, we had gained in confidence and had actually stormed every show. Although not discarding any of the other impressive concerts, Wembley Arena was the one that I really wanted to work more than any other. I walked into the auditorium while it was still vacant and the ghostly emptiness sent a shiver through me. While walking backstage I was greeted by an old security guard who showed me to my dressing room. He then went on to direct me as to where Marc Bolan had made one of the rooms his own when T.Rex played there in 1972 for the filming of *Born To Boogie* and their two sell-out concerts that had been incorporated in that one day. The old security guy who was working there back then saw and remembered all the commotion and hysteria that occurred. He told me that it was absolutely chaotic and total madness from start to finish and that he could hardly hear the band because of the constant screaming and shouting from the fans - he had never experienced anything like it before or since.

Before the tour began, I did various television interviews for shows such as *Good Morning With Anne And Nick* on BBC1, and others on MTV/VH1, mostly through November, all to help promote the dates. They were all great to do except that having to get up at the crack of dawn was dreadfully boring and tedious and not rock 'n' roll at all! Prior to one interview, Gary Glitter and I stayed at The Swallow Hotel in Birmingham. I remember that we were there early enough to have a meal, but as no one was that hungry, we just sat around chatting. Gary ordered some ice cream and strawberries, so we all decided to have some too. In the whole restaurant there was only Gary, myself, Jeff Hanlon, and Gary's make-up artist, who also looked after his wig as if it was a precious stone. It was the first time that I had seen him without his obligatory wig and he seemed very relaxed with just having a cap on his head instead of having to show off his usual persona of Gary Glitter - it was quite nice to see and speak to him as just plain old Paul Gadd, his real name of course.

A few months prior to the tour, I was lucky enough to be approached by Clive Jackson (the 'Doctor' from Doctor & The Medics fame) who owned the record label and company *Madman Records*. As far as I was concerned, who would want to sign up a tribute band and what would be the point? Clive's company did however want to record T.Rextasy and offered us a two-album and single deal. Little did I know at the time that other recording contracts, not only with *Madman Records*, but with other labels too, were just around the corner.

My previous experience with Tarazara had led me to jump at the opportunity to accept the offer and so we began recording our first single only a few weeks after I signed on the dotted line. Weird as it may seem for a tribute band, we actually recorded a self-composed song, 'Baby Factory'. I gave the band the recording that I had done a few years earlier with Blackfoot Sue and we just copied that version with a few added up-dates. *Madman* loved it so much and decided to use the song as the lead track, so we recorded a version of the Bolan track 'Planet Queen' (originally from 'Electric Warrior') as the B-side, or second track, depending on what listening format was being prepared.

On 16th December, in the middle of all the Glitter mayhem, both Neil and I were invited onto the *Johnnie Walker Show* for an interview about the tour. We talked about all things Bolan, and what T.Rextasy hoped to achieve. We had also taken our acoustic guitars along, so we played an impromptu acoustic version of 'Life's A Gas' before rushing off to Wembley Arena for our show that evening while Johnnie played out with our new self-penned single 'Baby Factory' that *Madman Records* had just released as a 7" vinyl limited edition with a replica T.Rex blue and red sleeve design and label to match.

Our appearance at Wembley was of course nothing like the madness the old security guy was talking about. However, we played on two sell out nights on Wednesday 15th and Thursday 16th December. To hear an audience of approximately 10,000 people all talking and shouting and screaming simultaneously while we were waiting behind the vast black curtain tabs to withdraw is a strange and surreal experience. One cannot hear a word from anyone in the audience, but can feel a massive presence of sound. It is like nothing else. It is very hard to explain the experience but it is one of exuberance, excitement, and adrenalin-fuelled emotion that I have never experienced since.

Our drum kit was placed in the middle of Glitter's two kits. Paul Thomas had made two backdrops out of two single white bedroom sheets, which hung either side of the stage; one had the face of Marc, and the other had our T.Rextasy logo. As our intro music of 'Theme For A Dragon' played, the curtains opened up to reveal the giant auditorium and the very loud and appreciative audience as we blasted into '20th Century Boy'. It was amazing to think that songs such as 'Telegram Sam', 'Get It On', 'Jeepster', and 'Hot Love' hadn't been played in this venue since that crazy day in 1972. Our thirty-minute spot appeared to end as soon as it began, but it was fantastic to hear thousands of music fans singing the choruses of 'Hot Love' with us.

After the second night I was told that Marc Bolan's wife June had been in attendance. She was a good friend of Jeff Hanlon who had invited her to the show. While I was sat in the VIP seats with Caron ready to watch Gary's performance, I was told that June was backstage and would like to have a chat. We both got up from our seats and made our way to the backstage bar. The first thing she said as we approached was "when I saw you on stage I thought I was going to have a heart attack. You reminded me so much of Marc. It was just an uncanny experience!" We sat around a table for a good while, just Caron, June, and myself. We talked about Marc a lot before Caron commented to June that she was surprised that she was still wearing the wedding ring that Marc had given to her. June took the ring off from her finger and showed it to us and talked about the good times she'd had with Marc. Before leaving she said to me and I do quote, "if there is anyone who I'd like to see step into Marc's shoes, I'd like it to be you." It is something that I have never forgotten. For a while afterwards, I used the 'heart attack' quote in our biography, but I decided to withdraw it when June actually died from a heart attack under a year later.

I had first met June at a Marc Bolan Convention in Doncaster in December 1991. She had been invited as a special guest by John Bramley who was then running the Marc Bolan Fan Club. He called Caron and I into a private room, where he introduced us to June. The three of us spent some time chatting about Marc and what we were all getting up to in the present day. Later, when we got up to leave, June looked down at my over-the-top cowboy boots (bright red and white leather, with side flaps and boot straps) and said, "My God, Marc would never have worn those!"

There were a few more incidents on the tour that were memorable. The first was our show on Tuesday 7th December. Ten minutes before show time the tour manager walked into our dressing room at The Westpoint in Exeter to tell me that the show will have to be cancelled, as Gary had just been taken ill! He said that if we wanted to, we could still play our set but he would have to announce first that Gary wouldn't be performing! Typical of me, I took the masochistic route and said that we would still perform.

From backstage we heard boos and chants of disapproval and disappointment as Jeff made his announcement, but I thought what the hell! We took to the stage with confidence and ended up playing a blistering set, which got the crowd behind us from start to finish. We played to the 4,500 capacity crowd for nearly an hour, which was double the amount of time we were booked to play for! I also recall a surreal moment when we played the Whitley Bay Ice Rink on Saturday 18th December. It was a freezing venue and we couldn't wait to go on stage to get warmed up. I always used to begin each concert with my back facing the audience in those days. As I turned around, a girl in the front row suddenly collapsed and fainted. I saw the *Red Cross* arrive and carry her away. After our performance and as I was walking from the stage, a first aider from the *Red Cross* came up to me and said that the girl had fainted because when I turned to face the audience I had reminded her so much of Marc!

One of the last radio interviews I did that year was on BBC Radio Scotland on 23rd December, where I had a chat to the DJ before playing live acoustic versions of 'Girl', and 'Planet Queen'. This was a period before 'unplugged' became fashionable. Many DJs at the time were asking me to come in and play a song or two on acoustic guitar as if it was something out of the ordinary. Just a year or so later of course, everyone was doing it, so it became quite commonplace. People forget that Marc used to do acoustic ditties just about everywhere he could, which proved yet again that he was way ahead of the game!

I did enjoy these very last dates on the tour, including those that took place in Glasgow's impressive SECC auditorium. We did three consecutive nights there but it didn't help matters when on the first night I greeted the audience with "Hello Aberdeen", just realising that that was the previous evening! It was the first time I had heard so many boos aired in my direction! Needless to say, I never made that mistake again. The last night in Glasgow was really exciting when Gary asked me up on stage to sing the second verse and choruses of his hit song 'I Love You Love'. Afterwards, Gary called me into his dressing room and as we were chatting about the shows he started singing "The things they said about the two of us were lies" (lines from 'I Love You Love') in a Marc-vibrato-type voice and said he had really liked the way I sang it.

Playing at these venues felt different to playing today's festivals or 'one-dayers', where four or five bands or more are on the bill and where people come along with their picnics or just for the day out not even concerned about who is playing. I can't put my finger on it, but I just feel that those venues did bring along a lot more people that were interested in music, rather than just 'going out for the day'. In the years to come I became saddened by the way stadium gigs and festivals became more of an outing and a day for laying out a rug for a picnic while the bands played and children ran around laughing and eating. I long for the time when real rock fans would congregate and totally appreciate the bands on the bill. Where the most they would bring along would be a large *Party Four* to down with their mates, or an old LP stuck under their arm in the hope of getting it signed by their favourite band or singer. I guess times change, but I know which I would prefer.

I was very grateful to Gary and Jeff for choosing T.Rextasy as their opening act, especially as they had always used well-known original acts in previous years. The tour gave the name T.Rextasy some kudos and we received some good reviews from the music press and media. Even the hard rock magazine *Kerrang!* gave T.Rextasy an excellent few paragraphs closing with "Probably the closest you could come to experiencing T.Rex." All in all we totalled that in December alone we had played to over 300,000 people in the UK. It was a great way to end the year.

We started off 1994 well, with a long interview on Radio West Midlands, which took place on 12th January and was broadcast live. The interviewer, Jennie Wilkes, talked at length with us all about the previous Christmas tour, and what we were likely to do in the forthcoming year. Since I had my acoustic guitar with me I strummed a live version of 'Girl' (from 'Electric Warrior') before the show played out with our forthcoming 'Baby Factory' single. I was also called in to do interviews on GLR Radio on 27th January and then a few weeks later on Radio GMR Manchester on 16th February, where I sang an acoustic version of the Bolan song 'Lofty Skies' (from 'A Beard Of Stars').

Between 17th January and 7th March 1994, *Madman* not only released 'Baby Factory' as a CD single, but also on 12" vinyl with an additional live version of '20th Century Boy'. We also had a party launch for the single at *Gossips* club in London where invited fans and renowned DJ Anne Nightingale came along to hear the single and to watch the band play a short set.

In just under two years, the tribute scene was starting to grow in popularity. The *News Of The World* got in on the act by including an article in its magazine supplement on 7th February 1994 about some of the most popular tribute bands on the scene. Although they printed a good photo and some complimentary comments they didn't really have much of a clue when it came to reviewing bands. The reporter actually placed T.Rextasy and The

Counterfeit Stones (a great Rolling Stones tribute band) alongside a Carpenters tribute and some guy wearing glasses trying to pass off as Buddy Holly!

The band hadn't been together for two years yet, but I was determined not to let the grass grow. We had been offered our first major theatre tour, which was a great opportunity to play around the UK in quality venues. Glasgow Pavilion for example, was exceptional, attracting a wild crowd of appreciative fans and to this day it has remained a stronghold for us. This period also saw us playing many shows at the prestigious Marquee Club in London (when it was located in Charing Cross Road after transferring from Wardour Street) before it closed down and relocated to North London a few years later. On one of our theatre dates, at the Worthing Pavilion, ex-T.Rex guitarist Miller Anderson came along to check us out and went away commenting that it was a "ghostly experience" and in his opinion, "no one would be able to take Marc off as well as Danielz." I have always kept that quote with me as I have a great respect for Miller as not only an ex-member of T.Rex, but an exceptional and talented guitar player in his own right.

Even though the scene was on the up, it was still an up hill struggle to obtain credibility. Many tribute bands were still seen as a kind of novelty value, an association of which I hated and strove to ignore and steer clear from. However, sometimes things worked out to my own personal benefit. Such as on 11th March 1994 when *Rock Circus*, the *Madame Tussauds* of the rock music world in Piccadilly, London, opened up one morning especially for me. Just so I could be interviewed by ITV for a forthcoming concert. I sat next to the waxwork model of Marc Bolan and sang an acoustic version of 'Get It On'. Unfortunately, a few days later catastrophe struck as our bass player's house caught fire and destroyed two rooms in his home. We had to cancel our planned Basildon show. Due to the fire, Paul lost many of his precious albums but he was quite touched when fans gathered round and sent him replacement T.Rex records to help build up his collection again.

Meanwhile, our drummer Nigel, had known and kept in touch with various associates of Joe Meek and in doing so, we were both invited by Screaming Lord Sutch to attend a special concert celebrating the life of the producer. The concert was held in a small pub called The Holloway, in Holloway, North London and was attended by guys and girls who were around at the time of Joe's success. Lord Sutch played a great live mad and bad rock 'n' roll set before spending a little time with us chatting about his days in the sixties and how it had all changed into the corporate jungle it now was. We didn't spend any time talking about his MP persona in the *Monster Raving Loony Party*. Sadly, only a few years later, David 'Screaming Lord' Sutch would take his own life, partly due to his serious bouts of depression.

Seeing how well we were doing as a gigging band gave two ex-members of the original T.Rex, Miller Anderson (rhythm guitarist 1976 - 1977) and Dino Dines (keyboard player 1974 - 1977) the impetus to form a band under the name of Ex-T.Rex. They tried to pull together a tour and auditioned for a frontman. They initially asked me if I would be interested, but I said that T.Rextasy was my baby and I preferred to carry on building up the reputation that we were slowly receiving. They tried out two guys for a time; *Stars In Their Eyes* contestant and Marc fan, Paul Feldon, and Darryl Reed, an actor and writer. For various reasons, neither worked out for them, and to make matters worse, the dates they had planned were not selling well enough so most were pulled.

Unexpectedly, I received a call from Dino asking me if would like to have a jam with them in a studio, no ulterior motive, just for pleasure. I wasn't quite that naïve, but I thought it would be fun all the same and a studio was arranged. I arrived with Caron and we sat and watched while the band played versions of T.Rex classics with Miller taking the lead vocals. Miller then asked if I would like to come up and play. I wasn't going to say no, so I slung a guitar around my shoulder and we played through various songs, such as 'Dandy In The Underworld', 'Get It On', 'Hot Love', and 'Jeepster'.

The band was a talented group of musicians that also included John Bentley, the original bass player from Squeeze. Although the band was obviously capable, they didn't have that special feel that was necessary to capture the T.Rex or Bolan spirit. It felt slightly uncomfortable playing the songs so tight without that T.Rex looseness. However, it was still great fun. Afterwards Miller asked again if I would be interested in joining but received the same reply as before. He then asked if I would be interested in standing in as frontman for the duration of the shows they were committed to, if there were windows in my schedule that didn't clash with any T.Rextasy dates. I thought about it for a few minutes and then agreed that it would be a cool and enjoyable thing to do.

One of the shows was at The Cliff's Pavilion, Southend on 31st March

1994. It was quite daunting playing with a group of musicians that I had never played with in concert before. However, I tried my very best to stay calm. Miller and Dino made me feel very at home and as we hit the stage with the 1977 version of 'Jeepster' everything fell into place. The crowd were wild, as they hadn't seen Dino and Miller perform together since the 'Dandy' tour in 1977. I was happy to take a backseat on this occasion even though I was still playing lead guitar and taking on the lead vocals. It was great playing tracks like 'Groove A Little', and 'Laser Love' with Miller on slide guitar, and 'Zip Gun Boogie' with Dino's keyboard sound. Although I didn't quite hit it off with the drummer, I found the bassist, John Bentley, very approachable and really into the music. Afterwards, we sat around talking for a while before shaking hands and wishing each other well.

A few months later in October, I received a follow-up call from Dino asking if I would do another one-off show in Preston, with him, Miller, John Bentley and their drummer. I said I would do it, but as I wasn't comfortable with the drummer they were using, we agreed that Nigel would step in for the show. The gig itself was quite a high class bistro, but it was such a pleasure playing with Miller and Dino again that I just had a world of fun that night. I have since kept in touch with Miller and his wife Fiona and although we are not what one might call the best of friends, we do speak on the phone now and then and exchange Christmas cards every year!

I was not in the habit of performing at too many benefit shows, but one that appealed was at Chats Palace in London on 30th April 1994. All profits were to go towards a statue of Marc Bolan to be erected in Hackney. The gig took place, but the statue was never commissioned. However, Dino Dines had agreed to play a few numbers with us, which made the evening quite exciting. Dino was pretty nervous, but nevertheless, at rehearsals he really got into it and played like the professional he was. He even got out one of his old hats that he used to wear, and threw himself into the Dino of old. Many fans have a soft spot for Dino as not only was he the third longest member of T.Rex, but he did always make a point of spending time talking to the fans after the shows. There was never any 'Dino-the-star' - he was always Peter 'Dino-the-friendly-musician' Dines, and he remained like that through all the years I knew him.

Mike Southon was a wealthy businessman and entrepreneur who had always wanted to be a rock star, and in his alter ego Mike Fab-Gere he could become just that. Mike made a mint when he sold his own business for a massive profit and set his sights on the world of pop music. He surrounded himself with good musicians and set about conquering the world. Well, he never did manage that, but through the next few years, he did arrange some great shows in the UK in which he called *Freak Out!*, and named the band Mike Fab-Gere and The Permissive Society. He always wanted two or three of what he called, "the top tribute guys in the country". And in his opinion, they were mainly myself, John Mainwaring (singer with the brilliant David Bowie tribute band Jean Genie), and a guy called Patrick, who took the part of Freddie Mercury very well indeed. Of course, I never thought of myself as "taking anyone's part as such" I always performed as Danielz performing in the spirit of Marc Bolan, and not actually mimicking him. Thankfully it worked then as it has done throughout my career.

I did plenty of 'special guest' appearances with Mike's band singing and playing just two or three T.Rex numbers with the added encore with Mike, John Mainwaring and me singing the Rolling Stones' 'Brown Sugar'. It was a bonus getting paid the same fee, and sometimes collecting more than I would have if I had performed a whole concert with T.Rextasy! Money didn't seem to be a concern for Mike as he was now spending his hard-earned fortune from his old computer related business and utilising it in anyway he wanted to. Mike was one of the good guy's who just wanted to have fun and play the pop star when he felt like it, and he did it well with the confidence he was gifted with.

Mike did many shows for charity events too, so it was lovely to be involved in those gigs, knowing that the money was going to a good cause. Years later, he wrote a best selling book about how to be a successful entrepreneur and also ended up writing a column for *The Times*. He was and is one clever corporate guy!

What had been a great few months ended with a sad footnote, as I was told that June Bolan had recently died from a heart attack while on holiday in Turkey. A strange twist of fate would happen a few years later when I would purchase an extra large and rare Marc Bolan mirror from a house in Baldock, Hertfordshire. Only four of these had been specially made in the USA for T.Rex. Marc had them shipped back to the UK, out of which it was understood that he had kept two of them. After Marc's parents had passed away, his brother Harry gained possession of one of the mirrors that had hung on the wall in their Putney flat. June had taken the second one with her when she split up with Marc in 1974 - this is the one that we had just purchased all those years later, which now hangs on our wall. As for the remaining two mirrors, I understand that Marc had given one to Ringo Starr, and the other was accidentally smashed during transit.

At the beginning of September 1994 we played a few dates with Andy Scott's Sweet, while also being interviewed for a thirty minute Glam rock TV special on MTV/VH1. London ITV did yet another interview with me for the daily *London Tonight* programme. The interview was to commemorate Marc's 17th anniversary on 16th September.

As summer rolled by, a Dutch film company called *Zest Pictures* approached me with a view to document a kind of 'day-in-the-life' of me with T.Rextasy. I was flattered and we began filming in what was to become a film entitled *Whatever Happened To The Teenage Dream*. The director, Peter Van Houten, was an excitable and energetic guy, full of enthusiasm for his work. He was a fan of T.Rex and was fascinated with what I was undertaking with T.Rextasy.

Peter filmed Caron and I at home in Holloway, North London, as I got ready to set out for the latest T.Rextasy gig. He interviewed me in taxicabs, filmed the band at sound-checks and at the actual gig. He also did additional interviews with fans and friends. He interviewed 'The Doctor' from Dr & The Medics, as well as one slightly unflattering or double-edged interview, depending on how one listens to his comments, from journalist and writer Mark Paytress. Before filming had started, I was told that the film would be about the fans of Marc Bolan, but as it progressed, the film slowly morphed into a video documentation of T.Rextasy, but I wasn't going to complain about that! The film got its first airing back in Holland at one of the country's film festivals, and then later it was shown on Dutch television. It is a shame that it never got a screening in the UK, but it was great to have been involved in a project so professional in such an early stage of the band's life.

I'd always enjoyed playing acoustic guitar and it was one day while I was strumming away that I got the idea for playing a few acoustic shows. I decided that I would try and obtain a few bookings under the banner of 'T.Rextasy Unplugged'. This was just Nigel (on congas) and me, before John Skelton took over from him a few years later. The unplugged shows are great to do as they are so relaxed, just playing a batch of Bolan songs on acoustic guitar, without the mayhem of an electric band playing at rock level! Ironically, one of the earliest of these shows took place at The Empire

Theatre in Halstead, Essex on Sunday 30th October 1994. Halstead is a very small town with a total population of only around 12,000 people. Unbelievably, little did I know that within ten years I would actually move there to live in part of an old quaint Victorian building that was previously a school for wayward girls in the 1880s.

I was altogether quite shocked when I received a call out of the blue from Jeff Hanlon offering us another three dates on the up and coming Gary Glitter tour, which would include two at Wembley Arena, and one at Sheffield Arena. The disco band Village People were due to play on the whole tour, but for some reason they couldn't make all the dates. As we had gone down so well the year before, Jeff offered us the dates they couldn't do! How could I refuse? I arranged the deal with Jeff and looked forward to playing both of those venues again. I couldn't believe that I was going on that Wembley stage for a third time in my career!

We took the audience for all it was worth and rocked hard for the thirty minutes that was once again allocated to us. Only this time around we actually got to play an encore at all three shows and with me wearing a Santa Claus outfit. I was never quite sure how much Gary's band liked us. Gary definitely did and thought we were a great group and did Marc proud, just like he said at nearly every gig we did with him. Unfortunately there was a little tension in the camp with one of his drummers. Martin 'Animal' Clapson was great and we all got on fine, but Gary's other drummer Andy Ebsworth took a dislike to me and we just didn't hit it off.

I remember on one of the last dates that we did, Gary went crazy in his dressing room because his band had played a practical joke on us. In front of thousands of fans, while we were playing our final number, a couple of Glitter's band started spraying me with cans of coloured spray-string until I was covered in it. They then tied Neil's legs and arms up while he was doing his backing singing. One of them walked alongside the stage in front of both us and the audience, in a builder's hat carrying a long ladder! We all thought it was hilarious, but Gary didn't see the funny side of it. As we walked into our dressing room all we heard was him smashing up the partition wall and other items in his room and at the same time shouting abuse towards his band.

We saw Gary every day and he was always very approachable and friendly. It was only shortly before the shows that we would leave him alone. He used to do a daily routine by having someone shine a torch in his eyes and then running up and down backstage and shouting the words "Leader! Leader!" It was his way of psyching himself up before he performed. Gary was quite a heavyweight guy and so everyone used to move out of the way when he did his 'running at speed' routine to avoid a collision.

Of course, all this had to end. We did think that there was a possibility in the future that in years to come we might have been invited back again, but due to the dreadful series of events that followed, Mr Glitter's Wembley days would be well and truly over. It was sad to see Gary fall from grace after knowing him, but if he did what he was charged with then he does deserve the punishment he has received and shouldn't return with any glory whatsoever.* His music however, should remain, if possible, as a separate entity allowing everyone to judge the songs and recordings for what they are worth. It may have been Glitter who sang them, but we should also not forget the people behind the songs such as Mike Leander (producer and co-writer), and The Glitter Band, who should not be chastised because of one man's actions.

Through the nineties we were still playing at some of the larger Marc Bolan parties and conventions, mainly the fan club parties that were held in Doncaster, South Yorkshire, or the ones held in London by the wonderfully named Marc Bolan Liberation Front (MBLF), an organisation set up by Martin Barden and Ros Davies. They were both very well arranged affairs with decent PA systems for the band and exceptionally well attended. Too much of a good thing slowly began to thin out attendances as smaller Bolan parties began springing up all over the country which ended up scattering sections of fans into less significant numbers. We were fortunate though as our fan base was consistently growing and developing nicely.

Many of the parties nowadays seem to be slightly cliquey and attract many of the same crowd that attends them all. I decided towards the end of the nineties that we wouldn't play anymore Bolan parties or conventions unless I felt it was really special or important to do so. I felt that not only would I be preaching to the converted, but also the challenge would be minimal, and after all, it is the general public that needs to be sucked into the church of Bolan. And the only way to do that would be to concentrate on upping our anti and getting into the theatre market and more established

---

*In November 1997, Gary Glitter was arrested after pornographic images of children were discovered on the hard drive of his computer that he had left at a store for repair. In 1999 he was sentenced to four months' imprisonment and listed as a sex offender in the UK following conviction for downloading thousands of items of child pornography.

venues.

Just before the end of what was a most exciting and pleasing 1994, *Britannia Music* requested T.Rextasy to play alongside Marcella Detroit (vocalist for Eric Clapton and Shakespears Sister), Kenny Thomas, Gabrielle, DJ Bruno Brookes, and Paul Jones (Manfred Mann) at the *25th Britannia Music Awards* at Alexandra Palace in London. This was one of the few times in my life that I was allocated a chaperone or bodyguard who stuck by my side throughout the whole evening, even though it was a corporate event and everyone was well behaved.

We played a thirty minute set of hit singles, which got everyone up on their feet before Paul Jones took to the stage... whereby many of the people returned to their seats. Not because they were not interested in seeing him, but because he was obviously a little more laid back than we were. Paul got extremely annoyed by their reaction and literally stormed off the stage and didn't return. So that was the end of his performance! It was a nice surprise to see a photo of the band included in the *Britannia Music Awards* brochure a few months later in their edition dated 5th March 1995, especially as the brochure was circulated around the country inside all the national newspapers.

After the tour and many gigs later, it was good to have some time to begin recording and mixing tracks for our forthcoming CD album. We already had two songs in the can and indeed out in the racks with 'Baby Factory', and 'Planet Queen'. In addition to the two songs, we recorded another ten tracks in Fortress Studios in London over a two-week period. I ended up producing and mixing the album (with the help of Neil Cross coming in as Executive Producer) in only a day or two as funds were running low after spending hours trying to obtain various sounds and ambience at the recording and in the control room.

I have always felt that in some ways, it is easier to record original material because there is nothing to compare it to. When one has to try and re-create a performance or studio recordings, it becomes more of a challenge, as one has to search through dozens of effects and old style studio tricks to try to come up with an original feel of songs that were recorded on equipment used twenty years previously. Having said that, I don't think anyone has ever mastered or re-created the sound that was created on those old albums. Even now, they sound fantastic and I still think that Marc and Tony Visconti were one of the greatest of combinations in the studio.

Recording the album did give me the opportunity to include two of my own compositions, 'Baby Factory', and the atmospheric 'Village'. The lyrical gist behind 'Baby Factory' is pretty straightforward but I do remember how those memorable words and catchy melody came to me. It was way back in the eighties when I was on a London bus travelling from where I lived at the time, in Feltham, Middlesex to the West End. I had no pen and paper to write anything down so I had to remember the tune and chorus for the whole day. When I got home I quickly scribbled the words down before working on the verse and middle eight. I kept the song close to me until I had my first chance of recording it, the first time of course being with Blackfoot Sue in the early eighties, and now again in the nineties with T.Rextasy.

With 'Village' I had always wanted to write and record a non-commercial number and I felt that this was maybe the one chance I had to do just that. I wrote the song in a minor key and the lyrics reflected the mood of being lost and alone in a small and densely populated village, late at night with fog and other-worldly sounds surrounding one's psyche... anyway that's what I had in mind when I wrote it! The recording had the sound of a branch snapping halfway through. I had wanted to record a live affect, rather than just taking a sound bite from one of those BBC Sound Effects albums, so I brought in a few real branches and did a few snaps into the microphone. I very nearly got the recording I wanted, and very nearly captured the late night, eerie effect, but I was happy with it overall. In my opinion, the best ever eerie effect on an album is the opening first minute or so on the first Black Sabbath album - if you've never heard it, then try and take a listen - fantastic.

It was decided that we would not include 'Planet Queen', leaving that as a UK only B-side. We had Lisa in to do some backing vocals, but she had decided to leave the band a little before the album's release, and although she parted on amicable terms we lost touch and have never spoken since.

In amongst the songs recorded was a track entitled '20th Century Baby', a song that Marc Bolan only ever got so far as to record as a demo with Dino Dines. I thought it would be interesting to make this track into a fully blown T.Rextasy song. I gave Dino a call and he kindly came down and played a lovely solo complimenting the track perfectly. He also stayed for the remainder of the recording session to put down keyboards on our version of the Bolan's 'Laser Love'. Dino and I stayed in touch off and on for the next few years until he actually joined T.Rextasy as a member of the band a few years later.

On the same lines as '20th Century Baby', there was another track that Marc had only recorded as a demo. It was 'Over The Flats', (lyrically brilliant as it was an insight into Marc's younger days) which we recorded with the full electric treatment. I gave it a kind of 'Dreamy Lady' feel and I was, in the end, pretty happy with the way it turned out.

I called the album 'Trip And Glide In The Ballrooms Of T.Rextasy' - It was a play on the lyrics from the song 'Ballrooms Of Mars' from 'The Slider' album. To tie in with the CD, Caron took some photos of me wearing a top hat for the cover sleeve, which *Madman Records* loved. My idea for the back cover was a pastiche of the 'Tanx' album, which included all mini photos of the band, and instead of pictures of tanks, we used electronic pictures of ballrooms instead, which was a little tongue in cheek, but worked well with the concept.

In the following months I went out looking to obtain interviews or publicity for the band and in doing so managed to get in touch with many local papers and radio stations willing to talk. This included *The News Shopper* in Kent, *The Commuter*, and a wealth of others including a very neat appearance on BBC Radio Wiltshire on 18th January 1995 where I did an acoustic version of 'Hot Love' with Martin Rushent in attendance - it was exciting as he was the original engineer on 'Electric Warrior'. After the performance, Martin commented on air, "That sounds as authentic as you're gonna get!"

Gary Glitter & T.Rextasy Wembley Arena concert banners - 1993.
Neil is at the bottom of the photo on the left with outstretched arms.

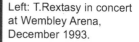

Left: T.Rextasy in concert at Wembley Arena, December 1993.

Below: Neil Cross and I after one of the Glitter dates.

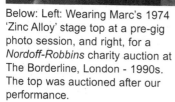

Below: Left: Wearing Marc's 1974 'Zinc Alloy' stage top at a pre-gig photo session, and right, for a *Nordoff-Robbins* charity auction at The Borderline, London - 1990s. The top was auctioned after our performance.

Below: Promotional photo I had taken for Ex-T.Rex. From left to right: Miller Anderson and Dino Dines.

Right: Performing with striped trousers under the name of Ex-T.Rex with Miller Anderson on guitar & Dino Dines on keyboards - 1994.

AOMITS 2.

Above left: 7" vinyl release of the T.Rextasy single 'Baby Factory' on *Madman Records* in replica T.Rex company sleeve. This was also released on limited edition 12" vinyl.

Above right: Record company party invitation for T.Rextasy's single 'Baby Factory' - January 1994.

Left: T.Rextasy promo photo. From left to right: Nigel Silk, Paul Rogers, Neil Cross, Lisa DaVinci, and me in the boa! - circa 1994.

BABY FACTORY

intro : Drums

G · Em · G · Em

① I want to be in your baby factory
I want to play in your baby factory

chorus : Do you want it
Do you need it
Do you feel it
Do you mean it
yea yea, yea yea

② repeat verse / chorus

mid 8 : I'll be your valentino on a cosmic trip
I'll be your soul survivor watch my honey drip
A fantasy child is a reality scene
The art of seduction a young man's dream

③ Repeat verse / chorus
(instrumental) : G · Em ·
G · Em

Repeat chorus

(outro) I want to be in your baby factory

(G · Em · G · Em)
(Em / Em · G ·)

Above left: My original handwritten lyrics for 'Baby Factory.'

Above: Promo photos - mid nineties. Bottom one with Neil. *(Colm Jackson)*

Left: 'Baby Factory' CD single released by *Madman Records* - 1994.

Left: Uncut sleeve for the 'Trip And Glide In The Ballrooms Of T.Rextasy' CD album on *Madman Records* (UK) & *Quattro Records* (Japan) -1995

58

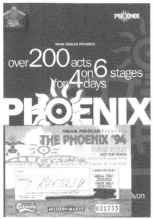

Left to right: Brochure & backstage pass for the Phoenix Festival, Stratford-upon-Avon - July 1994; *Freak Out* flyer - One of my many special guest appearances with entrepreneur Mike Fab-Gere for his seventies-based rock music show. I can be seen on the far left and Media press cutting for *Freak Out*. From left to right: Me, Mike Fab-Gere, and John Mainwaring (from the Bowie tribute band Jean Genie) - 1994.

Above: Ticket for a concert at Chats Palace in London featuring Dino Dines - 1994.

Left: With Screaming Lord Sutch at a Joe Meek celebration party in the nineties.

5

Europe To The Far East

Famous London venue The Camden Palace, presently called Koko, was due for a re-launch after various set backs and closures over the previous few years. On 1st February 1995 I was asked to attend as special guest alongside ex-Wings and ex-Moody Blues star, Denny Laine. I ended up for most of the evening chatting to him in a little cut-off booth we were given as VIP's for the night. We found that we both had something in common in that we knew Miller Anderson. It turned out that Denny was an old friend of Miller's from years back. As the evening went on Denny drank more and more until I couldn't understand what he was saying. Boy could this guy drink! Although we were treated as guests and given complimentary food and drink, we didn't really have anything to do and neither were we at any time asked to do anything. In the end we both spent our time hanging around, eating, drinking, talking, and then said goodbye to everyone and left! A strange night I guess, but we all left with very full stomachs.

With Lisa deciding to leave the band, I wasn't sure if I wanted a replacement backing singer. The problem was that for much of the gig, there wasn't that much that catered for a female voice. Especially as my favourite songs tended to be from the earlier T.Rex recordings that either had Marc and Tony Visconti singing backing vocals, or Howard Kaylan and Mark Volman (from The Turtles), with the exception of course of the girls on '20th Century Boy' and 'Solid Gold Easy Action'. In the end I thought I would give it one more shot so we recruited Michelle DePass. She had a great voice for a lead singer but not entirely suited as a backing vocalist. Nevertheless, we decided to keep her on the books for a while and in her short time with the band she did really well in her attempts to sing back up as opposed to scatting over my lead vocals.

Paul King (from the eighties band King) had become a high flyer and a much-respected VJ on VH1. At the beginning of March 1995 he phoned up and invited me for an interview and to play an acoustic number on air. I accepted and found myself being interviewed by one of VH1's regular VJ's on 27th March. A few days before the interview, I was sent the latest Duran Duran album 'Thank You', and asked if I would review it on air within the same session as the interview. The album was a selection of cover versions of mostly well-known songs, together with a few unlikely numbers such as 'Crystal Ship' (The Doors), and 'Success' (Iggy Pop), and of course the title track 'Thank You' (Led Zeppelin). I talked about and gave my opinion on each song, before moving on to chat about Marc Bolan and my ambitions with T.Rextasy. Directly after the interview, a pre-recorded acoustic session was shown of us in the studio playing 'Hot Love'. Alongside me on vocals and guitar, the session also included Neil (guitar and backing vocals), and Michelle (tambourine and backing vocals). The recording came across cool and easy. If I remember rightly we did a couple of takes, but of course they only transmitted the second recording and most likely erased the first take.

Most of our dates in April 1995 were taken up by playing in Germany, and mostly on the Eastern side. The shows were mainly with bands such as Les Gray's Mud, Slade, Bay City Rollers, Andy Scott's Sweet, or Suzi Quatro. It was strange at first to be playing alongside bands and artists that I had admired as a teenager, and now having to play the game and be as good as they were. Most bands are pretty easy to get on with, although some of them do tend to live in a seventies bubble and act like they are still at the top of the charts.

Mud was always a friendly bunch of guys and although Les Gray, the lead singer, was the only original member at the time, he remained down to earth and was always pleasant to me. It was a shame that drink got the better of him. Sometimes, such as one night after a show I was unlucky enough to have a hotel room next door to Les and his wife. They argued for ages about his drinking problem before 'smash', a glass shattered against the wall, and then another smash before all going quiet, and thankfully all were able to go to sleep. Sadly, Les lost his life in February 2004 while in Portugal, but I will always remember him as a nice and gentle guy.

Many people still remember Slade with Noddy Holder and Jim Lea and without them it has been a little bit of a struggle. When we first started gigging with them they were known as Slade II and were using a great singer and front man called Steve Warley. He didn't sound like Noddy at all, but made the songs his own and captured the hearts of many fans. After a few years, Noddy and Jim relented and agreed to them using the name Slade. Don Powell (the original drummer) and Dave Hill obviously have a bond between them although they don't let it show too often.

Right from the beginning Don was a welcoming guy, down to earth and all too ready to have a drink and chat. It took me a lot longer to get to know Dave Hill. He still to this day needs to be massaged into the roll of rock star image but he does play it well. I remember once in Germany he had a flight case that he used to stand on when playing guitar solos. When we took to the stage I stood on it and was later asked if I would "not stand on Dave's box", which I thought was a little laughable and unnecessary. This was all one-upmanship of course, and I learnt very quickly. Since then at all the shows we have played with Slade, I have asked the crew to move all the boxes out of my way so there is never a misunderstanding.

Dave and I get on pretty well now. I think in the beginning he thought we may have been a fly-by-night band, but since then he has given us respect and at times has even commented on the "excellent T.Rextasy" at various gigs that we have played with them. I suppose Dave comes from a time when one had to serve one's apprenticeship as he had done, playing the clubs all over the UK, and travelling up and down the motorway every week in their early days as Ambrose Slade. Because of that I respect both Dave and Don equally. A few years ago, I gave Dave a T.Rextasy t-shirt and he wore it too. I think that was his way of saying we were okay.

Across the water, thousands of miles away, the Japanese recording company *Quattro Records* had taken an interest after *Madman Records* had played them some of T.Rextasy's recordings. Before long, we were being offered a deal for our album to be released in Japan. T.Rextasy photos and articles began appearing in Japanese fashion magazines such as *Brutus*, *Spa, Popeye, Rockin' On, Parco, CDJ* and the HMV freebie magazines - all in the March to July issues in 1995. In spite of this, the Japanese company still wanted a bigger promotional tool to advertise the band. Between *Madman* and *Quattro*, money was advanced to produce a promotional video for the track 'Baby Factory'.

We congregated at a London video recording studio and spent the day lip-synching and miming to the track. For some of the recording, I actually wore Marc's blue lamé dungarees. I had a few props to use as well, such as a seventies peacock chair, and a full sized leopard made of china. I also used an old snake-headed walking stick that I had brought along with me. I loved making the video, and thankfully the companies that had paid for it were really pleased with the outcome. The video was shown in Japan many times on MTV and various music and television shows throughout the summer of 1995.

In the mid nineties television appearances were still reasonably easy to obtain as the age of *Pop Idol*, *X Factor*, *Britain's Got Talent*, and all the rest of those reality pop shows hadn't arrived en force. I was asked to film a series of Glam Rock TV ad trailers for Channel Four's up and coming *Glam Season* - I ended up recording around three or four short adverts which were broadcast numerous times during April and the first week in May. They had me dressed up in my stage gear posing around and self-consciously saying things like "be there with your corkscrew hair", and other short sound bites which they thought were "Marc Bolan-like." Channel Four also included me in its programme entitled *Glam Rock Top 10*. Broadcast on 8th May 1995, they talked to me and also ex-T.Rex members about Marc, before cleverly editing Marc saying "and now Bolan's tip for the top" and synching into a live clip of T.Rextasy! I was thrilled to find that we were the only tribute band included in the show amongst all the contemporary originals.

On 7th May 1995 I was flown to Japan for the very first time. I had no idea what to expect, and having to go on my own it was quite a daunting experience. I was met by Koichi Hanafusa, my Japanese interpreter and chaperone, plus a member of the *Quattro Recording Company*. The weather was absolutely stifling and quite unbearable. I had to keep my throat moist so that I could sing as well as project my voice for the many interviews I was flown out there to do. The Japanese people are quite remarkable and I fell in love with Japan from the first day. It is a fantastic part of the world with people to match. I love their professionalism in all things and their time keeping is impeccable. I was taken to a hotel and told that they would pick me up at a certain time every day. They were never late and somehow they would turn up at the very minute that they had told me to meet them. I am sure that they must have been hiding around the corner so as to be exactly on time, every day!

I was contracted to do so many interviews and solo acoustic and electric sessions that I have forgotten some of them. There are a few however that do stick in my mind, as they were either uniquely a little strange, or just good fun to do. One of which took place at a TV station inside a shopping mall on Thursday 11th May. The public sat gathered round before the programme went on air inside a selection of clothes shop, or some other kind of retailers. The show was called *Bubblegods*, which I thought was a brilliant title and something that Bolan would've picked up on. Just before my appearance, a couple of other English guys had just finished their interview. As they walked off stage, we said a mutual "hello" and went our separate ways. They were from a newish band called 'Radiohead' - I wonder whatever happened to them? The interviewer, Ken Kawashima, was a great guy and very interested in Marc Bolan as well as T.Rextasy.

I performed a live acoustic version of '20th Century Baby' directly before the interview. The talk went really well even though after every question and every answer he would interpret into Japanese for the audience. We actually got on so well that we later filmed a black & white television interview short that he called *5 Minutes With T.Rextasy*, which was transmitted on *Bubblegods* on 11th September 1995.

The promotional outing also included interviews and photo sessions with various music magazines such as *Guitar* and *Guitarist*. Afterwards, I was always taken to lunch and dinner. I had never eaten real Japanese food before, but it was also a weird experience for me to see *McDonald's* with adverts promoting 'Teriyaki Chicken Burgers' and such like. Japan was like another planet with a completely different way of life and culture and I should know as I lived and visited countries all over the world while I was growing up. I did like a lot of the food such as Shabu-shabu, which is a very thin red meat in which one cooks in a large communal pot for only a few seconds. It is supposedly called Shabu-shabu because it is similar to the sound it makes when it's cooking. I wouldn't eat it now though as I haven't eaten red meat for years. However, I wasn't over keen on some of the fish dishes on the menu as some of them were still alive and flicking their tails when served.

As the first promotional trip had gone so well, I was called back for a second time from 4th to 11th July as a run up for what was to be our forthcoming tour. My return trip was a little more enjoyable as I knew what to expect and to make the experience more relaxing I was booked into the same hotel as the previous visit.

A day or so after my arrival, I was asked to perform an acoustic concert in *Tower Records* in Tokyo. They had a small auditorium on the 8th floor of the building in which they held live gigs. I was given an acoustic guitar and told that a limited number of fans, of around 100 in all, were allowed tickets for the event. I didn't know what to expect, as I had never appeared in front of a proper Japanese audience before. I made sure I had lots of still water before I walked onto the stage, as the air was so dry. They start their concerts very early in the evening. So at 6pm on the 8th July 1995 I performed my first ever concert in Japan. I tried to talk slowly so that they could understand me better. When I asked they called out that they could understand me perfectly! I sang a selection of songs including 'Solid Gold Easy Action', '20th Century Baby', 'Metal Guru' and '20th Century Boy' amongst others - just me and an acoustic guitar. The fans sang along and applauded with great enthusiasm while they mostly all sat crossed legged on the floor, or on the seats provided.

After around fifteen minutes or so, a Japanese Glam Rock singer called Akima joined me. He is quite well known in Japan and very well known in the Japanese circle of Bolan fans for his previous band Marchosias Vamp. Tsuneo Akima was and still is an obsessive Marc Bolan fan. He is dare I say it, Japan's equivalent of more or less what I do, although he has made his name with original material and has hosted many special Bolan concerts through the years, playing a selection of T.Rex tracks with various special guests. They call this event 'Glam Rock Easter' as they have suggested the meaning comes from when Bolan is born again.

Akima brought along a conga player of exceptional standard and we played as a threesome for the next twenty minutes with Akima also playing acoustic guitar and singing alternate lines on the songs 'Spaceball Ricochet', 'Children Of The Revolution', 'Hot Love' and a few others. After the concert I remained inside the building for around an hour or so chatting and getting myself together. I was then introduced to three girls from a Japanese management company who presented me with an elaborate bag that had printed pictures of Marc Bolan and me. I looked into the bag and took out the most amazing leather guitar strap, which had photos of every T.Rex album imprinted on it. What a wonderful gift.

A Japanese fan who called himself 'Jerry' also gave me a beautiful black and brown one-piece striped satin jumpsuit, which had originated from the collectable *Mr Freedom* shop in the 1970s. I tried it on and it fitted perfectly. On this trip I was given many presents, such as a talking Tyrannosaurus alarm clock, models of a Japanese super hero called *Zinc Alloy*, from which I was told Marc had got his inspiration for his concept 'Zinc Alloy and the Hidden Riders of Tomorrow', and a stash of Japanese lucky charms. When I was finally shown from the *Tower Records* building, I was stunned to see so many fans patiently waiting in the rain just to obtain an autograph or a photo.

The next day I was taken to one of the MTV stations on the outskirts of Tokyo. The VJ came across as a Japanese/American and spoke both perfect Japanese and English with an American accent. I did a reasonably long interview while holding an acoustic guitar, which was really just a prop. Before the interview ended he asked if I could sing a song live on air. I didn't have a song prepared, so I asked him if he had a song in mind. In the advert break he asked if I could sing 'Solid Gold Easy Action'. It wasn't a song I had played acoustically very often, but as I didn't want to say 'no', I obliged. On hearing it back I was pleased to hear how good it sounded, and since then, T.Rextasy have played this song acoustically many times.

Along with the MTV appearances I was called on to do a few television interviews on programmes for Nack TV, TV Tonight, and NHK TV. I also did interviews and photo sessions for more of the music and fashion glossy magazines such as Cutie and TJ. I counted nineteen in all, but there are probably some that I have forgotten about now and have never seen. The *Quattro Record Company* arranged for me to play and promote in some weird and unusual settings around Tokyo, Shibuya, and Ikebukuro where I was given an electric guitar, an amplifier and microphone and asked to do a fifteen minute set at each location. This was all to be performed outside shop fronts, stores and music shops. It was a little surreal and it took a while to get used to it all, but I had to knuckle down and just get on with it. A crowd gathered each time I performed, but I suppose they would out of curiosity, as it must have seemed strange to see some European guy with long curly hair, make up, wearing satin trousers and bat-wing jacket playing and singing outside their favourite shop!

I was glad to see that our CD album was being sold in the shops. The promotion in *Tower Records* was superb and helped to sell 3,000 units within the first two weeks of its release. As I walked into the giant superstore I came face to face with an almost life-sized cut out of me advertising the album. We were also on the play-loop, so every so often I would hear one of our recorded tracks over the speakers.

The album sleeve was a little more elaborate than the UK version. It came with a thick booklet of lyrics and photos. The Japanese had also asked for two bonus songs for inclusion, so it was decided to include the B-side 'Planet Queen' and an acoustic version of 'Girl' (that I had originally recorded for a live UK radio show). An inspired move saw *Quattro* also release 500 copies of a special 3" CD sampler single of '20th Century Baby' c/w 'Baby Factory' with a black and white card cover advertising the release of the album on 21st June 1995. This promo has since become a quite sought after collector's item.

Before leaving Japan, I was invited to the home of the Japanese superstar Tomoyasu Hotei. Due to the extreme high cost of accommodation in Tokyo, very few people actually own houses in the city. Hotei didn't have a house he had something like a three-storey mansion. Walking into his hallway I was greeted with two magnificent and genuine statues of horses sculpted by my favourite artist Salvador Dali. Small spotlights with alternating colours shone down from above onto the horses, giving a most spectacular effect. Hotei had a beautiful guitar room in his shag-piled carpeted basement where he had a collection of instruments behind glass. The room was atmospheric and plush and kitted out with top notch studio equipment. His living room was white, with large white sofas, white carpet, the works, with an absolute top of the range hi-fi system, which filled the room with sound. He had a lovely roof top garden, which looked over Tokyo's impressive skyline. I spent a couple of hours with Hotei and even though he is a superstar in Japan, he still retains that humble and yet proud side that so many Japanese people possess.

It had been a most unusually fantastic experience and although it was over for the time being, I knew that when I returned with the band for our tour in September, it was going to be magnificent!

Shortly before my trip to Japan, Miller Anderson and Dino Dines had been in touch again to ask if I would front another show that they had planned and were still contracted to do. As we were shortly touring Japan, I didn't have any T.Rextasy gigs booked within that period, so I agreed. The show took place at The Embassy in Selsey on Saturday 15th July. It was great to play with both Miller and Dino again, but I felt that they both knew that they couldn't really take the band any further and they finally decided to call it a day and 'Ex-T.Rex' folded for good.

Being in T.Rextasy did have a few other perks such as getting on guest lists to see other bands. During a weekend summer break Caron and I were staying at a *Holiday Inn* in Birmingham. While going down in the lift, it stopped on a floor below and who should walk in but Geoff Beadman, a PA engineer that I had used on various occasions, along with the ex-Rainbow drummer Cozy Powell! He said that we should come along to the local *Ronnie Scott's* as Cozy was doing a gig there that night with the ex-Fleetwood Mac guitarist Peter Green. I had always loved Peter's guitar playing and also Cozy Powell had always been one of the great drummers in rock 'n' roll, so how could we refuse?

Our names were put on the door and we attended the show later that night. Peter's voice wasn't too hot, but his guitar playing and Cozy's drumming were, as expected, exceptional. After the show I purchased a signed copy of Peter Green's biography. It was then that I remembered a little story that Marc Bolan had once told about when Peter was at a low ebb, wandering around South West London with no shoes. He invited him back to his place, gave him a meal and a drink and also gave him a pair of shoes to go back out in, and Peter went on his way. One never knew just how many stories Marc conjured up, but if this was true, then it is quite a touching story, especially as we all know that Peter did go through some rough times with his health.

The next morning we were at breakfast in the hotel and Peter came in still wearing his pyjamas! Everyone pretended not to notice. I said to him "I really enjoyed the gig last night" and he just looked at me almost with a kind of blank expression and said "uh, thanks." I realised that he was still not all that well. You'd never have guessed it though when he put on that *Gibson Les Paul*. He played the most awe inspiring and sweet lead guitar that he was always famous for, back in those grand days in what I call the genuine line-up of Fleetwood Mac.

I've never met Peter again, and sadly, I never got the opportunity to meet Cozy Powell again either, as he would die in a car crash in just a few years time, in 1998. I guess that I will have to remember that few seconds in that lift where we both just said 'Hi' to each other.

Before the summer was out we appeared on another couple of UK television shows. The first was an interview with Paul Ross for the ITV show *Big City* followed by the BBC programme *The Punt And Dennis Show*, which was shown on Thursday 7th September. We recorded a version of '20th Century Boy', which went over the allocated four minutes in length, so they had to edit it down to what they considered suitable. At the time, this show was considered quite cool and aimed at a slightly arty and cultured audience. I do think now that it was a show of its time as I have very rarely seen it repeated. I also did a very substantial interview for *Strangled* the official Stranglers Fan Club magazine, which appeared as a double page spread in their quarterly glossy publication. I hadn't a clue what connection, if any, The Stranglers had with Marc Bolan, but they were very interested in T.Rextasy, so I was able to promote not only my band in a Stranglers magazine, but also Marc as well.

One morning I picked up a call from a company called *Prism Leisure*, a budget CD company that specialises in cover versions and sells them through various outlet stores. They asked if we could record a few tracks for a compilation album that was being based on a 1970s CD they were compiling. Well, it sounded like a fun idea at the time. We recorded around five parts of Bolan songs, such as 'Get It On', '20th Century Boy', 'Hot Love', Telegram Sam', and 'Metal Guru', that would blend into other tracks - a kind of megamix I suppose. It was pretty dreadful. We basically ran through the songs almost like a soundcheck or rehearsal and before we knew it, the engineer said, "that'll do". We had only arrived in the studio a couple of hours before hand! I couldn't believe it when I actually saw two separate CD albums with the tracks that we had recorded, officially released and in the shops a few months later. It was one of those things that I feel must have surely been a dream. To date, there are quite a few versions floating around, as it appears that selected tracks are included on various releases.

Our UK shows were slowly gaining larger audiences. We were getting quite a reputation in some areas of Germany too, playing in Eissenhuttenstadt and Waren (Müritz) to around 10,000 people in total. Due to our recording deal we were also in the major CD retailers such as HMV and Virgin. However, we were to take a break and fly out to Japan for our first tour outside of Europe. As we would be in Japan from 15th - 21st September it would be the first time I missed going to Golders Green Crematorium on the 16th September, (the day that Marc Bolan had that fateful accident) to pay my respects to the one person who had given me the opportunity to make a living from playing his music. I would have to pay my respects to Marc when I got back in just under two weeks time. I was also proud to find out later that T.Rextasy would be the first ever, British tribute band to tour Japan.

Meeting at Heathrow airport, it was all very exciting although we were all trying to be cool about it, but inside I know that the adrenaline was kicking in. On our arrival we were met by Koichi (our guide, interpreter, chaperone, and member of the *Quattro* Company) and driven to our hotel in a luxury air-conditioned tour bus that had been used only three days previously by The Stone Roses. Once again the way we were treated, people would be forgiven for thinking that we were some major rock band and not a tribute band that were still trying to make a mark in their own country, never mind halfway around the world.

The day after our arrival on Saturday 16th September, we were all invited to the 9th Japanese *Glam Rock Easter* at The Nissin Power Station, in Tokyo. A group of fans handed me a box of chocolates and a great Marc Bolan t-shirt that had been printed especially for the evening. We were told that the 850 capacity venue had already sold out in advance. To celebrate Marc Bolan's passing, rock star Tsuneo Akima had arranged a group of musicians to play Bolan songs. On this occasion, I would be one of the special guests. The rest of T.Rextasy and Caron mingled and chatted to fans in the club while I spent my time backstage with Akima and the rest of the musicians. We rehearsed the songs that Akima had asked to perform but as he did not speak English, everything had to be relayed via an interpreter.

The concert was full of over excited fans and when I came on stage to perform 'Cadilac' and 'I Love to Boogie', the crowd literally went crazy. I couldn't believe it. Girls started to scream and some began to cry with emotion. This wasn't what I had expected from a Japanese audience as I was always led to believe they were reasonably subdued. I was asked to stay on stage for the duration of the concert and luckily I knew the rest of the material. It was all great fun and a thoroughly enjoyable experience of playing with musicians that didn't speak English but spoke through the power of music alone. After the concert I was presented with more presents from fans, that included a framed painting of the T.Rextasy CD cover, a Japanese flute, and an origami set. On our return to the hotel I was given bouquets of flowers and 'Welcome to Japan' letters from another group of fans.

What surprised me was how outrageously the fans in Japan dress, and how they sing so loudly to the electric numbers. In the acoustic section however, they sit and listen with respect but then go absolutely wild at the end of each song. It felt quite honourable and humble, as there was so much respect for Bolan, not only for his music, but also for Marc as a human being.

Our tour would be on what was known as the 'Quattro' circuit covering Tokyo and Osaka, which are two of the major areas in Japan's rock market. Our first gig took place in Tokyo on Sunday 17th September where we were booked to play two consecutive nights at the 500 capacity club. It was great to know that both nights had already sold out. On arrival for our soundcheck at around 3.00pm, we were amazed to see that even though gigs in Japan start very early in the evening, fans had already begun to queue. Inside the entrance to the venue a large cardboard display of the 'Trip & Glide' album hung on the wall. As I walked into the dressing room a large bouquet of flowers was presented to us with bottles of saké wine and a room full of food. We were told that some of the gifts were from a popular Glam band in Japan called The Yellow Monkey.

A short while later Hotei arrived. He was to be our very special guest for our encore. As soon as he strapped his guitar over his shoulder we knew that this guy was special. He is as tall as Neil Cross, which is quite unusual for a Japanese man. Hotei and Neil stood side by side and used the same microphone for the backing vocals. I had decided that we should get him to play 'Get It On' and 'Hot Love' as they have always been our final numbers. Hotei agreed and we went for it. The soundcheck and rehearsal went well and the venue's sound system was first class. Hotei didn't speak too much English, but the language of music yet again was all that was needed and we all worked well together.

Fans appeared to arrive out of nowhere and by 6pm the venue was already full. There was tension in the air and a sense of trepidation too. Although we had heard that Japanese fans tended to be very quiet but appreciative, after my experience at the *Glam Rock Easter* show I was unsure what would happen. We walked on stage to a sea of screaming fans and people calling out my name and shouting "T.Rextasy!" with such enthusiasm. It was truly exhilarating and quite emotional. We rocked into 'Chariot Choogle', 'Midnight', and 'Baby Factory' and they appeared to know every single song we played. However, when I introduced Hotei onto the stage, the audience went almost silent. I think they thought I was joking -

how could Japan's biggest rock star be here? But when he walked onto the stage the reception was unbelievable. People were screaming and crying in disbelief! We immediately shot into 'Get It On', and then followed it with 'Hot Love' where Hotei played a few rock 'n' roll ad-lib guitar riffs and sang the choruses.

By the end of the evening I think the audience were as emotionally drained as we were. After the show we went with Hotei to a nearby restaurant and had a few drinks and something to eat. Strangely enough although I am not a drinker of alcohol, I did get a taste for sake, and drank my fair share while I was out there! After a couple of hours we ventured outside to make our way back to the hotel. I was talking very loudly and walking down the middle of the road a little worse for wear. About twenty or so fans were still waiting for photos and autographs at the hotel. We ended up spending a little time chatting to them before saying our goodbyes. However, most of them were back the next day for the following concert.

As we had played at the venue the evening before, our equipment was already set in place so we had very little pre-production to do. For the encore numbers this time, we had invited Akima as our special guest. We rehearsed 'Get It On', and 'Hot Love' in which Akima would play guitar and sing some of the vocals just as Hotei had done the night before. Once again a group of fans were already waiting by the stage door for autographs and photos and in the queue to get the best position in the venue. The show was practically a carbon copy of the previous evening with fans screaming and singing all the songs and making us feel extra special. Akima strolled onto the stage for the planned encore and was received rapturously by the crowd. After the show, I received a massive tin of sweets with a squeezy Tyrannosaurus Rex on the top. I was also given a beautiful jewelled photo frame, together with fan letters and cards of well wishes. As this was the last show in Tokyo, we were thrown an after-show party from inside the venue. I was asked to make a short speech of thanks to the promoters before the party was allowed to commence. Once again, when we left the venue hours later there were still fans waiting outside for us.

The next day we caught the Bullet Train to Osaka. This is one of the world's marvels in travel. I had never been on a train that was so futuristic. The doors open up exactly to the inch of where one is told to stand on the platform. The carriages are on two floors with some of the seats made of luxurious soft leather that could turn full circle so that one could take in the scenery from any angle. Although the train travels at amazing speeds, the sound from inside is just a comforting hush. Ticket collectors and train supervisors are smart at all times in their uniforms and white gloves. One could also check on the speed, as there is always a digital speedometer to be seen at the end of each carriage. The food section is also immaculate and everything is in perfect order and wrapped to perfection. On the journey itself we travelled past some of the more desolate parts of the country, which looked a little like shanty towns and villages. We also passed by beautiful countryside and even saw the famous Mount Fuji in the distance with snow on the top peaks while we were baking in the heat down below, although inside the carriages the air conditioning kept the temperature just right.

When we arrived at Osaka I was convinced I was in the set from *Bladerunner*. It was the most futuristic city I had ever visited. It had a stronger and tougher feel than Tokyo and was a little more westernised. I must say that in all the time we spent in Japan I never felt threatened or uneasy. Everyone seemed to be friendly and hospitable to us all. When we arrived at the hotel, I couldn't believe a couple of fans were already waiting for autographs and photos. Later that evening I was asked to do a promotional interview for Radio 802FM and play a few songs acoustically live on air. The show in Osaka, on Wednesday 20th September, was a little more hard-edged but we played exactly the same set. It was a slightly larger venue that held 600 people, but once again, the show was sold out by the time of the gig. When we arrived at the club, I was given another large bouquet of flowers and we were treated to some lovely food and drink in true Japanese tradition. We took to the stage at the usual time of 7pm and the audience's enthusiasm and reaction was quite astounding. So much so that I had to shout many of the count-ins to the songs as Nigel couldn't hear over the screaming.

After the show, a large group of fans gathered outside the venue to ask for photographs and signatures. It took nearly half an hour to finally get everyone to disperse. We were taken to a lovely restaurant for our final evening meal in Japan before retiring to our hotel in the early hours. Before we knew it, it was all over. We were told that many bands only visit Japan once, mainly because of the cost and the distances involved. We felt privileged to have been asked out there at all and to have had the opportunity to play and see just what went on in that part of the world. The main thing was that it had been a major success. Even a Japanese Fan Club formed and began publishing regular fanzines dedicated to T.Rextasy in conjunction with the Japanese Marc Bolan Fan Club.

Although it had been a great experience abroad, it was comforting to get back home to all the things that we were used to like fish and chips, English chocolate, our own tea and biscuits, the slightly cooler weather, English speaking television programmes, the quaintness of our towns and villages, and things that we all take for granted. I can fully understand when people decide to emigrate and go off and live in foreign lands only to return to the UK - there is definitely something that draws us back here to this green and pleasant land!

Our next newsletter featured a four page Japan special with a yellow front cover and an ambiguous Marc/Danielz in a Japanese kimono drawn by Paul Thomas. The newsletter detailed the tour day by day and relayed a diary of events, as we all thought it was an important time not only in our career, but also to prove just how popular the name of Marc Bolan was in the land of the rising sun. Within the next few weeks, I was sent copies of reviews of our short tour in Japan and was happy to see favourable and five-star write-ups from top music magazines such as *Music Life*, *Rocking F*, and *Rockin' On*.

Left: Playing my newly acquired cherry red *Gibson Les Paul Standard* - 1990s.
(Sharon Thompsett)

Below: Promo photo used for our first tour of Japan - 1995. *(Koichi Hanafusa)*

Promotional photo. From left to right: Neil, me, Paul, Nigel, and Michelle - 1995.

Above: A group of Japanese fans waiting outside the Club Quattro in Tokyo - 1995

Below: Together with some of the Japanese fans after the same gig.

Above: Japanese magazine article.

Below: Tsuneo Akima (from the Japanese T.Rex inspired band Marchosias Vamp) and I being interviewed by *Guitarist* magazine in Japan - 1995.

Left: Japanese promotional flyer for the "Trip & Glide" album released on *Quattro Records* - 1995.

Below: Japanese magazine article.

Below: Japanese promotional flyers for the "Trip & Glide" album released on *Quattro Records* - 1995.

Left: 3" mini-cd promo single for 'Baby Factory' c/w '20th Century Baby' released by *Quattro Records*, Japan - 1995.

Above and left:: Japanese magazine article.

6

Joey Ramone Calling

Amongst the many different types of venues we were playing, none other than the *Butlin's* Holiday Camp venues gave me cause for anxiety. I was never that keen on doing them even though I knew that thousands of people flocked to the events. I just didn't think it gave the band kudos in any shape or form. When we first started playing there in the nineties, they were fine, but as the years went by the seventies weekenders especially, began to get more and more cheesy and lacked a sense of quality control, seemingly taking any band as long as they played music that fitted the bill. I know many decent bands still play at these events, and that's fine too - it's just not for me on a regular basis.

Mercifully a few years later when we were getting more than enough invites and bookings to play other venues around the country, I eventually pulled out altogether from the holiday camp circuit. I also used to find it invariably unsavoury. For instance, after one of our performances, I saw one of the members from Black Lace who were on before us, doing unscrupulous things with a young lady in the backstage toilets - the only thing that went through my mind at that moment was that it was so sad that the young woman in question only had aspirations of going that far with a member of Black Lace! When we used to play the camps, we mainly arrived, did the show and never stuck around for too long - it really wasn't my kind of set up.

Early one evening while we were walking around the chalet areas with nothing to do, Nigel was playing up a little and so the rest of the band decided it would be a good idea to pick him up and throw him inside one of those giant green industrial bins. After he was thrown inside and the top closed, he couldn't get out! He began shouting and rocking the bin from side to side so hard that it collapsed and crashed over on it's side with Nigel dropping out looking dirty, greasy and a little worse for wear with his coat all stained, smelly and grubby.

Back at home; a call came through from Hotei's UK representative. Hotei had decided to record his next album in the prestigious *Abbey Road Studios* in London and had asked me to guest on backing vocals on one particular song. As Hotei had come on stage with us in Japan as a friend, I decided to reciprocate and go along for the experience of recording in one of the greatest and most famous studios in the world.

When I got there John Miles was in the control room. He'd had a big hit in 1975 with 'Music' and was quite a talented musician in his own right. He had known Hotei for some time and was also booked to play on some of the tracks being recorded. Hotei shouted out a loud "HELLO DANIELZ!" and gave me a big hug from his six-foot frame. After a coffee and a chat we got down to business. He played me a song called 'Captain Rock' and explained that he wanted me to sing on the choruses and also shout out a Bolanic "Yea!" at certain sections of the song. I made my way down into the gigantic recording room which had to be cordoned off as it was so intimidating to be singing in there alone in such a vast cavern of a room.

The track played through the headphones and I sang along with the choruses and did my "Yea!" at the places that Hotei guided me to. I did it very quickly and within three takes it was all in the can. John and Hotei were quite struck at how quickly I had not only learnt the tune for the choruses, but also getting the timing and lyrics in synch with a track I had only heard twice through the studio headphones a few minutes beforehand. I have always been better when I'm thrown in at the deep end and have to learn fast, rather than if I have weeks of rehearsals, as I tend to get bored quickly and it can all end up very stale.

A few days after the recording sessions had finished, Neil Cross and I were invited to *Air Studios* in London for an 'after mix' party where we met up with the band Jesus Jones, and members of Sigue Sigue Sputnik. 'Captain Rock' was included and released on Hotei's CD album 'King & Queen' in Japan and the Far East in February 1996. It sold in mega quantities and went straight to the No.1 position. It was terrific to have been given the opportunity to be involved in a No.1 album and especially recording in the *Abbey Road Studios*!

It was around October-November 1995 when Veronica Kofman from

The Ramones Fan Club had a season of coming to see the band. She ended up interviewing me on one occasion and included it in the November edition of *Loudmouth*, the official Ramones magazine. She enjoyed the gigs so much that she told Joey Ramone, who was an avid Marc Bolan fan, all about us. Joey was intrigued and interested enough to arrange for me to receive a copy of their then latest album, 'Adios Amigos'. Particularly as it had one song written by Joey that was based around Bolan's lyrics to 'Life's A Gas'. Although it had nothing to do with the famous track from 'Electric Warrior', the feel and the run down of the guitar pattern, was very reminiscent of T.Rex. He said the deal was that if he sent me his album that I would send him the latest T.Rextasy CD, which of course I did.

As Christmas approached we embarked on a tour with Andy Scott's Sweet and Slade, and played a good lot of theatres throughout the UK. I managed to get a ten-minute interview on Radio West Midlands with DJ Jennie Wilkes to help promote the dates. My favourite gig on the tour took place at Wimbledon Theatre in London. It was smashing to play 'I Love To Boogie' knowing that the last time any band had played that song live in the venue was T.Rex back in 1976 on the televised *Rollin' Bolan* show.

I had the surprise of my life on Christmas Day when the phone rang at near midnight. It was The Ramones secretary saying that Joey would like to speak to me from New York to wish me a Happy Christmas and New Year. We ended up speaking for nearly half an hour or so talking about his favourite things about the UK such as Stonehenge, Glam Rock, and seventies music, which he loved. We also chatted about T.Rex and about when he had met Marc in 1977, and how he had suggested that Marc should re-issue the track 'Solid Gold Easy Action' because it was so 'punk'. We also talked about the music scene in the USA, and how much he so wanted to visit England again. He said that he really liked what we had done with some of the Bolan tracks on the album, and really loved the song 'Baby Factory'. He said that he had planned to speak to three people that evening, the first one was I, the second was Noddy Holder, and the third was Roy Wood.

I didn't know if he managed to speak to the other two that night, but I was very flattered that he had even bothered thinking of me and taking the time to call. On 15th April 2001 Joey Ramone sadly passed away and became another star that leaves a great musical legacy behind him. I never met Joey face-to-face, which was a great shame, but I will always remember that call on Christmas Day.

Shortly before the end of 1995, Caron received a telephone call from Gloria Jones. She had been speaking to Lenny Zakatek, Hotei's manager, who had told her how well T.Rextasy had gone down in Japan. Gloria said that she would like to get T.Rextasy over to the USA for some dates and that she was so pleased that we were keeping Marc's music alive and respectable. Unfortunately, her good intentions never came to fruition. She was always concerned that as Marc only ever had one Top 10 in the American charts, 'Get It On', or 'Bang A Gong' as it was known in the States, that it may not have worked out as well as she would've liked it to. I was nevertheless glad that she had given her support and her endorsement, which made the call all the more worthwhile in the end.

We began the New Year gigging again as usual but at one particular show on Friday 8th March a guy approached our roadie and said he wanted to speak to me as he was producing a radio show about the tribute band phenomenon. The man in question was John Walters who had worked with John Peel for years on Radio 1. He was now working on his own show on Radio 2, *Yesterday Once More*. I was always a little sceptical of becoming associated with various bands on the scene, but he told me that he would be interviewing the likes of The Bootleg Beatles, and The Counterfeit Stones, so I thought if they were doing it, I would be in decent company!

The programme eventually aired on 1st June 1996 at 5pm and although in places it was a little tongue-in-cheek, we were treated with respect. My interview with John Walters was affectionate and reasonably serious enough as he had known Marc Bolan personally and knew that I was taking T.Rextasy as seriously as if it was an original band. Although he played various snippets from our recordings such as '20th Century Boy', I was incredibly happy when he played a segment from my song 'Village'. When I met up with him for the interview, he brought along various presents that Marc Bolan had given to him. Amongst the items he showed me was a lovely signed single with an inscription dedicated to John from Marc. On 30th July 2001 John sadly passed away and left a gaping hole within the confines of the BBC network where he had made his name, mostly of course synonymous with John Peel.

One of the more respectable indie venues in Southsea, just outside of Portsmouth was The Wedgewood Rooms. We began playing there twice a year and received rave reviews from the fashionable glossy music magazine, *Venue*. They had already placed my photo on the cover and interviewed me quite substantially over the last couple of years but it was a shame when a few years later the magazine folded, even though The Wedgewood Rooms still marched on. It was always a pleasure to see Mick O'Halloran in the audience at our shows. One of the first he came along to was The Wedgewood Rooms on Friday 1st March 1996. Mick was not only Marc Bolan's long standing friend, but he held the position of Marc's personal roadie for the duration of Tyrannosaurus Rex right through to the final end of T.Rex. I really wanted Mick to like the band and I knew he would be completely honest with me too. After the show he came backstage and said, "I thought the band was excellent, but I can't get over how much you remind me of Marc." I sighed with relief, as this was a guy who was with Marc for almost nine years and knew what he was talking about.

After the success of the 'Trip & Glide' album in both the UK and Japan, it was gratifying to know that a follow up CD was being requested. As our gigging schedule was pretty tight, we had little time to record, so I drew up a list of tracks that I wanted the band to learn so that when we did enter the recording studio the process wouldn't be so demanding. I also wanted to include another two tracks of my own, so within the next few weeks, I organised the track listing and gave some thought to the sleeve design.

It was a bolt out of the blue when I received a call from Clive, from *Madman Records*, saying that the Japanese were so happy with how our dates had gone that they wanted to 'up' the anti and organise another tour, only this time much, much bigger, with more bands and in larger venues. I couldn't believe it. I thought that was it for Japan, but if we were going to be given another chance to play there, then I was going to grab the opportunity with both hands.

The plan was for T.Rextasy to headline at various substantial venues, but the promoters wanted another two bands on the bill that the fans would know. Queen and Kiss were two bands that'd had mega success in Japan so it was decided to fly over a Queen band called The Royal Family and a Kiss tribute called Dressed To Kill. I accepted this so long as both bands played live without the aid of any backing discs. To make the package work even better it was announced that another two UK bands would play, but on different days. The Bootleg Beatles and The Counterfeit Stones would play on one night, and then our package would play on either the evening before, or the evening after. It was a great concept that worked out perfectly.

While the tour abroad was being organised we had decided to put together a VHS video of the band as so many fans had been asking for such a release. This was still before the age of DVD, so quality wasn't exactly at a premium and because of the transfer of some of the tapes from the NTSC system, the picture quality suffered heavily for some of the recorded performances. When we finally released the VHS Video in April 1996 we were immediately inundated with orders that we had to have 100 copies run off at a time by the manufacturers. We sold out over various runs and then had it deleted. I decided to call the video 'Wind Of Illusion'. The title was taken from a Bolan lyric from 'Casual Agent'. I thought the word 'illusion' kind of summed me up in a way as I felt that T.Rextasy and what I did in my performance was always a kind of a rock 'n' roll illusion.

The video was mainly compiled of Japanese appearances with a total playing time of about one hour. Strangely enough, although a lot of the footage wasn't much to be desired compared to today's standards, it retains a quaint bootleg quality of old - a throw back to a time when one bought one of those scratchy bootleg albums that sounded as if it had been transferred three or four times down the line before making it onto vinyl!

In the second week of May I had to fly out to Japan once again to promote the tour. I was put up in a beautiful hotel and used that as a base to be picked up and dropped off on most days. I did a variety of television and radio shows throughout my visit and what made it all the more enjoyable was that so many people remembered T.Rextasy from our last tour.

We had performed a gig in the West Midlands on 11th May and I had to fly to Japan from Heathrow Airport the following day. It was nerve racking to say the least, as I had no time to pack properly or to get myself in the right state of mind. Added to that, my return flight to the UK had been booked for 16th May, to get me back in time for a concert at the Glasgow Pavilion the next day! The problem arose when I found out that there were no direct flights to Glasgow Airport from Japan, so I had to fly to Paris and then onto Glasgow all within twenty-four hours. When I arrived in Glasgow I was absolutely shattered. Luckily I had time for a few hours sleep before having to get up for sound checking. If that wasn't rock 'n' roll, then I don't know what is!

The Glasgow Pavilion was the first of a nine-date tour of Scotland. Following on from Glasgow we played venues in Seton Sands, Bathgate, Falkirk, Greenock, Wemyss Bay, the Lemon Tree in Aberdeen, The Venue in Edinburgh, and the wonderfully named Lucifer's Mill in Dundee. The Scottish audiences, it has to be said, must rate as some of the most appreciative in the UK, Glasgow in particular.

I remember Bolan once saying in an interview that two of his most favourite places to play in the UK were Birmingham and Glasgow. Although I was able to fit in a couple of radio interviews to promote the tour, I was most grateful when I heard the DJ John McAuley on Radio Clyde say that "T.Rextasy is the finest tribute band around", which I am certain must have helped push a few ticket sales.

In the midst of all this, my good friend in Germany, Jorg Günther had arranged for me to go there to appear on a TV music show called *Kuno's*. I did an interview with *Kuno's* of which every sentence I uttered had to be translated into German and relayed to the television audience. I then played a couple of acoustic songs live, which carried on for ages afterwards when the TV cameras stopped rolling, playing an impromptu set for the invited guests who were part of the studio crowd. Detlev Flohr, another German friend and photographer also managed to take a few photos of my time there, of which one shot actually ended up on the cover of the forthcoming T.Rextasy CD 'Savage Beethoven'.

)PS ✶✶ SNIPPETS

COSMIC CHRISTMAS HAPPENINGS

✶ MORE FROM ATN ✶

http://www.addict.com/ATN/

Remember how we learned about the discovery of Marc Bolan's hand-written note mentioning Joey Ramone? Well, it was a big surprise for Joey too, and he decided to give Danielz from T-Rextasy a Christmas Day phone call.

In his Christmas Road Report for Addicted to Noise, Joey tells the story:

"I began the day making phone calls. First I called Roy Wood, then I called Veronica Kofman from the RAMONES UK Fan Club, and then proceeded to contact Len Tuckey, who used to be married to Suzi Quatro but now manages Slade. I wanted to wish Noddy Holder a Happy Christmas and to tell him what a big Slade fan I've always been.

Then I spoke to Danielz from T-Rextasy, who's formed a tribute band, keeping Marc Bolan's spirit alive. I called to wish him a Merry Christmas, which turned into a pretty cool conversation about Stonehenge, the current music scene and cool '70s glitter bands. While we were talking Danielz exclaimed "I don't believe it, the Ramones are on "The Simpsons" right at this very second! How cosmic!"

Left: Extract from the Ramones Fan Club magazine about Joey Ramone's Christmas day telephone call to me - 1996.

Below: Tomoyasu Hotei and I at Abbey Road Studios, London after recording vocals for his album 'King & Queen' - 1995.

T.REXTASY!
WIND OF ILLUSION...

✶✶Live acoustic sessions
✶✶Japan convention
✶✶Live in Japan
✶✶Promo-video
✶✶Interviews

Right: Cover of the VHS video compilation entitled 'Wind Of Illusion' which included TV and live performances from Japan and the UK - 1996.

Left: Talking to a reporter at Golders Green Crematorium - 1990s

Below left: Catching up with Herbie Flowers (T.Rex bassist) at The 12 Bar Club, London - 1990s.

Below right: Harry Feld (Marc's brother) giving me a bear-hug backstage at The Wedgewood Rooms, Portsmouth - 1990s.

Right: Promotional photo; left to right: Neil, Nigel, me, & Paul.
(Miam Davidson)

Above: Live at The Marquee Club, London - 1995.
(Unknown)

Right: A T.Rextasy Christmas concert at JB's in Dudley - 1990s.

Below: German photographer and friend Detlev Flohr took a few shots while I was appearing on the German TV show *Kuno's*. This shot was later used for the front cover of 'Savage Beethoven' - 1996.
(Detlev Flohr)

Below: On the German TV show *Kuno's* - 1996.
(Detlev Flohr)

Right: Chilling out shortly before my appearance on the German TV programme *Kuno's*. From left to right: Unknown TV guy talking to my friend Jorg Günther, Caron is talking to me - 1996.
(Detlev Flohr)

7

Japan 1996

All five bands congregated at Heathrow Airport looking forward to the trip as well as playing in a country that was alien to most of them. We stepped off the plane on 6th June 1996, it was humid and sweltering and the heat made it a little uncomfortable. The plane journey had been long and not without a little heavy turbulence on the way. It freaked out one of the guys from The Counterfeit Stones who began shouting very loudly and punching the air with his fists. Caron, who is not the keenest of flyers, was allocated a seat next to him, which made her even more nervous. On the flight, drinks were handed out by the stewardesses at an abundant rate and by the time we were only halfway through the journey they had run out of alcohol! It seemed that between the two of them, Nigel Silk and Paul Rogers had consumed most of the booze and Nigel was the worse for wear. He threw an empty can over his seat, which landed in my lap. I took the can and crushed it hard over his head but he was so out of it that he didn't even feel it!

On our arrival the promoters and sponsors, who happened to be the giant *Heinz Ketchup Company*, met us. We were told that they had actually commissioned a couple of special guitars that were made in the shape of *Heinz* ketchup bottles specifically for promoting the tour! We hurried onto the coach, mainly to get out of the blistering heat that hit us as soon as we stepped out from the air-conditioned airport. The traffic was at a standstill and it took ages to arrive at the hotel. It was unusual for us to have a couple of days off before our first show, however, we soon found out that we were booked to do a whole stack of interviews and promotion for the press, media, and television appearances.

One of the interview sessions we were contracted to do took place at

The Nikko Hotel in Tokyo on 7th June 1996. A press conference was held and televised. All five bands had their seated section and were interviewed as a group one by one and were asked questions about the tour and what the fans could expect from the gigs. As expected, the main bulk of questions were aimed at The Bootleg Beatles and The Counterfeit Stones, but we still had our fair share of TV time. After the session, I was asked if I would perform an acoustic song to close the proceedings. I agreed and Neil accompanied as we fittingly closed the evening with a rendition of 'Hot Love'. We were also interviewed for the TV channels NHK, WIN, TX TV, CNN, and WIDE TV, and others that I just cannot recall as we were always being whisked from studio to studio, all very tightly scheduled, but all so well organised.

Our first major concert was at the City Hall in Nagoya on Sunday 9th June. Playing at this venue probably meant more to me than some of the others as T.Rex had actually played there in 1973. This was the first concert of the tour and it felt so exciting that I even placed 'Buick Mackane' into the set, as it was one of the non-single tracks that Bolan had played in the hall back then. Some of the audience were too young to remember T.Rex and some who had come to see the other two bands, reacted better to the well known singles, such as 'Telegram Sam', 'Get it On', 'Hot Love', and 'Jeepster'. However, we were determined to include 'Buick Mackane' and the odd album track, if not for anything else, for our own enjoyment and the die-hard fans.

From Nagoya we travelled to Osaka to play Melparque Hall on 11th June before moving onto Hiroshima's Aster Plaza Hall. We arrived in Hiroshima early on 12th June and were later escorted to and around the Museum of Peace, a large imposing building which was an awful reminder of the destruction of Hiroshima. Relics of the bombing were on display as well as photos of the aftermath showing the devastation, death, illness, and poverty that occurred at the time.

Outside the museum there are more reminders of the atrocities of war, and I found the people there discerningly different from those I had met in every other part of Japan. It was as if Hiroshima, at least the part that we visited, had remained in some kind of time capsule. It was the first place I had been to in Japan that I hadn't felt totally comfortable. Our Japanese guides advised us to wear our Union flag backstage band passes while walking through the streets to show that we were British. We were told that there was a possibility that we could receive abuse from the locals if they thought we were American. I felt very subdued and depressed on our return to the hall. It remained quiet in the dressing room for some time as the visit did affect us. Later on we had something to eat and by sound-check it was back to business. All in all though, it had been an unusual and solemn experience but I was glad not to have missed it.

On our way back to Tokyo we reflected on the terrible tragedy and what some of the people there still have to cope with in living within site of that museum. A few hours later, the mood lightened as we arrived to face the most lavish and futuristic hotel I have ever stayed in. The Tokyo Bay Hotel was gigantic and beautifully first class in every way. Our rooms were terrific and we were looked after like true rock stars. In the morning I made sure I had the sumptuous large prawns with oversized fresh cherries for breakfast, all paid for by those wonderful *Heinz* sponsors!

From our hotel window we had a balcony view, which looked out onto the beautifully constructed Rainbow Bridge. I never found out if this had any connection with Jimi Hendrix or not, even though an album was released with the same name after he had died.* The ground floor of the hotel consisted of a selection of shops that sold clothing, jewellery, and fashion accessories. It also had a choice of cafes, restaurants and chill out zones. Surrounding the hotel were gardens and fishponds that contained rare giant carp and other exotic fishes.

Our next appearance was at the Ariake Coliseum in Tokyo on Saturday 15th June. This was the largest venue we would play on the whole tour. It was like a smaller version of Wembley Arena I suppose, holding a capacity of around 6,000. We had sold around 2,000 tickets for the concert so I was pleased enough with that. Also, NHK TV was to film the whole show and broadcast it over their network. Rail tracks were laid out below and in front of the stage for the film crew to set their cameras on moving tripods. Songs from the concert such as 'Children Of The Revolution', '20th Century Boy', and 'Telegram Sam' together with a pre-gig interview was eventually shown on NHK TV in August of that year. The PA sound was big and crystal clear and filled the auditorium. I sang a few lines on the microphone before we

* Rainbow Bridge - Original Motion Picture Soundtrack LP was from the 1972 film of the same name directed by Chuck Wein that features footage from a Jimi Hendrix open-air concert held on 30th 1970, on the island of Maui, Hawaii. However, for contractual reasons and due to the original music soundtrack being of substandard quality because of strong winds, the album doesn't actually include, any of the live material from the film, but does include the featured studio tracks.

sound-checked and my voice echoed with the natural reverb of the large empty room.

As the venue slowly filled with the sound of that eerie hum that one only hears in a large auditorium, the lights went down as the evening began. The organisers asked if I would play one of the 'Ketchup-style' guitars that they had made. As I knew the gig was being filmed neither me or Neil accepted the invitation as we didn't think it would look too cool on the TV screens. I also thought that the pick-ups fitted on the guitar might not have been as powerful or as high quality as the ones on my *Gibson Les Paul*. Instead, one of the other bands agreed to use them. The cameras rolled and The Royal Family hit the stage followed twenty minutes later by Dressed To Kill - both bands went down really well.

Another twenty minutes break and then we sauntered on stage. A whole section of the audience sprang into action as we had the reliable Japanese T.Rex / T.Rextasy fan club in attendance. They had made a large T.Rextasy red and white banner, which they held aloft for the whole show. Throughout the gig they waved, screamed, sang, and shouted. It was quite a spectacle, and of course it made an even better display for the cameras. For the duration of the tour Akima had kindly lent me his 100 watt HH IC100s amplifier head so that I could achieve my usual sound, or at least as close as possible to it. When I saw some of the concert footage on television later on, I noticed that, although it was close, my guitar didn't sound exactly how I had anticipated it to be. As I had to use the HH through a Marshall Cab, the sound was a little more 'metal' and perhaps too hard. However, there were no complaints as everything else was handled to perfection. The stagehands, the roadies and the staff couldn't do enough for us and were always on call the split second they were required.

For this visit to Japan, I had decided to get hair extensions. Even though my hair was naturally of good length, I wanted something a little different. The hair extensions were really long and photos from that period show my hair way beyond shoulder length, and now, in retrospect may have been slightly too much. In the heat they really got on my nerves and having to wash it after every show made my head feel like it was being pulled down by heavy weights, but I had no option. I had to endure it until I had flown back to the UK.

At The Tokyo Bay Hotel, we were met by a group of fans, some of whom had formed the fan club. Yuriko, Yumiko, and Reiko had been fans of

Marc Bolan for as long as they could remember and had decided to form both the Marc Bolan Fan Club and T.Rextasy Fan Club after seeing us perform in Japan the year before. There hadn't been a definitive Bolan Fan Club in Japan for some years. We spent ages chatting over a drink or two in the plush foyer seating area about all things T.Rex. I was intrigued and surprised that no one appeared to own any Japanese video footage of T.Rex in concert. I was told that in the 1970s especially, the parents of Japanese children were very strict, and attending concerts or even watching rock or pop music on television, was considered out of bounds to many.

The next day we travelled to Fukuoka to play at Crossing Hall. It was Sunday 16th June and the area was buzzing. There seemed to be a touch of rock 'n' roll about this place, and the venue didn't disappoint either. The next day we played at the unusually named Izumity 21 in Sendai, before moving on to Niigata, to a venue called Telsa on Tuesday 18th June. The last three nights felt more rock 'n' roll and I enjoyed them all. There was even standing room at some of the halls, which made it all the more rock orientated. I do like playing venues that are seated, but I also like the fans to have the opportunity to stand if they prefer.

In between shows we sometimes had the use of an air-conditioned coach, and other times we travelled by Bullet Train. On one occasion travelling back to Tokyo and while waiting to collect our tickets who should walk past us but David Bowie. Out of pure coincidence, David was travelling on the same train, on tour and on his way to Russia after being diverted, due to an accident at the airport. When we reached the platform I went up to him and said, "Hi, I'm Danielz and I'm touring with T.Rextasy." To my astonishment, he said, "I know who you are, I've been reading about you," which broke the ice a little. It was fortunate that we had received quite a lot of media coverage and I guess that David had seen us in one or two of the magazines and papers. I had a brief chat about our stay in Japan and then mentioned Marc Bolan to him, to which he said "I still miss him." I then asked if we could have a photo together and he was most obliging. Caron had the camera and clicked the shutter just as David's manager purposely walked in front of us! David then said to her, "it's okay, these guys are cool," and then Caron did a second snapshot of us together. He was very friendly and willing to chat nonchalantly before the train arrived. We all boarded the same train, but I decided not to approach him again and gave him the respect of privacy that I'm sure he wanted.

When we got home to the UK, we had the film developed and it was great to see that not only had the second shot of Bowie and myself come out well, but the first photo as well - it appeared that David's manager had actually missed walking in front of the shot after all.

We'd had a fantastic trip but it was time to go home. When we arrived at Narita Airport in Tokyo the following morning it was touching to see a whole group of our fans with the T.Rextasy banner unravelled over the separation fence. It was a lovely gesture, especially as no fans of any of the other bands had bothered to turn up. I felt quite emotional that anyone had even bothered to do this for us. I went across to them and had a chat and said goodbye before being called away to the ticket barriers clutching a suitcase full of CDs, photos, books, videos, jewellery and other wonderful gifts that had been given from fans.

Caron and I decided that when we got back to England we would tie the knot, and on 25th June 1996, we were married at the Westminster Register Office.* We kept the attendance down to a minimum and so only family, the band, and very close friends were invited. I wore a green and black satin top - a replica of the one Marc Bolan had worn on the TV show *Get It Together* in 1977, with black PVC trousers. Caron looked stunning in a red with orange tint two-piece raw silk suit and hair extensions that she had had woven in especially. It was a sweltering day, but as we approached the River Thames, where we had hired a restaurant barge for our reception, the water and river breeze made it all the more of an exceptional day than it had already been. Afterwards, we were chauffeured by our friend Gavin down to Sussex where we spent a beautiful time surrounded by lovely countryside at the Copthorne Hotel.

Before we knew it, we were back on a plane heading for Denmark's Midtfyns Festival on Saturday 6th July 1996. Although there were a few British tribute bands on the bill, the majority of acts were original and it was terrific to be included in the same programme with the likes of ZZ Top and Iron Maiden. A few days later on Friday 12th July we played at The Kent Custom Bike Show supporting Eddie & The Hot Rods. We all had to use the one dressing room and because we had arrived a little early the drinks rider was already in place. By the time The Hot Rods arrived all the alcohol had

---

* Formerly known as the Marylebone Register Office.

been disposed of. They were pretty furious about it, but everyone kept cool and by the time they took to the stage, we had packed up and left before their last number!

It was always a pleasure to play a gig on the Isle of Wight, as I knew that we would also have the honour of Mick O'Halloran's company, as he had lived there since the 1970s. On one occasion, Mick invited me to his home after soundcheck. Over a cup of tea, he told me various anecdotes about his time with Marc & T.Rex and showed me the famous 'Pan' statuette, which belonged to Marc and featured prominently on the lyric sheet of the 'A Beard Of Stars' album.

Pan is the Greek god of creativity, music and poetry, amongst other things and I'm sure Marc was attracted to this connotation. Mick told me that he had told Marc that he had always admired the ornament and if anything drastic ever happened he would like to own it. I was absolutely stunned at the height of it - it was a lot taller than I had imagined it would be, around twelve inches in height at a guess, and the colours were a vibrant green and yellow. Even after all the years that had passed by it was quite astounding that time had not blemished or diminished the vibrancy of this unique sculpture.

The next time I saw Mick was at a show in Portsmouth. This time he brought along a suit that Marc had designed and had made for Marc's chauffeur (and sometimes bodyguard) Alphi O'Leary. Alphi told Mick "Danielz is the only person I want to give the suit to. Marc designed it for me and chose the material for it." I was quite shocked that someone that I didn't really know felt that I should be handed over something so special. I telephoned Alphi later that week to thank him for it. He said something on the lines of, "to be honest, I never really liked it. Marc insisted that I should wear it and I did those kind things for him because I loved him. He had the ability to persuade people to do things that they wouldn't normally do for anyone else!"

The garment was of course made for a very big man, and Alphi was at the time, quite a giant of a guy. It was a well-made two-piece suit, cut from fine cloth. When I was given it, it still had the original brightly coloured purple/pink handkerchief in the top jacket pocket. Somehow I just couldn't imagine Alphi wearing it!

After our return home from our second tour of Japan I decided that it was time that I should obtain a replica of Marc's *Gibson Les Paul Standard* guitar. I had used and owned various electric guitars throughout my time with the band, such as a *Gibson The Paul*, a *Gibson Sonex*, a Japanese *Fender Stratocaster*, and a wine coloured *Les Paul Standard*. However, as I had recently been given a beautiful 1960s re-issued white USA *Fender Stratocaster* from *Arbiters*, thanks to the help of a big Bolan fan called Chris Etherington, and a bass guitarist called Dave Glover (who both worked for *Fender*), I felt that my wine coloured *Gibson*, lovely though it was, and almost identical to the cherry red guitar Marc had used in 1977, was still not the absolute.

I sold the wine coloured guitar and purchased a sunburst *Les Paul Standard* instead. On picking it up from the *Gibson* dealer in London's Charing Cross Road, I immediately took it around the corner to the famous Andy's workshop in Denmark Street. I had talked to the guy that worked there at length a few weeks prior and we had discussed exactly how I wanted the guitar to look. I had also taken along the 'T.Rex' album cover, or the "Brown" album as it is sometimes known, which had a great photo of the guitar I wanted replicated.

I decided that it had to be stripped down totally and re-sprayed with a semi-opaque orange colour. I also gave instructions that it should not be fully lacquered so that it would retain the original slightly matt appearance. Adding to that, I had the pick-ups replaced with the black and white zebra design. The neck on my new *Les Paul Standard* was fitted with the *Standard* neck of course, and not the *Custom* neck, although it is debatable as to which one is preferred - as either could be considered correct. Marc only had the *Custom* neck fitted and replaced a couple of years after he purchased it with it's original *Standard* neck. Marc had the neck replaced no fewer than three times over the course of about six years! The one thing I didn't ask them to do was to drill holes in the body of the guitar in those strategic places to imitate where, on Marc's original guitar, someone at sometime used a *Bigsby* whammy bar and then had it removed.

Marc's guitar was always rumoured to be a model from the late 1950s and it was Mick O'Halloran (Marc's personal roadie) who actually picked the guitar up for him in 1970 after seeing it in the window of a guitar shop in either *Top Gear* in Denmark Street or in *South Eastern Entertainments* in Catford, just outside Lewisham where Marc purchased his now famous *Vamp* amplifiers - Mick's memory has faded a little as to exactly which shop it was purchased from as there are two stories in existence. Marc loved the look and the colour, as it reminded him of the guitar played by his idol Eddie Cochran. Marc actually purchased the instrument in all its concocted and mismatched glory, in that it had already been re-sprayed together with that strange blend of mixed pick ups and drilled body before he had bought it! He must have been inconsolable when his pride and joy was eventually stolen. In 2011, *Gibson* finally recognised Marc's original and very special guitar as the iconic instrument many people always knew it was, and released a collector's limited edition *Signature* model. However, they decided to issue the guitar with a *Custom* neck and not the original *Standard* neck, which Marc would've used when he recorded the 'Electric Warrior' and 'The Slider' albums, but I guess that's nit picking to an obsessive like me!

Andy's workshop completed my guitar in just a few weeks. When I saw it I couldn't believe my eyes. I felt it was perfect! All I had to do now was wear it in slightly as it looked a little 'too new'. The best looking guitars in my eyes are those that look battered, used and worn, like Rory Gallagher's *Stratocaster*, or Francis Rossi's *Telecaster*. I felt as if I was pretty complete now that I had the *Gibson* and the *Stratocaster*. In time, I even managed to purchase an additional *Les Paul Standard* that had been doctored and finished like Marc's just to use as a spare!

The record company *K-Tel* had released various T.Rex albums in the past, including a very well received double album entitled 'The Best Of The 20th Century Boy'. The company had booked us to play at their 25th anniversary celebrations at The Mean Fiddler in London. After our show, presentations and speeches took up a lot of the time, but it was interesting to hear that their T.Rex album had sold more than any other product released on the label. While at the party I was introduced to a guy called Mark Esgain a cousin of the Feld family. The next day I telephoned Marc's brother Harry and passed on his telephone number. Harry was so pleased, as he had lost contact with him years ago. It was a nice feeling to put the two family members back in touch with each other.

Corporate bookings were never that common for us, and those that we did partake in could be quite starchy affairs. But we did do one that was a little more memorable than some of the others we had done in the past. We were booked to play for a private company at a golf club alongside Suzi Quatro, Andy Scott's Sweet, and Alvin Stardust. The line-up was kept hush-hush from the guests so as to keep the evening a surprise. We were on first and the show went well. As I said "'thank you and good night", I added without thinking, "I hope you all have a great evening with Suzi Quatro, Alvin Stardust, and The Sweet!" As soon as I said it I realised what I had done. When I came off stage, the organisers were not too pleased that I had given the game away, but Suzi, Alvin, and Andy all thought it was a great laugh and took it in their stride... and people wonder why I don't accept too many corporate events!

Just before 1996 closed, I was informed that the Japanese Fan Club had issued its first magazine dedicated to T.Rextasy, which they had published in November. It featured interviews and reviews and a personal biography on each member of the band. It took the shape of a slim A5 sized fanzine and had a slight punky feel to it. The magazine would run for a few years siding parallel with their Marc Bolan magazines, which were sent out simultaneously. They were of course always written in Japanese, but every few months, maybe twice a year, they would religiously send out copies to me to peruse and add to my collection.

At the pre-tour conference in Tokyo.

Left: Neil & I performing 'Hot Love'.

Below: Neil and Paul (top), Nigel and me (front).

Below: Awaiting to be picked up by our Japanese touring company and chilling out in a Tokyo restaurant. Left to right: Nigel, Neil, Caron, Paul.

Left: David Bowie and I on a platform awaiting the Bullet Train - "I know who you are!" he said to me.

Below: The view from my Tokyo hotel window.

Above: Caron and I signing our marriage certificate,
Marylebone Registry Office, London 1996. *(Nigel Silk)*

Below A live shot with my newly acquired,
Marc Bolan replicated *Gibson Les Paul Standard. (Unknown)*

Above: A great rock'n'roll live shot captured just right!

Below: Taken shortly before one of our corporate summer shows.
From left to right: Andy Scott (Sweet), Alvin Stardust, Suzi Quatro, and me. *(Unknown)*

8

A Bolan Commemoration UK Style

It felt that throughout the nineties small television channels were popping up all over the place and were sending out scouts to find anyone who would agree to appear on television. We were still at the stage where I was just happy and grateful to be asked. I didn't think too much about whether or not it was the right thing to do or whether the programme had any kudos or not. So when I was approached by a satellite channel called Live TV to take part in a pop quiz, I agreed immediately. The show was called *The Sham Rock TV Show*. Two bands took part, a Queen tribute called The Bohemians, and T.Rextasy. The show was broadcast on 11th March 1997. Both bands had to face each other and each member was asked individual questions about pop and rock. The Bohemians won the quiz getting one more question right at the very tail end of the show. However, we still closed the show performing a mimed version of 'Metal Guru' taken from our own recording of it.

Ever since I became a fan of T.Rex, I have always felt that Marc was treated unfairly by certain aspects of the media and specifically by some of the music press. As Marc's 20th Commemorative Anniversary approached I felt that someone should make a stand and talk about Marc the musician, Marc the poet, Marc the songwriter, Marc the guitarist, Marc the performer. There was a short programme that featured on London ITV every so often entitled *Your Shout!* whereby, if selected, one could make a short three minute programme about one's grievances. I phoned the TV channel and told them about Bolan's up and coming anniversary. They took an interest and straight away agreed that I should record one of their mini features.

A film crew from ITV arrived and started recording from a script that I had written and pre-arranged. Other than a few edits, they used most of what I had to say. They filmed me talking about Bolan in my Holloway flat, in London, before taking me to the outskirts of Golders Green where, for some reason, they had me walk across a zebra crossing while talking about 'The London Boy'. I wore my replica of Marc's black and green 1977 *Get It Together* top (the programme where he performed 'Dandy In The Underworld'.) *Your Shout!* received its first airing at lunchtime on 7th April 1997 and then repeated just before 6.30pm in the evening and was shown at least five or six times after that over the next couple of weeks.

A few days later out of the blue, I had a call from Marc's first girlfriend, Terry Mosiac (sic), her real name was Terry Whipman, but Marc had always called her Terry Mosiac. She had seen the *Your Shout!* programme and felt that she needed to see me. As I didn't drive, Caron picked her up in our car. We met at Charing Cross station and then drove back to our flat. Terry was a very spiritual human being and got very nervous when she thought we were taping her conversation as she said that recording her voice or photographing her image would take away or steal part of her lifeline. When she was happy that we were not taping her, she settled down and began to chat quite freely.

Terry reeled off a poem that she had memorised that Marc had written for her in the sixties before she said, "I was the 'Woman of Gold' in the song 'Hot Love'." She followed that by telling us that she had lived on the Torquay coast in the sixties. She insisted that Marc had written the song about her, i.e. with the lyrics 'She lives on the coast', etc... Terry was a very frail looking woman, who strangely enough reminded me of a slightly older looking June Child, who Marc would later marry. Afterwards, we dropped her back at Charing Cross. I saw her just one more time when we performed at the Lewisham Theatre, in Catford.

Lewisham Theatre was a venue we had played previously and like so many other theatres in the UK; it was nice to return there. This time was a little different though as I knew that Terry was in the audience. The concert was very well attended and the crowd were pretty rowdy. Terry didn't like it. I think she thought that it would be quite a serene affair and retain some of the old hippy ideals. I think of Marc as a rock 'n' roller and that's the way I perform - as Marc did in his hey-day. Terry had other ideas and felt that perhaps the show was too brash - too Marc in his 1972 or 1973 Glam Rock period. After she told me that it wasn't what she had expected, we didn't speak again, not a falling out or anything, but we just didn't have anything in common.

I have never been one to jam with musicians, as I like to rehearse and be as tight as possible. So it was unusual when I accepted an invitation, in a little pub somewhere in Essex, to go up onstage with Legend, featuring Len Tuckey, guitarist from Suzi Quatro's band, and Bill Legend, to sing and play guitar on a couple of Bolan tracks. Len called me up from out of the blue to play 'Jeepster' and 'Get It On'. I felt that I couldn't refuse, Len passed me one of his guitars, and we were away! It was a somewhat strange experience having Bill behind me playing drums as it was for him watching me singing and playing those songs in front of him. I was shocked that Bill had remembered the long version of 'Jeepster'. Marc always used to play an extended guitar solo live and out of habit; I had gone into automatic mode and carried the song into the extended version.

One of my favourite band's of the seventies was Mott The Hoople, so I jumped at the chance when I was asked to play support to Mott front man and chief songwriter Ian Hunter. I always felt that Ian was one of the few remaining guys from that era of what was termed Glam that had kept his kudos. He had never relented into buying into the Butlin's/holiday camp market that so many of the other bands have ended up doing. I am convinced that Marc Bolan would never have contemplated going down that road either.

T.Rextasy and Ian ended up playing only two shows together, but I had a great time. I don't ask too many people these days to sign CDs, but I got him to sign a couple of things at the end of our last show together at The Spa Pavilion Theatre in Felixstowe on 9th May 1997. He told me that, in not so many words, "I was never a great fan of T.Rex, although I did have the greatest admiration for Bolan. I think that he was an amazingly prolific songwriter."

To that, he walked off, and came back two minutes later from his dressing room with a great pair of trousers that he had bought in Los Angeles. They were black, made from a stretchy material and had skulls down the sides of each leg. He held them out to me and said, "Here, you can have these if they are any good to you - I won't wear them anymore!" I took them from him instantly with a smile and said, "Thanks - they're great." I haven't met up with Ian since, but those couple of days were to savour.

Around this period there were those who began to take an interest in what I would call my 'formative years'. Although I didn't want anything to get in the way of our forthcoming album, I thought it would be a nice idea to release an album of my previous original work. I ended up issuing a ten track cassette only album, 'Out Of The Silent Planet.' It was fun to compile and it gave fans another insight to material I had recorded in my life before T.Rextasy. I advertised the album in the July 1997 newsletter and in only a couple of months they had sold out completely... I wonder where they all are now?

By the spring of 1997, we had our second album in the can. I called it 'Savage Beethoven', after one of the Bolan-penned tracks that we had included on the CD. Once again, I included two of my own original tracks - 'I Wouldn't Lie' and 'Voice From A Silent Heart' - one rocker and the other a ballad. I was really pleased with "Silent Heart" as I wanted it to sound as if it was based on Bolan's 'Whatever Happened To The Teenage Dream.' I got a friend called Jim Berry up from Cornwall to put some piano on it. He did a perfect job, and played exactly what I asked him to do. I also recalled that Noel Gallagher, from Oasis, had mentioned that his song 'Cigarettes And Alcohol' was loosely based on 'Get It On', so I thought it would be a novel idea to record our version of 'Cigarettes And Alcohol' but in the style of 'Get It On', which we did, and I think it worked extremely well.

On this album, as we did for our previous release, I thought it would be a good idea if we recorded more of Bolan's unreleased and unfinished songs, so I gave the band various Bolan demo-tapes to listen to. We ended up recording 'Savage Beethoven', 'Classic Rap', and 'Sanctified'. We also decided to do songs with a slight twist to the originals, such as 'Buick Mackane', 'Children Of The Revolution', and 'Magical Moon'. The only songs where we stuck strictly to the original versions were 'Metal Guru', and 'Hang Ups.'

Madman Records did a great job of the label - a pastiche of the retro *Fly* label that 'Electric Warrior' was released on, and the black and gold sleeve colouring, turning it into a real and genuine play on the original album design.

I was happy to be notified that the major label *Columbia Records* wished to distribute the album in the Far Eastern territories. We were asked to include two additional bonus songs for that market only, which included Japan, who always wanted extra bonus tracks for their releases. We ended up including a single length edited version of 'Children Of The Revolution', and an acoustic recording of 'Dreamy Lady'. The album was finally released in the UK and the Far East in the summer of 1997. *Columbia Records* released the album with the same sleeve design as the UK version, except that they incorporated a foldout insert with lyrics and notes, in both Japanese and English.

Germany beckoned. The shows there are completely different to those in the UK or Japan. In Germany they seem to prefer lots of varied styles of music at one show, which has always been difficult for me to grasp. I like my concerts to have a theme, by which one knows if it's a rock night, a pop night, or even a bubblegum night, although there were some shows more in line with my own taste.

One of the most memorable was in Barmstedt on 13th June 1997. Ray Dorset from Mungo Jerry was placed in as support, even though some of the adverts actually stated that Mungo Jerry would be appearing, as many people used to think that that was Ray's actual name! I had never met Ray before and he came across as a lovely guy. The show was a sell out and we both received rave reviews from the local press. It made my evening all the better when Ray agreed to perform the encore with us, playing out with 'Hot Love' and a rocking version of 'Tutti Fruitti' where Ray sang alternate verses and also played harmonica.

Most of our concerts in Germany were either a contained package deal with other bands, such as Sweet, Slade, Uriah Heep, or even Middle Of The Road, The Glitter Band, or The Bay City Rollers, but sometimes we managed to get our own shows such as the Stadtsaal in Solingen on 31st October 1997, where we had the opportunity to play for longer than our usual one hour routine and able to include a few album tracks and B-sides that many fans wanted to hear.

I have always had a soft spot for Status Quo, even though I've always preferred the original line up with Alan Lancaster and John Coghlan. Therefore I jumped at the opportunity when I was asked to perform at an open-air festival in Rügen in the summer of 1997 with the Quo on the bill. As the show drew closer and closer, day by day, I was looking more forward to it but Quo's Rick Parfitt had a heart attack and the band had to cancel the concert.

It was such a shame as I was so looking forward to meeting both Parfitt and Francis Rossi. However, all was not lost as another one of my favourite bands from that period was to take their place. I had loved Uriah Heep in the early seventies, especially when David Byron sang lead vocals - sadly another star that has passed away. Their original guitarist Mick Box, and drummer Lee Kerslake were still in the band and it was great to be able to chat about the Heep and just hang out with the guys for a while as I had grown up with their music, playing it loud from my hi-fi.

Opening the evening was The Glitter Band with Gerry Shepherd on guitar, yet again, someone else who is sadly no longer with us. Gerry was a tiny guy, even smaller then me. I always found him quite shy but always complimentary towards us, which was nice. After The Glitter Band's gig, I was asked if I would come out onto the stage shortly before our performance to read out numbers for their lottery! I found it all very unusual, but I did it anyway, all in front of around 2,000 people at an open-air concert! We did however have a cracking show, and it was great to hear Mick Box and Lee Kerslake comment at how good they thought our performance had been. In the morning we all met up for breakfast. Mick left a piece of toast on his plate. I told him for a joke that we would take it back to England as a roadie of ours was a big fan and he would probably have it framed! In fact, we did take the toast back to the UK and gave it to our old roadie, and I wouldn't be surprised if he didn't frame it!

Before now, T.Rextasy (as a full band) had never given a complete 'Unplugged' performance. It was still a time when not too many bands were doing such things. We decided to play our first ever acoustic show at London's 12 Bar Club in July. It wasn't exactly difficult to sell it out, as the venue was so tiny that when Neil stood up he could actually see the people face to face in the balcony! We ended up playing for nearly two hours and it was pleasant to see that we had attracted legendary folk star Bert Jansch, and television presenter Katie Puckric, who stayed for the whole evening.

September 1997 was indeed a very special time for all Bolan people as it wasn't only the celebration of Marc's 50th Birthday, but also the commemoration of his twenty years of passing. To celebrate and commemorate Marc's achievements, the *Performing Right Society* (*PRS*) was to unveil a special memorial stone in Barnes at the spot where Marc and Gloria Jones had that fatal accident in the early hours of 16th September 1977.

I was honoured to have received an invite from the *PRS*, along with Caron and Neil Cross to attend the occasion, held on 15th September. We all arrived on time and mingled with other guests that included Siouxsie and Budgie (from the Banshees), Tony Visconti, Mick O'Halloran, Tony Howard,

Chelita Secunda, Mickey Finn, Jack Green, Bill Legend, Andy Ellison, Rolan Bolan, Geoffrey Bayldon (the *Catweazle* actor who also starred as the waiter in *Born To Boogie*), Harry & Sandy Feld, Eric Hall, and Keith Altham, amongst others.

While mingling, I said, "Hello" to Geoffrey Bayldon. We began chatting and after a couple of minutes he suddenly turned and said, "You know you are very much like your father..." As he carried on, I realised that he could not have met or seen a photo of Rolan, and was under the impression that I was Marc's son. It all got a little embarrassing so I had to tell him who I was before I pointed out Rolan to him! We laughed about it later, but for that one moment, it was a little difficult. I moved on and introduced myself to Tony Visconti, with whom I had been liasing via emails, but had not yet met face-to-face. He was with his wife at the time, May Pang, who was well known for being associated with John Lennon and his 'lost weekend'.* I introduced myself as Danielz, to which he immediately said to May, "May, this is Danielz" after which he gave me a big hug. We chatted for a while before the ceremony began.

It was a touching few minutes as Geoffrey Bayldon recited word-for-word the 'Union Hall' poem (reminiscent of how he had performed it in *Born To Boogie*) plus an additional poem that he read out from Marc's *Warlock Of Love* poetry book. Both John Logan and Nicky Graham from the *PRS* gave speeches of gratefulness and gratitude regarding Marc's generosity towards musicians and *PRS* donations, before Marc's old work colleagues Eric Hall and Keith Altham took to the stand to recall some wonderful anecdotes and stories about him.

Rolan then unveiled the plaque donated by the *Performing Right Society*. After milling around a little longer we all made our way to Olympic Studios for food and refreshments where we chatted further about Marc's achievements and successes, while Jorg Günther from Germany rolled his video camera discreetly for posterity. It was also nice to see Marc's old friends Bruce Welch (from The Shadows), and Mike Mansfield, the director of the TV music show *Supersonic*.**

Since Tuesday 16th September 1997 when we played a one-hour

---

* This was a period of eighteen months between 1973 - 75 when Lennon separated from his wife Yoko Ono and spent his time in Los Angeles in the company of Pang.

** Mansfield persuaded Bolan to perform on a giant swan during one particular performance.

show at a special London commemorative convention, I had taken a stand not to play on the actual day of Marc's demise. It was a strange feeling because neither Tony Visconti nor Rolan Bolan had seen T.Rextasy perform before, so it was all a little daunting to say the least.   Afterwards, I was slightly coy when they came into the dressing room, but both Tony and Rolan immediately said how fantastic they thought the gig was. I think it was a little more nerve racking playing in front of Tony than Rolan in a way, because Rolan had never seen his dad perform and has only video footage as both a memory and a taster. But Tony had seen and heard Marc so many times, so it was absolutely brilliant when he not only gave complimentary comments, but in time became a friend as well.

Over the years, I have appeared on many different television shows, but I always enjoyed doing the VH1/MTV programmes. I did one on 20th September for *Saturday Brunch* where I talked about Marc's influence on the music scene and what he had meant to me. I was also able to chat about the 'Savage Beethoven' album too. It was a nice touch when they pictured the album cover on the screen, and ended the interview playing out with Marc and T.Rex performing 'I Love To Boogie' from *Top Of The Pops*.

Friday 26th September saw Rolan's twenty-second birthday and as he was still in the UK he had decided to ask a few guests who he had now considered friends, to join him for a party at the *Planet Hollywood* restaurant in London. The seven people that attended were myself, Caron, Martin Barden, Ros Davies, Noel Hammond, Harry Feld, and a friend of Gloria's, whose name sadly eludes me now. We all had a great time sitting around one very large table where we spent a few hours talking about Rolan's mum and dad and what the future held for the growing lad. Everyone had bought him gifts; Caron and I presented him with a framed photo of Gloria and Marc holding him as a baby. It was a shot that he had not seen before, as it had remained unpublished, so he was really excited to receive it.

Marc Bolan's 50th Birthday Anniversary was rapidly approaching. I had been in talks with Mick Gray at The Cambridge Corn Exchange over the past several months attempting to arrange a special concert for all the fans. We both thought that it would be a great idea for a Marc Bolan Anniversary Concert to be held there. Mick used to be a T.Rex roadie in the 1970s - he was re-named Mickey Marmalade by Marc due to Mick's past involvement with the band Marmalade.

I got in touch with people such as Andy Ellison and Chris Townson from

John's Children, Akima from Japan, Paul Fenton (a drummer who had recorded sessions and overdubs with T.Rex) and Rolan who at this time had never performed live in the UK. Mick got in touch with Jack Green (T.Rex rhythm guitarist in 1973/4), and Mickey Finn (the original conga player). I also managed to get VH1 on board as Paul King was interested in not only filming the event, but also performing with us as he was also a Bolan & T.Rex fan.

I was a little disappointed with a few people that let us down at the final hurdle. Steve Harley suddenly had a German tour, Boy George had to attend a studio session, and at the last minute Dr Robert from the Blow Monkeys was producing Beth Orton. For some reason Dino Dines u-turned and decided against attending after seeing everyone at the *PRS* plaque unveiling. And Bill Legend became nervous that 'past' relationships might turn up on the day. But I was focused into getting the show sorted out as best as possible.

The stumbling block was with Mickey Finn. When in 1992 Caron and I had written *Wilderness Of The Mind*, we had got in touch with Bolan's manager, Tony Howard. He visited us at our home and spent the evening chatting and giving us the lowdown on T.Rex, together with stories about Marc. Tony ended up kindly writing one of the forewords. In our conversation, he told us that he had been given instructions from Marc to sack Mickey Finn from the band, but he had also been told to keep it quiet from the general public, leaving Mickey to say that he had "left" instead. We printed what Tony had told us, as we believed it to be true, especially as we had heard from another reliable source that this had been the case. I later heard that Mickey had found out that we knew what had happened and was wary of talking to me. Thankfully, Mick Gray talked him round and got him to agree to perform.

The concert took place on Marc's birthday, 30th September 1997. He would have been fifty. Nothing like it had ever taken place at this level before, so it was a joy to be a part of it. It was billed as 'T.Rextasy In Concert with Special Guests.' The evening was full of anticipation and excitement. Mick O'Halloran and Alphi O'Leary both turned up for the event.

Before the show and in the midst of soundchecking, Paul King interviewed all those taking part for a VH1 television special. The sound-checks were dreadful and took hours to get a satisfactory mix. The PA was powerful, but the guys in charge of it seemed to take forever and everyone began to get irritated with nothing progressing. At last, after what seemed like hours of hanging around, everything was set in place and we began to rehearse with each special guest.

The concert began with over 1,200 fans in attendance - the biggest gathering of Bolan fans since 1977. Akima from Japan had flown over just to be part of the event and performed 'Children Of The Revolution' with such gusto and to the total bewilderment of the many Japanese fans that had also flown over especially. I accompanied Paul King on acoustic guitar who sang a beautiful rendition of 'Cosmic Dancer', his voice not faltering at all since his days as a consummate pop star with King. Andy Ellison (on lead vocals) and Chris Townson (on additional drums) came on to perform the very early Bolan track 'Desdemona' with all the energy of a teenager, and Mickey Finn and I did a duo-version of 'Spaceball Ricochet'. Mickey sat down and played bongos, while I stood and played acoustic guitar. It was a fine and proud moment.

Rolan Bolan then came on stage to sing 'Dreamy Lady' a track that he introduced and dedicated to his mother. After my introduction Rolan came on and presented me with a flower. The fans were ecstatic, as very few people in the UK had actually seen Rolan as an adult, having lived most of his life in the USA. Rolan's voice was shaky and nervous, but he kept his cool and got through it. As the song reached its closure, one could sense his relief as he threw flowers to the audience.

The flowers were actually from a giant bouquet delivered to the Corn Exchange for Caron from a Japanese fan. But without reading the card inscription, no one knew and were just helping themselves to the odd flower to either throw out to fans, or wear behind their ears, or for a make-shift vase in the dressing room.

I had been spending some time with Rolan off and on while he was in the UK, and he had decided that he would like to travel with the band to the gig. On the way, Rolan and I went over and over 'Dreamy Lady.' On each run-through he asked if I could sing another line, then another verse. I said that the fans would love him to sing the whole song, but as time went on, he became more anxious, and I thought at one time he may have even pulled out from performing. Therefore, to keep things as calm as possible, we ended up singing alternate verses and singing together in the choruses. I was still very happy that he came along and did the show. It was an extremely brave thing to have done, as he knew that all eyes would be on him, more than anyone else.

I invited Mickey Finn, Jack Green, and Paul Fenton on stage for a few numbers including 'Jeepster', and 'Telegram Sam'. I tried to keep everything as orderly as I could and everything worked out well. It was an absolute success and I still couldn't believe that it had all gone so smoothly. For the encore numbers I had plenty of people to re-introduce, but I surprised even myself by remembering everyone in order. The big encore featured all the performers. We played a long extended version of 'Get It On', before leaving the stage, only to return again for the finale of 'Hot Love'. By this time the stage was soaking wet with spilt water. Andy Ellison had poured a glass of water over my head and then lifted me onto his shoulders, then slipped over causing both of us to go arse over tit. I still carried on playing guitar while lying on my back. It was a great rock 'n' roll ending to a one-off evening that could never be repeated.

We all went to a hotel across the road for an after drinks party, but disappointingly, the mood changed after a little while and some people got into little cliques, which I didn't care for too much. Even though the concert was a spectacular event, I felt that some people had forgotten why they had been invited in the first place. We decided to give it up while the going was good and just remember what a great night it had been for all. So we said goodbye to everyone, and made our way home. I was so happy that I had given my all that night and hoped that if Marc had been looking down, he would have been proud...

マーク・ボラン生誕50周年記念トリビュート企画決定盤！

T.REXTASY

Savage Beethoven

オアシスの「シガレッツ＆アルコール」もシニカルにカヴァーしたT.REXトリビュートの決定版アルバム！　マーク・ボランの生き写し、ダニエルズを擁するT.REXTASY。マークを今偲ぶならこれを聴くべし。

T.レックスタシー
サヴェージ・ベートーヴェン
CD:COCY-80679　¥2,548(tax-in)
シガレッツ＆アルコール、メタル・グゥルー、チルドレン・オブ・ザ・リヴォリューション
他全13曲（日本盤ボーナス・トラック2曲含む）

好評発売中！

マーク・ボランの生誕50周年という記念すべき年に発表となった、T.レックスタシーのセカンド・アルバム。特に7曲目（タイトル曲サヴェージ・ベートーヴェン）は、すばらしい。T.レックスのアルバム「フューチャースティック・ドラゴン」に入れても、見劣りしないぐらいだ。　秋間経夫（マルコシアス・バンプ）
ライナー・ノーツより抜粋

ダニエルズの凄い所は、壇実に前作より極みを増してるのが手に取るようにわかる所。ここまで愛情を持って真剣にトリビュートされているマーク・ボラン鍵匙本人も、天国で相変わらずのラメラメなメイク＆コスチュームで微笑んでくれるはず・・・、がんばれ、ダニエルズ！
廣瀬洋一（THE YELLOW MONKEY）
ライナー・ノーツより抜粋

マーク・ボラン
ゲット・イット・オン
CD:COCY-80680
¥2,548(tax-in)

9/21発売
マーク・ボラン生誕50周年記念盤！
レアな別テイク集
全22曲収録
（日本盤ボーナス・トラック含む）

会員募集中
T.REXTASY FAN CLUB
SOLID COMPANY
COLUMBIA RECORDS

発売元：日本コロムビア/洋楽制作オフィス　tel:03-3584-8223

Above: Japanese advert for 'Savage Beethoven' - 1997.

Below: Ian Hunter and I backstage after our Spa Pavilion show in Felixstowe - 9th May 1997, and a magazine advert for the gig.

Above: T.Rextasy live at the Rügen Festival, Germany - 18th May 1997

Below: By the Berlin wall, Germany in 1997.
From left to right: Neil, Paul, Me, and Nigel.
(Jorg Günther)

Left: An advert for a concert in Barmstedt in Germany with T.Rextasy and Ray Dorset (Mungo Jerry) - June 1997.

Below: Rolan Bolan visiting our flat in Holloway, London in September 1997.

Left: Caron, Rolan, and I at his 22nd birthday party at Planet Hollywood restaurant, London - September 1997.

117

SET LIST AND ORGANISATION FOR 30TH SEPTEMBER 1997

FIRST SESSION: (BEGINS AT 8.00PM)

1.   CADILAC (T.REXTASY ONLY)
2.   BABY STRANGE (T.REXTASY ONLY)
3.   DESDEMONA (T-REXTASY, ANDY ELLISON,CHRIS TOWNSON) (ANDY - LEAD VOX)
4.   CELEBRATE SUMMER (T.REXTASY ONLY)
5.   BORN TO BOOGIE (T.REXTASY ONLY)
6.   CHILDREN OF THE REV. (T.REXTASY WITH AKIMA) (AKIMA ON LEAD VOX)
7.   RIDE A WHITE SWAN (T.REXTASY)
8.   BUICK MACKANE (T.REXTASY ONLY)
9.   METAL GURU (T.REXTASY & PAUL KING) (PAUL ON LEAD VOX)
10. LIFE'S A GAS (T.REXTASY ONLY)
11. I LOVE TO BOOGIE (T.REXTASY ONLY)

ENDS APPROX. : 21.15PM)

(INTERVAL)

SECOND SESSION: (BEGINS AT 21.45PM)

<<ACOUSTIC SESSION>>
12. SPACEBALL (DANIELZ WITH MICKY FINN)
13. SARA CRAZY CHILD (ANDY ELLISON ACOUSTIC SOLO)
14. COSMIC DANCER (DANIELZ & PAUL KING) (PAUL LEAD VOX)
15. DREAMY LADY (DANIELZ & ROLAN) (DANIELZ & ROLAN SHARE VOX)

16. 20TH CENTURY BOY (T.REXTASY ONLY)
17. TEENAGE DREAM (T.REXTASY ONLY)
18. TRUCK ON (T.REXTASY WITH JACK GREEN & PAUL FENTON & MICKY FINN))
19. THE GROOVER (T.REXTASY WITH JACK GREEN & PAUL FENTON & MICKY FINN)
20. ZIP GUN BOOGIE (T.REXTASY WITH JACK GREEN & PAUL FENTON & MICKY FINN)
21. TELEGRAM SAM (T.REXTASY WITH MICKY FINN, JACK GREEN & PAUL FENTON)
22. JEEPSTER (T.REXTASY WITH MICKY FINN, JACK GREEN & PAUL FENTON)

23. GET IT ON (1ST ENCORE - EVERYONE ON STAGE)

24. HOT LOVE (2ND ENCORE - EVERYONE ON STAGE)

Above: My draft set list for the T.Rextasy 'Birthday Concert for Marc' at the Cambridge Corn Exchange on 30th September 1997.

Below: T.Rextasy & guests at the Cambridge Corn Exchange. From left to right: Paul Rogers (bass), Jim Berry (keys), Mickey Finn (congas), Jack Green (guitar), me (guitar), Paul Fenton (drums), Andy Ellison & Chris Townson (John's Children), Rolan Bolan, and Tsuneo Akima (guitar).

Above: Mickey Finn and I performing 'Spaceball Ricochet' at the Cambridge Corn Exchange - 30th September 1997.

Right: Japanese magazine review of the gig. From left to right: Mickey Finn, Jack Green, and me - September 1997.

Below: Rolan handing me a flower as he came on stage to perform 'Dreamy Lady' at the Cambridge Corn Exchange gig.

Viewfinder

Tレックス復活？

マーク・ボラン没後20年の光景

9

A Bolan Commemoration USA Style

A few days later, I received a request from Tony Visconti. He had been invited to an anniversary event in New York City that was being dedicated to Marc. He suggested that I should also be involved, and that if I flew over to New York for the event I would be welcome to stay at his studio apartment. I told Tony that I was interested but that I didn't want to make the trip on my own, so I asked if I could bring a couple of people with me. Tony agreed, so Neil and Gavin Ingels (a friend who also later became the webmaster for the T.Rextasy Internet site) flew across with me.

Tony picked us up from Kennedy Airport in a spacious people carrier, with his wife May and his two children Sebastian and Lara, and drove us to their New York apartment. Tony and May actually lived out of town and used the apartment for studio work and when they needed to be a little more central. After settling in, we chatted and just chilled out before Tony and May said goodnight and left us until the following day.

There were only two beds in the apartment. Gavin had the single in one room, and Neil and I decided to share the double in the other room. It wasn't a standard double, but the biggest I had seen in my life. May had acquired it from John Lennon. May Pang had worked for Lennon and Yoko Ono as a personal assistant in the seventies and had had a widely known eighteen month affair with Lennon. In that time, she acquired a few a bits and pieces including the Emperor bed, which, could have easily catered for at least five people! Neil took one side and I took the other. It was almost as if we were on different sides of the room. In any case, we all had a good night's sleep and ready for the next day's event.

In the morning we thumbed through some of Tony's record collection and came across a few excellent pieces of vinyl including some old BBC transcription discs and a couple of very rare records. When Tony arrived, he said that he had a few things to do before he could return to pick us up, but in the meantime we could play with his studio-mixing desk if we felt like it. He put on a multi-track of 'Jeepster', and 'Get It On', and left us to play around with both tracks, in which we were able to solo Marc's voice or listen to the guitar tracks, and basically rough mixing T.Rex on Tony's desk! I felt that leaving us alone with something so valuable and rare was a lovely trusting gesture and in turn we of course treated his studio equipment and apartment with the utmost respect. Afterwards, Tony gave me a special mix of the two songs on a DAT tape, which I still have in my collection.

Later in the day, he drove us to the club where the gig was to take place. It was quite a small venue and only had one dressing room. I could see that it was going to be quite cramped. I sound-checked one or two numbers, with Tony playing bass and Clem Burke (from Blondie) playing the drums. Lloyd Cole whose biggest hit was in the 1980s with 'Lost Weekend'* turned up later as did various other musicians who were taking part in the event, such as Richard Barone, who used to be in a band called The Bongos. I didn't really know what to expect, but although Bolan fans surrounded me, no one seemed to know all the correct words to some of the songs, such as 'The Groover' for example. I began correcting them but as time went on other lyrics were also being sung incorrectly. I got the distinct impression that they didn't want me to interfere and were quite happy to sing words that they thought were correct, so I backed off.

I hadn't heard of many of the people who were involved, although I remembered the name Joe Hurley as Tony had mentioned him in some of our recent conversations. He helped organise the event as well as singing a couple of songs. The show was quite an intimate affair but I was made very welcome in front of the 200 capacity audience. One of the most interesting aspects of the evening was when Tony did a Q & A session. I was amazed at how little knowledge some of the people in attendance had about Bolan, especially as some of the questions were quite basic. It was an insight to see and hear fans from another country talking about Marc and getting so much information incorrect at the same time. It proved that Marc was really still a cult figure in the U.S.A., and that fans, although obsessive

---

* 'Lost Weekend' reached number 17 on the UK charts in 1985.

and desperate to get the facts, were still reasonably starved of real information about T.Rex.

The concert was great fun and some of the performances were interesting to watch. Such as Lloyd Cole's slurry and alcohol induced version of 'Mystic Lady'. He had been drinking whisky throughout the day and was quite affected by the time of his appearance. Richard Barone is most certainly a genuine fan, of that I have no doubt, and he performed very well. I felt he was really in his element singing Marc songs. In some parts of the show I would describe it as organised chaos, but all in good spirit and I could see that everyone involved had a lovely warm feeling and love for both Marc and Tony. For my part in the proceedings, I performed the two songs that I had sound-checked earlier with Tony and Clem and then for the encore everyone squeezed onto the tiny stage and sang 'Hot Love'. The song carried on and on as no one wanted to stop what was such an enjoyable time. I was so glad that I had made the decision and effort to attend such a lovely intimate evening. The next day Tony and May dropped us off at the airport and we said our goodbyes. We all agreed that the trip had been well worth it.

Back in England I received a call from Paul Fenton, the on/off session drummer hired by Marc, asking if I would be interested in fronting a band that he was putting together. He was going to call it Mickey Finn's T.Rex. I told him I was very happy fronting my own band and that I had already captured much of the UK market place, so I didn't see the point in quitting something I had spent so much time building up. I also was totally against him using the name T.Rex. As far as I was concerned, even though Mickey had been an original member, without Marc Bolan, there would've been no T.Rex.

I have always respected the other musicians, but it has to be said that Marc was T.Rex - the name will always be forever associated and linked to Marc Bolan. In my opinion, no one should ever have the right to blatantly use that name. To further the argument, I could've easily called my band T.Rex, or Dino Dines' T.Rex, or something similar, but it would've been totally wrong, and derogatory towards Marc's memory.

The majority of real Bolan fans were just as disgruntled with them using the name as I was. Paul did however end up playing in Germany with his new band, although I found out later he had been fortunate as he had earlier roadied for Smokie there. He had made contact with one of their promoters who just happened to be Suzi Quatro's German husband, Rainer Haas. Ironically Haas had offered T.Rextasy dates in Germany just a couple of years previously but only on the condition that we took Mickey Finn along with us. I had graciously refused, as I knew Mickey was not in the best of health. I didn't think that he would be totally reliable, and I was not one for babysitting anyone. I was also worried that he would let us down by not turning up, or expecting to be picked up, which he was prone to do from time to time due to his alcohol problems.

I do not hold any malice towards Paul Fenton. I, like many others, have only felt aggrieved by the name of the band, especially later, after Mickey died*, when Paul still retained the name T.Rex in large lettering deleting the words 'Mickey Finn's' but including the phrase 'A Celebration of Marc & Mickey' instead. It made no real difference as they were still being advertised by many promoters as T.Rex!

On 1st November we were back in Germany again with Andy Scott's Sweet in Recklinghausen. Beforehand, both Andy and I were driven to Radio FTV to promote the show. In the ad break the interviewer asked if I would perform an acoustic number. I thought 'Hot Love' would be a good song that everyone could join in with. I asked Andy to clap along in the outro and he did so, which was probably the only time anyone has ever got him involved in a Bolan song. I think he was a little self-conscious though, at least he looked as though he was, but he was a good sport and it made the radio session all that more interesting.

Over the years Andy's 'Sweet' and T.Rextasy have gigged together many times, although our paths have crossed with some damaging effect too. Both of us have our stubborn side which has been a little detrimental to our relationship as acquaintances go. Therefore it was pleasing to hear when a couple of years later, John Skelton, our drummer from 2007 onwards, attended a friend's wedding reception and saw that Andy was also there. John had a brief chat to Andy whereby he asked after me and said that although he thought that I did a great job in T.Rextasy, arguments always occurred because of the previous drummer being left-handed, as the kit had to be re-set and re-positioned for The Sweet's right-handed drummer and turn-over time was always at a premium. I gather that one of the

_____

*Mickey Finn died on 11th January 2003 in hospital in Croydon from suspected liver problems, as a result of his alcohol dependency.

instances that Andy was referring to was a trip we had all made to Sweden in 2006 where because of the lack of depth of the stage our drum kit couldn't be set up in front of the Sweet's and Andy refused, due to time restrictions, to remove theirs. Because Nigel was left-handed it became a catch 22. In the end after a much-heated discussion, we didn't play that night and were only able to play the second of the two gigs that we were booked to do.

The Recklinghausen concert had an 'interesting' line-up including Ohio Express who'd had a bubblegum hit some years earlier with 'Yummy, Yummy, Yummy'. I felt it was inappropriate to support T.Rextasy and Sweet, but that is how some of those dates in Germany took shape. The promoters like to use the term 'Oldie Festival' and it seems that anyone who was able to have had just one hit can get to play at these concerts to around 1500 people.

Throughout December, with Andy Scott's Sweet we toured the UK playing theatre venues from 3rd-24th. Although the line-up worked out well, it wasn't to last as the headline band for the Christmas tour for the next few years would shortly be taken over by Slade.

Just before the year ended we received a batch of press coverage from the likes of *The Sunday Express*, which remarked that "T.Rextasy are the most dedicated tribute band on the scene today", along with *The Sunday Mirror,* which mainly covered my relationship with Caron, and featured a whole double-page spread on us both. *The Birmingham Evening Mail* copied the story in detail with the additional headline "Telegram Sam - He's My Main Man!"

Although the Cambridge Corn Exchange concert was a big success, the monthly music magazines mostly ignored it. However, a beautifully produced Japanese monthly *Dig* decided to cover the event in full. It included an in-depth review of the concert, colour photos of the band and guests, and some very nice and previously unseen photos of Marc himself. Another Japanese magazine also included a lovely double-page colour spread and photos of the evening and a special shot of the Japanese contingent that had flown over especially for the concert.

There were of course one or two Bolan magazines that thankfully did give it their full consideration. A glossy publication *Rumblings* gave the anniversary concert a very detailed and descriptive analysis and contained some good photos, as did the Marc Bolan Fan Club magazine *Interstellar Soul*. Thank goodness there are records and reviews out there that did document such an important event. It was a shame that some of the majors didn't feel it was significant enough to cover, but as always it was the fans that made it what it was.

Apart from T.Rextasy, any alternate life in music and songwriting had become practically non-existent, not that there were any complaints, but my own original work had generally taken a back seat. Other than being able to include a couple of tracks of original material on each T.Rextasy album, my original output had stopped. Therefore, it was a nice surprise when I received a certificate of merit from *Unisong-Amnesty International.** I had sent them a song that I had written a few years earlier called 'Woman In The Gallery', just out of interest to see if it would be included in their choice of 3,000 received songs. I managed to make the top 300, but was just happy to get some kind of recognition for my own work.

For some reason, television and radio latched onto us for a while and breakfast TV was no exception. GMTV invited me onto the Lorraine Kelly TV show shortly after hearing a twenty minute interview with me on her Talk Radio show in January 1998 where we spoke at length about the band and my fascination with Marc Bolan. As I had my acoustic guitar, I ended the interview with a short burst of 'Jeepster'. I ended up going on her show a couple of times, which were always enjoyable. Lorraine is a very amiable and friendly lady who tries to make everyone feel welcome into her studio home. When I appeared on her show later on in May, I had a short chat with her on air before walking over to a small stage to lip-synch to our recorded version of 'Metal Guru'. Embarrassingly, the technicians started the track before I was ready and I had to jump into the song missing the intro - I guess that's live TV for you.

Just a few days after, a call came through from another producer for a television show that Noddy Holder was hosting. The show was called *Electric Ladyland* and was aired on the cable network on the Granada Men and Motors channel. I appeared on this surreal show in May and it was broadcast just a couple of weeks later. The premise was that the programme's special guests, which included members of the The Cult and The Alarm, were blindfolded and then had to touch my hair, and other parts of me (!) and guess who I was supposed to 'be'. At first, one called out, "I

---

*Unisong was an International song contest, helping to raise more than $7500 for *Amnesty International*.

reckon it's Leo Sayer", and then someone else shouted out "is it Robert Plant?" until one of the guests asked "Is it 'Marc Bolan'?" I then had to run over to a stage and with the house band play a short, but live version of 'Get It On'. This was supposed to be a quiz show but it all used to collapse into a state of anarchic impossibility every week! The show was short lived, as was the TV channel.

After I had just completed one of my TV appearances, I had some time to kill, so I decided to visit an old bookshop in Camden Town. While looking through one of the poetry sections, I heard an eloquent, but recognisable voice from behind me say, "would you mind if I take a picture of your shoes please?" I turned around and it was BP Fallon, Marc's old publicist and good friend. He had seen my shoes and thought that they were unusual and wanted to take a few shots of them - for some reason, I never asked why! He took two or three photographs and then a couple of head and shoulder shots. This was actually in the bookshop, so God knows what they must have thought! Afterwards, we had a brief chat and "Beep", as Marc used to call him, talked about how he still missed Marc and wished that he was still with us. I wonder what he did with those photographs?

At the start of the summer season, I was invited by Birmingham City Council to attend the opening of the UK's largest ever dinosaur exhibition at the Birmingham Museum. The publicity officers at the council wanted photos of me standing next to and around the giant model of a Tyrannosaurus Rex for the West Midlands newspapers. I had to dress up in my stage gear and pose in front of museum on-lookers who must have wondered what the hell was going on, and who that weird looking person was having his photos taken alongside a prehistoric model of a dinosaur. No doubt all would've been revealed if they happened to pick up a copy of the *Birmingham Evening Mail* or one of the other papers circulated around the West Midlands the following week.

On 13th September 1998 Caron and I were invited to *The Disco Royale*, Manchester as Rolan Bolan was performing a showcase for the BMI (British Music Industry) with his current band, Brothers Bounce. We were given a promotional CD of two tracks - 'Classic Conversation', and 'Possibilities', both of which sounded extremely current and commercial. Rolan performed well with his band, with his urban edge and soulful vocal, a trait obviously from his parentage. It was unusual for Gloria Jones to be in the country, but she had flown over to be with her son for his initiation into the UK pop world.

Caron had known Gloria since the seventies so when the chance arose I was introduced to her - "You look so much like Marc" was one of the first things she said to me. Alvin Stardust also attended that day to see not only Rolan perform, but to reacquaint himself with Gloria, as he hadn't seen her since 1977. Alvin and I had a brief chat before a few photographs were taken with us all. Rolan was in good spirits as the gig went well.

Unfortunately nothing transpired from the showcase but I was personally really happy to have met Gloria at long last. Rolan did record a few more original tracks, including a song called 'It's All Right' on a CD that was available at a concert he performed at Shepherd's Bush on 18th November 1998, and also, amongst others, a 4-track promo CD in 2004 with the titles 'I Believe', 'You Really Love It', 'Something Beautiful' and 'People Get Ready' that he kindly passed on to me. Sadly again, no deal came to light and Rolan eventually settled back in the USA.

We were never a band to work heavily in the summer months, so in between our gigging schedule, and while some of the band had taken a summer break, I decided to write and publish an A5 magazine dedicated to T.Rextasy. It included features about individual band members, a discography, facts and stories, and anything that I felt that was of interest that had happened over the past few years. I called it *Cosmic Rock*. It ran for a few issues and was published twice yearly for the next couple of years or so via the T.Rextasy Fan Club. I had to stop it when our gigs and the sheer amount of work involved prevented me from the time required to put the magazine together.

One of the more interesting radio interviews I remember doing took place on Talk Radio London on 1st November 1998. Much of the interview was based around a discussion about the Glam feature film *Velvet Goldmine*. The ring of interviewees also included Noddy Holder, the writer Patrick Humphries, and Tony Visconti. There wasn't much critical analysis going on as most of the panel liked the film and were reasonably gentle with their comments. I thought I would stir things up a bit and said that I didn't think the film would relate too well to a British audience, and that in my opinion it came across too much like the "American film producer making a film about a British rock star" and getting so many factual things incorrect in the process.

I felt that it would have been more realistic and acceptable if it had been based on an American Glitter rock star instead of a British Glam rock singer. There has always been this thing in the United States that confuses USA Glitter Rock with UK Glam Rock and although I do not wish to completely generalise, the feel and substance is quite different. In the USA one had the shallowness of the Kiss imagery for instance, and in the UK we had of course Marc Bolan, who made Glam actually part of his make up and not just for the advent of stage. I felt that *Velvet Goldmine* was too stagey and unreal in every shape or form and even if the purpose was to obtain surrealism, or otherworldly it just didn't work for me on any level.

The discussion carried on for a few more minutes, mainly going in circles and not reaching any conclusion, so DJ and interviewer Nicky Horne, asked if I would play a song. I played out with an acoustic version of 'Jeepster', which helped conclude the programme quite nicely.

In the late nineties, a television show called *Nightfever* became a popular, albeit slightly kitsch programme, where mostly B-list celebrities would come on the show and sing karaoke style to backing tracks. There would be a panel of girls on one side and a panel of men on the other. Lyrics would also appear on the screen when songs were played for those watching at home to join in the fun. It was supposed to be a show whereby points were given to whoever sang the song the best, but really it was just mayhem every week, with Suggs from Madness trying to hold court.

T.Rextasy was asked to appear on the show on three separate occasions between 1998 and 1999, the only band to be asked back more than twice. Each time however, we were asked to play the same song, '20th Century Boy', and each time we had to mime to our own recording of it, although I did have a live microphone, so I was able to put in the odd ad-lib and pretend it was *Top Of The Pops*! On one of the shows, they had two guest bands - one was T.Rextasy, the other was The Wombles! It was fun to do, although it was a shame that Mike Batt, the originator of the Wombles tunes, wasn't inside any of the costumes!

One thing that was always being asked of me by fans was when a live recording would be released, and also if any of my posthumous recordings would ever see the light of day. In the spare time I had, I managed to do both. I decided to call the live album 'The Crack Of Dawn' - for no particular reason except that it just sounded right for the time. The album featured various live recordings and sessions from Germany and England. The quality was one of a decent bootleg, but I liked the rawness of it all and so, it seemed, did the people who bought it, as I had to do three separate pressings before I had it deleted.

The second album consisted of tracks that I had recorded in my formative years and covered my recordings throughout the eighties. They included songs with Tarazara, and solo recordings including those that were held under the guidance of my then manager Adrian Miller. The album was titled 'Out Of The Silent Planet' and, like the live T.Rextasy CD, was issued on the *Solid Baby Records* label. I had released these songs a few years previously with the same title on cassette, but it was now time to update them to compact disc. I chose the title from a CS Lewis book I was reading at the time. I have always had a soft spot for the author, so I thought it would be a nice tip-of-hat to him. Again, I was surprised at how well it sold - not in the thousands, but I still had to get it re-pressed a couple of times.

I was pleased to receive a telephone call from Chris Etherington who ran the North of England *Fender* Guitar Club. He rang to tell me that he had put my name forward to receive an honorary endorsement for membership and it had been accepted. Mainly on the grounds that I had been presented with a complimentary USA 1960s re-issue *Fender Stratocaster* a couple of years earlier from *Arbiters* (the guys behind *Fender*). A few weeks later I was interviewed and photographed for their official magazine, *Frontline*.

It was this year that Marc's official Japanese photographer from the early seventies, Masayoshi Sukita, had decided to visit the UK and had heard about T.Rextasy. He arranged to attend our show at The Standard Music Venue in Walthamstow. After the concert he came backstage with a beaming smile and although not being able to speak English, we communicated through his interpreter. He said that he enjoyed the show as it had brought back many memories. He said that he would like to take a few photographs of me before he left and that he would send me a few of the best shots. We ended the evening with Sukita (as he likes to be called) taking various photos backstage of me wearing a silver top and satin dungarees.

Just before leaving he said that he would like to give me a present. He delved into his bag and took out a couple of beautifully oversized black & white badges of Marc that were originally used as promotional items for the 'Marc Bolan 1972 Exhibition' held in Tokyo that year. Many fans in the UK were unaware that some of the photos used on the back cover sleeve of 'Tanx' were actually shot from that exhibition and that most of the photos were taken by Sukita.

Towards the end of the nineties, we gigged more and more, playing venues up and down the country, and never slowing down. It was great to headline The Boston Gliderdrome in Lincolnshire before the end of 1999, especially as so many fans remember this venue from the clips and photos of when T.Rex played there at its peak in the early seventies. Nearly 1,000 turned up for the show, many I feel out of nostalgia, and some out of curiosity.

I recall looking around the large dance hall and thinking that it hadn't really changed much since Marc's heyday. After the show, the manager presented me with a 68-page A5 booklet, which told the story about the venue's glory days. This was a lovely piece of nostalgia as it contained photos and write-ups of many of the acts and bands that had played there, including a whole page about Marc Bolan & T.Rex.

A while later we began to play, what became for years to come, our yearly December Christmas concerts with Slade II, featuring original members Dave Hill and Don Powell. I decided that from the start of the new millennium, I would become more particular in my acceptance of venues and bookings. There were now a few more Bolan related bands coming on the scene so it was important to keep our standards high.

I have always liked being seen as out on a limb, on my own, doing my own thing, which is one reason, why I am sure T.Rextasy has been considered by some to be slightly aloof. I also took the decision not to become a member of any club, or association, while in the band. I have never been that good at mixing with people anyway, and even though some people have seen me as outgoing and sometimes perhaps a little pushy, I am basically quite a shy guy, so I mostly prefer to retain the company I keep, and keep myself to myself, meeting up with only close friends and family.

It was time to aim towards the more up market venues, such as theatres and art centres and the better quality rock venues. We wanted to cut out the lower end gigs with their dodgy PA systems and bare bones lighting rigs with some of their non-qualified engineers. It wasn't an ego thing at all. We were just getting more and more bookings from better venues, it was as simple as that. If I had kept many of the old venues I would not have had the opportunity to raise the bar, and I am, if nothing else, ambitious.

I was stunned one day to receive an email from Sylvain Sylvain, one of the original members from the seventies US Glam/Punk band The New York Dolls. He told me that he had found me through going to Tony Visconti's website. It was of course a pleasure to hear from him. He wrote that he thought, "It would be so cool to do a rock 'n' roll tour together." He also told me that the first time he remembered seeing Bolan was at the Roundhouse in Camden in 1970 when it was only Marc and Mickey Finn on stage. He also commented that he thought, "Marc wrote the best songs in pop history," ending with, "You're doing a great job and I would love to hear your music." We ended up sending each other our latest releases - I sent him the 'Savage Beethoven' album, and he sent me a copy of a great album called 'Sleep Baby Doll'.

This was of course before The New York Dolls got back together again and before Morrissey managed to tempt them back over to the UK to appear at the famous *Meltdown Festival* in 2004. In the meantime we corresponded for a good while over various emails chatting about what each other was doing. He talked about his solo tours in the USA, his recording plans, his love of Bolan, his wanting to tour the UK, and the money he was getting, or sometimes not getting, as was the case. Strangely, his email phrasing was almost British in a way, calling me 'mate' for instance, which used to make me smile... You just never know who will get in touch next.

Left: In Tony Visconti's studio apartment in New York City. Left to right: Me, Tony, Neil Cross, and Gavin Ingels - October 1997.

Below, left: Playing acoustic guitar in Tony's apartment.

Below: Advert for the New York Marc tribute concert.

Right: My Certificate of Achievement from *Unisong* for supplying the track 'Woman In The Gallery' - 1997.

Above: Performing at the Bolan tribute concert at The Fez Club, New York - 3rd October 1997.

Left: Performing the encore at The Fez Club. Left to right: Sax player (from Dexy's Midnight Runners), me, Joe Hurley, Tony Visconti, Richard Barone (Bongos).

Right: Promo photo taken by Marc Bolan's Japanese photographer Masayoshi Sukita backstage at The Standard Music Venue in Walthamstow, London.

Below: Issues 1&2 of the T.Rextasy magazine *Cosmic Rock*.

'Out Of The Silent Planet' - my CD of original material compiled in 1999 but released in 2000.

Right: Dave Hill wearing a T.Rextasy t-shirt while Slade and T.Rextasy were gigging together in Germany.

Below: Pictured on a rare holiday in Portmeirion, Wales - 1990s.

10

Acquisition Of Bolan's Tapes

In 1999, I had to take some time out from my T.Rextasy life as something of vast importance to the Bolan world had come up. I was approached by entrepreneur Mike Southon who told me that he knew of a producer in Northamptonshire who had gained possession of most of Bolan's master tapes. Some later ended up in the auction houses of London but did not reach their reserve price. Caron and I approached a few fans and people we knew to ask if they would be interested in joining us to save Marc's original precious recording tapes from being scattered and distributed around the world.

We couldn't believe the knock-backs and rejections we received from certain people who could afford them or at least obtain the relevant funds but were just not interested. We decided that if they were not interested, then it would be down to us. From the people and friends we had at the time, only Gavin & Sally Ingels, Paul & Judi Thomas, and Marc Arscott and Karen Hirst proved passionate enough about acquiring the tapes and saving them for posterity. We all gathered together a ridiculous amount of cash, from loans and our savings, and whatever means possible to purchase the cream of Bolan's two-inch multi-track tapes and quarter inch demo and master recordings.

With our large bounty of cash (that was the deal - no cheques), Caron and I together with Paul Thomas drove up to a house in Northampton and cherry picked the best of the tapes that we wanted for our conglomerate. In time it ended up as *Thunderwing Productions Limited*, a name taken from the Bolan B-side composition of the same name. In those days, Caron had a purple *Nissan Micra*. The boot, the backseat, the floor in the front and back, and every spare inch of space was filled with original Bolan tapes and their boxes. It was a remarkable feeling to suddenly think that we were now the owners of the majority of Marc's personal master tapes.

We knew we were not able to release original Bolan product in the UK due to the legal restrictions from *Wizard Artists*, *Edsel Records* and the *Westminster/Universal Group* - all companies who held the rights to T.Rex with a tight reign. I therefore approached Bolan's record company in Japan - *Teichiku/Imperial Entertainment*. I had been able to establish some good contacts because of my recent tours there. I flew out to Japan with a few well chosen recorded extracts to play to one of the company's directors. On my return to the UK and in no time at all a deal was struck between *Thunderwing Productions*, *Teichiku* and *Wizard Artists* for us to mix and master two CD albums of original Bolan product.

We called the first album 'Bump 'n' Grind'. It contained fifteen tracks and was released in 2000 in a beautiful mini-LP designed open-out card sleeve with a comprehensive booklet. Duncan Muir, from *Sunshine Designs*, was a great help in the design of the album cover. The CD consisted of extended singles mixed down from mostly multi-track master tapes, including an un-faded six minute version of '20th Century' Boy' which had never been heard before, together with an amusing and what sounds like an alcohol induced twelve-minute minute jam of 'Children Of The Revolution'.

We followed it up about a year later with 'Shadowhead', which contained eighteen tracks and was again primarily mixed down from two-inch multi-track tapes and consisted of extended versions of exceptional quality. But this time it was mostly album tracks and unreleased versions of songs and studio sessions, including tracks such as 'Rapids', 'Baby Boomerang', 'Big Black Cat', and 'Precious Star'. Once again the album received critical acclaim from both sides of the Atlantic obtaining rave reviews, which made us all feel that we had done Marc proud. All of this felt surreal in a way but of course gave me great satisfaction, but I really had to get back to my livelihood, which was of course T.Rextasy.

The start of 2000 began well with the band being asked back yet again to appear on *Nightfever*, where once again we performed '20th Century Boy'. Suggs, was still the host and welcomed us back. One of the guests on the show who had been a longstanding friend and colleague of the DJ and TV star Kenny Everett, Cleo Rocos, took a shine to Neil Cross. They spent most of the waiting time and in-between takes, chatting to each other.

I did think that there may have been a little chemistry there, but nothing was taken any further.

Before long, we were back on the road playing one of our more memorable shows at The Talk Of The Town in Kent. Members of the punk band Eater came along to see us play. They had broken through with their fifteen minutes of fame in 1977 when they released a rough punk version of 'Jeepster'. They were all very young children at the time so when they introduced themselves we didn't recognise any of them!

The feature film *Billy Elliot*, about a young Northern boy who dreams of becoming a ballet dancer, helped boost our stature even more so. Not only were there Bolan songs in the film, but also the producer had made it quite clear that he was a fan of T.Rex. Therefore, it was pretty cool when I received a call asking if we would be interested in playing at the film premiere party that was to be held in an exclusive club in London's West End. I was delighted and accepted immediately.

We played a set of T.Rex hits, and then had a great time mingling and star-spotting while eating and drinking all that had been provided for everyone. Stars such as Julie Walters, Jamie Bell, Hugh Grant and Kathy Burke were in attendance. We all stayed ligging about until the end of the evening as we had to wait until there was a convenient time for all our equipment to be stripped down and loaded. On the way out Paul Rogers and I saw Kathy Burke standing in the exit doorway swaying a little and looking a bit worse for wear. She said to us with a slur, "I really enjoyed your show." I smiled and said "thanks", then Paul said something like "I think you've had a little too much to drink haven't you?" She laughed, swung her handbag around and whacked him over the head with it and shouted "bloody cheek!" It was good-natured fun and banter.

A few months into the year a scout approached me from BBC Television asking if T.Rextasy would be interested in appearing in a forthcoming one-off special programme called 'Battle Of The Fantasy Bands'. The criteria was that every band would have to play totally live without they aid of any backing discs, which immediately cast aside a wealth of tribute bands on the scene at the time. I rejected their invitation at first, as I didn't think that in the scheme of things we would be popular enough to win a satisfying position, but in the end and after various telephone calls from the BBC, they persuaded me to accept.

On the day of the competition I began to regret it. Bands such as The

Counterfeit Stones, a Beatles band, an Abba band, a Bee Gees band, and a U2 band called Achtung Baby, all groups that had mostly outsold T.Rex were appearing on the bill. I didn't think we stood a chance. Terry Wogan and Ulrika Jonsson hosted the show and before hand I did a filmed interview with Ulrika where I talked about Bolan, T.Rex, and T.Rextasy.

Every band was allocated around ten guests each, while the rest of the audience were made up of journalists and the general public who had written in for tickets - the studio was packed to the rafters. All the bands had to play just one number and all performed well. We were due on last and we took to the stage with our chosen song 'Jeepster'. As soon as we started, 'twang', a string on my guitar snapped. Recording had to stop while I had it changed. I decided that the best thing to do was to try and keep the audience from getting irritated or agitated so I sang a quick solo version of 'Life's A Gas' without any instrumentation.

A few minutes later, which felt like an hour, my guitar was re-strung. and I plugged it back into the *Orange* 4 x 12 speaker cabinet stack behind me which *Orange* had kindly couriered to me personally for use on the day. We kicked into 'Jeepster' once again before another setback occurred. This time the producers had decided that the camera angles were wrong, so we had to start yet again. By the time the cameras started rolling again, nerves were getting the better of me and I had to get myself into a state of confidence. Thankfully, we got through it without any further hiccups and I was relieved when it was all over.

We all made our way back down the stairs to our dressing room to get changed thinking the most we would get out of the day would be a good live promotional video from the recording. We then went back upstairs to hear the voting. Terry and Ulrika began announcing the winners. The U2 band was given third place with 'Best Musicianship', and then the Beatles band were announced second for the 'Best Look'. Just as the position of first was being announced, Steve Elson, better known as Nick Dagger, the main-man behind The Counterfeit Stones took a step forward, as Ulrika and Terry announced that the "overall winner" was T.Rextasy! Steve looked just as surprised as we were. We had already got changed back into our regular clothes believing that we didn't have a chance. All filming had to stop again as we had to hurry back to the dressing room to change back into our stage clothes.

Because of this we had to film our amazement and elation again in our stage clothing, pretending that we had just heard the result. It was contracted that the overall winners had to play an additional number at the end of the show, so straight after the announcement we jumped back on stage and played 'Children Of The Revolution' before the end captions rolled. It had been, in the end, a definite and worthwhile programme even though I don't think I would ever do something like that again!

Afterwards, we all attended a BBC TV after-show party. Everyone was in good spirits. Steve, from The Counterfeit Stones, joked to me, "surely the result must have been a fix!" Terry Wogan didn't stick around for any amount of time, and after getting his share of food and drink he left without speaking to hardly any of us. He jumped ship as soon as the programme was over, which we all felt was a little bit rude and not at all in the way his persona is publicised, although It didn't stop us from having a good time as we buzzed in glory for the next few hours.

Prior to the programme being shown on 19th January 2001, I had my photo in just about every TV listings magazine in the country. I was interviewed by Stuart Maconie for the *Radio Times*, by the *Sunday Mirror*, and a horde of other publications, all while having to keep the outcome of the programme a secret. I was very happy with the filming when it was finally shown at peak time on BBC1. It was great to be able to publicise on our posters and advertising that we had been 'Voted Best Live Tribute Band in the UK on BBC1', for years ahead.

In 2000, a special 'invitation only' Marc Bolan convention was arranged by hard-core Bolan collector George Rab. Although Caron and I had been invited, I wanted to add something special for the evening, so a few weeks beforehand while Tony Visconti was in the UK I invited him to our flat to do an interview about Marc and his recordings. As Tony had become a friend of mine, he didn't refuse and we ended up talking on camera for nearly two hours. Paul Thomas did the recording while I interviewed. We ended up editing it down to just one hour for the convention.

George, in the meantime, had also asked if I would do a talk on the recent acquisition of our Marc Bolan multi-track master tapes and recently formed company, *Thunderwing Productions Ltd.*, of which by that time I was made Company Secretary. In front of the specially invited audience, which included Mickey Finn, Eric Hall (Bolan's record plugger and friend) and Mick Gray, myself and Marc Arscott talked about the tapes, how we had acquired them, the state and condition of them, what was included on them, and what our future plans were. It was an unusual and extremely interesting day with plenty of original Marc costumes on show and additional talks by the other guests.

Towards the end of the evening, Mickey Finn was sitting alone and called me over for a chat. He said that he would really like to do some work with me, not with the band, but just the two of us playing some music together. He said that he thought I did a brilliant job, which I found heart-warming and endearing. I said that it would be great and we should get together at a later date and sort something out. I was also really surprised because Mickey had by this time joined Paul Fenton's band and I had heard stories from certain stirrers that he didn't want to work with me again. So it was with great pleasure that he had approached me with his offer.

It was quite surprising how some things happen when one least expects them to. One evening in 2000, I received a phone call from a producer called Brian Adams, the same guy that had signed me up in the eighties at Shepperton Studios! He had heard about T.Rextasy and wanted the band to record a series of T.Rex backing tracks with a view to recording a selection of artists to sing lead vocals on the individual songs.

We only had two days to record twelve tracks, so we didn't have the luxury of numerous takes, or run-throughs in the recording session. I was also not allowed to get involved in the production. The powers that be wanted to make the backing tracks sound Bolanesque, but not altogether like T.Rex. They wanted to adapt some of the recorded instruments to create a sound as if it wasn't exactly T.Rextasy playing on every track. I did however make sure that I was contracted to sing at least one number, so I was left to sing lead vocals on 'Get It On'. Other artists that appeared singing lead vocals included Doogie White (Ritchie Blackmore's Rainbow), Ray Dorset (Mungo Jerry), Steve Overland (FM), Chris Farlowe (of 'Out Of Time' fame), Davie Paton (Pilot), John Matthews (Undercover), and Jill Saward (Shakatak). It was a diverse bunch, but it was yet another enjoyable experience having so many varied singers on top of the tracks we had recorded.

The album was eventually released on *Cleopatra Records* (a division of the *Anagram* and *Cherry Red* label) in 2001 and titled 'The Music Of Marc Bolan & T.Rex - Legacy'. I only found out about the title after I had received my complimentary release of the CD through the post. The cover was cheaply produced and the production and mixing could've been so much better. It was a shame that more money couldn't have been injected into the project because the idea and concept was well thought out, although It was annoying when I checked through the credits to see that not only my name was spelt incorrectly, but they had also spelt T.Rextasy as T.Rextacy!

However, I was pleased that just a couple of months later I was sent another re-packaged version of the same album that had been released in Russia. The sleeve was quite absurd as the front cover artwork was a direct steal from "My People Were Fair..." but with the words 'A Tribute to T.Rex & Marc Bolan - Legacy' printed over the original Tyrannosaurus Rex sleeve. I was much happier with the credit information though, as whoever had re-designed the sleeve had noticed the spelling errors and corrected not only my name, but also the spelling of T.Rextasy.

My time in T.Rextasy has always been one of excitement and one of never knowing what may happen, and just one of these incredible times happened in January 2001 when we were asked to travel all the way to Marrakech in Morocco to play a one-off concert! What an amazing experience it was. On our first day we were shown around the market places and souks and taken to the town by an allocated chaperone. He seemed to have brothers, sisters, and cousins all over the place who owned shops and stalls selling products from wood carvings, clothing, and various nick-knacks for unassuming tourists!

At the time, we were using a roadie called Colin, although we all called him Bugsy. For some odd reason, we were taken into a rug and carpet house, whereby the owners dressed him up in full local regalia and suddenly transformed him into a passable Arab. As we walked through the souk market we saw some very odd things indeed, such as a giant mound of second hand false teeth, which were, all for sale as individual sets while people were trying them on to get a good fit! Another stall had chunks of raw meat hanging up on large hooks that was hounded and surrounded and being crawled on by thousands of flies. I am sure that health and safety was not in the vocabulary of the owners or traders in this section of the market place.

In the afternoon, we were all taken to the desert, where we rode camels that were owned by; yes you've guessed it, the cousins of the chaperone. It was all great fun and we had photos of riding camels and sitting by the side of camels, you get the picture. It was unbearably hot, so on our return to the hotel, which was amazing in itself being partly constructed from pure marble, it was a relief to enter a building that was so cool. Food was in abundance, but I hoped that they hadn't purchased any from the market stalls that we had seen earlier, as was the drink, which was in full supply. I was surprised to see that even though the locals were not supposed to participate in alcoholic beverages, one would never have guessed it as they drank just as much as any of the hotel guests!

The gig itself was an evening corporate affair, playing to a host of people that were not really interested in live music at all. We kind of guessed as much, as corporate events tend to be made up of people who are only there to promote themselves, and for the free food and drink with the hope that they may also walk away with an award or two - the bands tend to become a bit of a sideline or novelty. However, the experience over the previous twenty-four hours alone made up for the damp squib of a show. In the morning there was a hold up in leaving the hotel, as a couple of the band hadn't paid for their additional drinks not included in the rider and had to settle up their bill before they were allowed to leave. It was hit-and-miss whether they would get to the airport in time. Being stuck in a foreign land without sufficient funds or support would not have been any fun. Luckily for them, they just managed to reach the terminal in time for check-in.

The year had begun in a pretty cool fashion, but then out of the blue I received a letter from someone claiming to be the long lost daughter of Peter (Dino) Dines! It appeared that this 32-year-old Norwegian woman called Agnes had been sent letters from her mother Ashild claiming that Dino had had an affair with her some years previously and that Agnes was his daughter! She told me that she wasn't after any money from him and that she only wished to see him to make contact with no strings attached. I told Dino, who was obviously taken-aback and shook up. He then told me that he remembered Ashild as a lovely woman whom he did have an affair with and was stunned that he could have a daughter that he had never known about! I passed on Agnes's details to Dino and after various conversations and some intimate and personal knowledge was exchanged, Dino told me that she was definitely his daughter! Over the next few years Dino corresponded and spoke to Agnes and established a good relationship with her, even arranging to meet at a later date. I was quite touched to think that without T.Rextasy, they may never have found each other.

Every now and then I was approached to write the liner notes for the odd CD album. One of which was for the CD 'T.Rex Rocks', issued and released by *Crimson Records* in 2001. I enjoyed writing the notes as most of the tracks were not the usual hit singles, but included, as the title suggested, the rockier side of T.Rex. 'Buick Mackane', and 'Chariot Choogle' (from 'The Slider') and 'Plateau Skull' (a track only released posthumously), were three songs that I loved and made it quite easy for me to rave about them in the notations. The CD even included photos from my personal collection.

Of course not everything runs smoothly and on 13th April 2001 we were informed that Richard Jones, the brother of Gloria Jones had died of a heart attack. I had previously been invited to Richard's house and had met him on various occasions. He was a very big built guy but like a gentle giant and hardly ever seemed to take off his beloved 10-gallon cowboy hat when he ventured outside. He had a soft speaking voice and kept his hand in writing, singing and producing. I liked him and found him very approachable and always willing to chat. Richard was of course the guy driving in the car following behind Marc's *Mini* on that fateful day of Marc's and Gloria's accident.

Gloria invited Caron, and I (together with friends Ros Davies and Martin Barden) to the remembrance service. It must have been a custom of their religion to line up and walk around the open coffin, and touch the head of the deceased. Not wanting to appear rude, we did the same. Afterwards, Gloria asked us back to Richard's house, where on arrival, 'Crimson Moon', and 'I Love To Boogie' were played to lighten the mood. We all spent some time with Gloria and her husband Chris, before taking our leave. We didn't want to out-stay our welcome as Gloria had to prepare for Richard's funeral.

Glutton for punishment for long distance travelling, we had accepted and headed off for another one-off gig, this time it was in Abu-Dhabi! Once again the show was for a special corporate event and although we were treated exceptionally well, the actual concert itself was once again mediocre, playing in front of a group of people who were not very interested in what we had to offer. Before the gig I went around the town with Neil. It was so hot that I thought the ground would burn beneath me. In fact the heat was so intense that when I pressed down hard onto the pavement I easily made an impression in the tarmac. Workmen seemed to be everywhere, building up the surrounding areas for future luxury apartments and even more hotels. Just like Marrakech, the drinking situation seemed to be lax to say the least. All laws and talk of non-alcoholic beverages for the locals seemed to be in place out in the public arenas, but as soon as the Arabs entered the gates of the private sectors, they really knew how to put it away!

In the sweltering afternoon, we all took a walk by the sea. I remember sliding my arm into the water and feeling the warmth coming from it. It was a strange sensation as it really felt like it would burn if I had left it there for any length of time. We wandered about for a while as there wasn't too much to do as so much building work was taking place everywhere we went. It seemed such a long way to go for a corporate gig, but it yet again was another opportunity to give us an insight into another way of life. We had a great couple of days in a country that we had never been to, and to prove to some extent how hypocritical people can be about certain aspects of religion and lifestyle. As great as visiting different countries had been, we decided from this point that if we could get enough work in the UK from now on, then travelling abroad would become the exception to the rule.

For our Bolan Anniversary Concert on 15th September 2001, I invited Dino Dines to join us for the gig. Although Dino had played with us before, this was the first time he would actually play a full concert. Playing at my side, it made the songs feel and sound more like how Marc had played them around 1975 or 1976, rather than 1971 to 1973. When we played 'Jeepster' for instance, it sounded like the live version from 1977 instead of the original song from 1971 or the *Born To Boogie* Wembley version. But it did make a great change and how could we not bring Dino into the fold when he was so enthusiastic about playing with us? He loved every minute of it and asked if he could start playing more dates with the band. He told one interviewer, "I wouldn't have considered joining T.Rextasy if I thought that they were just a normal tribute band."

I have never thought of T.Rex as a keyboard-based band, as my favourite line-up had always been the quartet of Marc, Mickey, Steve, and Bill. However, I always understood why Marc had to change direction. As a writer one does have to take on alternative styles and explore different forms of music. I doubt very much if I would've accepted another keyboard player as a permanent member of the band - I wanted Dino on board, because it was 'Dino Dines from T.Rex'. Playing some of those songs live with him made it feel like a T.Rex band circa the later years, and for that period, while he was in the band, I really enjoyed it. He told us stories about the way Marc would suddenly change from being Mark Feld into 'Marc Bolan' as soon as he came into contact with the fans, or if he was around other musicians or people from the media. Dino said that, to him, Marc was "just a geezer" who he got on really well with, musically and socially.

Dino took rolls of photos of Marc, especially around the 1976 period, and one day he decided to give us a screened photo exhibition in his kitchen with his film projector. Many of the photos were interesting because they were casual shots of Marc in the street, outside the venues, pulling faces, and generally goofing about. Altogether we saw eighty or so slides and photos, so it made for a good evening. Dino also showed us a silver belt that Marc had given to him, along with a couple of Futuristic Dragon t-shirts, a couple of promotional 'Dandy In The Underworld' paper jackets, and some quarter-inch tapes that he had been working on in 1977. He also mentioned how happy Marc had been and how he was looking forward to following up the tour and album. He felt that after Rolan was born, Marc calmed down quite a lot and became one of the nicest guys he had ever worked with.

In late January 2002 I was offered a couple of associated jobs, one of which I took up, and the other I declined. The one I liked, or at least I was more interested in, was for a modelling session for a glossy monthly magazine *Arena* - a 'guys' fashion magazine. They wanted me in my Bolanesque guise to have photos taken in various designer clothing that they had supplied. I had to change into various outfits of which they had to adapt as all the clothes were mainly made for models of around 6' tall with a 40" chest, while I am only 5' 7" with a 36" chest! As with most sessions, whether they relate to music, fashion, or film, there was a lot of hanging around and people whispering and pointing about camera angles and lighting. This took up most of the afternoon but they decided to use the one photo out of the session which they were happiest with, and that I was very pleased with too. It depicts me in a very expensive black satin jacket designed by Andrew Mackenzie, a sleeveless white t-shirt with turquoise detail by *Energie*, and a black waistcoat by *Exte* - the photo was used as promised and printed on one whole page in their April 2002 edition. I was also wearing a lovely pair of metallic trousers too, but sadly they were out of shot.

The invitation I rejected was for appearing in the music video for 'Bad Cover Version' by Pulp. I was asked if I would be prepared to dress up and basically prance about as Marc Bolan. I didn't take it any further and turned the whole idea down. I think in the end they just got someone/anyone to dress up a little like bit like Marc, and they did what I was initially asked to do. I doubt very much if lead singer Jarvis Cocker, had even been involved in this decision, as it had been an idea of the film company that had been trying to arrange the score and storyboard. It was a shame really because I thought Pulp was a cool band and had a lot going for them, but this just wasn't my scene as I didn't want to come across as someone mocking Marc just for the sake of starring in a music video.

Amongst many of the special guest appearances that I did for Mike Fab-Gere, one that stands out on it's own was for a charity event at The Palace Theatre in London. I was asked to perform 'Get It On', 'Hot Love', and '20th Century Boy', and then later join in for the encore of The Rolling Stones' 'Brown Sugar'. Mike's band that day consisted of members of the Colin Bluntstone Band, Wishbone Ash, and Don Airey from Rainbow and Whitesnake - all in all, a great backing band! The whole evening was a blast and made an absolute mint for charity.

After our 1997 Cambridge Corn Exchange show, I had kept in touch with Alphi O'Leary. Unfortunately, he had been fighting cancer for some time and I was sad to hear of his death in February 2002.

A name synonymous with the late seventies and eighties punk and new wave scene was a band called Swell Maps with their lead singer and protagonist Nikki Sudden. He later branched out as a solo performer and obtained credibility from critics and punks alike when he released a wealth of original material over the years. In 2002 he began recording an album entitled 'Treasure Island'. Nikki had always been a die-hard Bolan fan and never lost sight of his influences, which also included Keith Richards from The Stones. For this album he had written two songs that were specifically Bolan influenced entitled 'Hanoi Jane', and 'Treasure Island'. He wrote to me asking if I would contribute my guitar playing and backing vocals to both of these tracks. I agreed, even though I knew that it would be difficult to arrange the scheduling. Nikki was based in Germany and every time he returned to the UK, I was away gigging somewhere. In the end, we had to cut our losses as we were never able to arrange any amount of suitable time together but said that we would make sure that we would record with each other on the next album.

Unfortunately even before the album was released, Nikki died from heart failure while on tour in the USA in March 2006. Caron had first met Nikki at a T.Rex gig in Hastings in 1975 and became a good friend of his and saw him progress as a performer and songwriter. I got to know Nikki years later as a friend and musician. It was so tragic that it had to end in that way. We attended his funeral in Leamington Spa on 19th April. One of his songs, 'Stay Bruised' (this was actually how he signed off in his last letter that he wrote to me) was played during the service. Nikki looked and lived like one of those real old time rock 'n' roller's in the Keith Richards style. He never had any time for tribute bands and I seemed to be the only one he ever accepted - I think he knew and felt that I was genuine and treated my career as though I had been handed the baton of Marc's music to be carried on, and that was fine by me.

At the end of May 2002 Tony Visconti had flown over on another visit to the UK. When he arrived in England I spoke to him on the telephone whereby he said that although he had come over on a business venture and that leisure time would be at a premium, he would still like to see me. He told me that he would like to introduce me to an old and interesting lady friend that he had known for many years.

A couple of days later I received a call from Tony inviting me for an evening meal with him, his friend and her family. I was given an address and an early evening arrival time to a large and imposing house in Surbiton in Surrey. Tony's friend, a lovely woman called Roshan who he had known since his early days in England in the sixties, greeted me. After our meal, Roshan took me on a tour around her beautiful house. Amongst the various and luxurious antique furniture and lavish surroundings, there, on the wall was a very large photo of her standing with ex-British Prime Minister, Margaret Thatcher - this was a woman with very influential friends and acquaintances!

Afterwards, a few of us sat at a large table and Tony played us a CD-R of the new David Bowie album he had recently been producing, but I couldn't hear it very well as everyone was chatting. One interesting little story came about when Roshan said to Tony, "Do you remember years ago when you and Marc came to my house to put up some shelves when I lived in Putney?" She turned to me and commented that, "the very first time I ever met Marc he was wearing a blanket with a hole cut in the middle where his head popped through!"

It was such an enjoyable and fascinating evening. It was amazing to think that Roshan had known and met such influential people throughout her life. I know that Tony was truly upset when a few years later Roshan passed away. She was obviously someone that had meant a lot to Tony and who had helped look after him when he was still discovering his own path in the music business.

Mistakes can sometimes be comical as was a Russian CD-Rom release that included various Marc Bolan albums all on one disc. On the actual sleeve, they had erroneously printed a photograph of me instead! Unbelievably, a short while later, this happened again, on the Russian release of 'Electric Warrior' where a live photograph of me was included in the accompanying booklet alongside photos of T.Rex.

2002 was a year that was mixed with happiness and great sadness. My youngest brother Gordon had worked as a roadie for T.Rextasy for about seven years before we parted company. On 23rd September, he committed suicide by taking an overdose of prescribed pills. He was suffering from depression but appeared to be getting himself together as he had only recently moved into a rented flat with a friend. As with so many manic-depressives, they can take a turn for the worse at any given time, and Gordon was found in his bed with a suicide note by his side.

I read out a few words at the church service but couldn't withhold the tears, and my voice cracked on more than one occasion. As we laid Gordon to rest in the nearby cemetery in Crayford in Kent, we blasted out a couple of tracks from a CD of his favourite band, AC/DC. In the note that Gordon had written, he had asked for 'Highway To Hell' to be played as a final number. I was angry that the priest overriding the funeral said that he wouldn't allow it as he didn't feel it was appropriate. I didn't think that it was any of his business what he felt was appropriate, and so while he was walking away after laying Gordon to rest, I pressed the play button and turned the volume up high - whereby Bon Scott's lead vocals screamed out "We're on the highway to hell" throughout the cemetery. I wasn't prepared to let someone in a dog collar dictate or refuse my brother's last wish.

Earlier in the year I was approached by a record company in Japan, elegantly named *Eggtoss* who wanted permission to release three T.Rextasy recorded tracks on a compilation album that was to feature a selection of Marc Bolan cover versions. I sent over the songs, '20th Century Baby', a live version of 'Jeepster', and the version of 'Get It On' that we had recorded for the "Legacy" album, that wasn't available in the Japanese market place. On 11th September 2002 the album was released with the title 'Universal Love' - a title taken from the B-side of the Dib Cochran And The Earwigs 1970 single 'Oh Baby' which had originally featured both Marc and Tony Visconti. The sleeve and packaging was marvellous. It came with a beautiful 24-page black and white photo booklet, which contained a wealth of photos of T.Rex and Tyrannosaurus Rex taken by photographer Pete Sanders. Separate from that was a large foldout inner sleeve, which had doctored photos of all the artists on the album, including Nikki Sudden, Johan Asherton, and Akima. My personal shot was morphed into the famous *Keep Britain Tidy* poster that Marc had campaigned for in 1972.

As another September rapidly approached I was pleasantly surprised to receive letters from Steve Harley, Tony Visconti, and Miller Anderson wishing us the best of luck for the 2002 Memorial Anniversary Gig - I even had a telephone message from Bob Geldof saying, "Hope it all goes well and the best of luck for the evening." The gig sold-out not least because Dino Dines had come along to play, but also because Rolan Bolan had agreed to sing a song or two with us. Dino sat in nicely and was rapturously welcomed as he always was by the crowd. As was Rolan when he came on to perform '20th Century Boy' and the encore of 'Hot Love', sporting his latest image with a dreadlock hairstyle.

So many years had passed by with the current line up of T.Rextasy that it was inevitable it would have to change at some time. Paul Rogers, our regular bass player had had enough of the gigging schedule and wanted to spend more time at home. He had missed seeing his first child growing up through her infant years and as his girlfriend Bev was pregnant again, he didn't want to miss out a second time. Initially, Paul was going to give up playing the bass guitar, but if one is a true musician, it can be tough.

After leaving T.Rextasy he began playing every now and then in a pub band in Crayford performing punk standards, while returning to his building job - his profession before he joined the band. Paul's leaving was a completely amicable separation. In all the years he had been with the band he had never let us down and had given around ten years of his life to playing around the UK, Europe, Japan, and Africa. On his last day we presented him with a CD box set of The Jam, another one of his favourite bands, as a leaving present before we finally said goodbye.

Sadly, due to my work schedule, the chat with Mickey Finn at the 2000 convention about working together was never to be, and I never saw him again. He died on 11th January 2003. A couple of days afterwards, I spoke to Mick O'Halloran on the phone as he had made arrangements to come over from the Isle of Wight to meet up with us to attend the funeral in South

London on 5th February. I told him that I could no longer go, as the day before was the inquest for my brother Gordon's suicide and I was just too upset to attend another funeral. However, Caron went along with Dino Dines, Mick O'Halloran, Paul Thomas and Nigel Silk and in doing so represented me in my absence. I was a little shocked to hear later, that Bill Legend, and Mick Gray had not attended (although Mick did turn up later at the pub for Mickey's Wake). It was depressing to think that three out of the four original members of T.Rex were no longer living.

Above: Inner sleeve design for the Marc Bolan compilation CD album 'Universal Love'.

Left: Neil and I on a camel ride in Marrakech a few hours before our gig!

Below: A selection of Marc Bolan multi-track two-inch and quarter-inch master tapes acquired from a producer in Northampton.

Left: Dino Dines backstage before a T.Rextasy gig.

Below, left: My brother Gordon wearing a T.Rextasy t-shirt, who roadied for the band in the nineties. That's me in the smock.

Below: The Russian release of the 'Legacy' tribute album - 2001.

Below, left: The Marc Bolan & T.Rex CD album 'Bump 'n' Grind released officially in Japan on *Imperial Records* - 2000.

Below: The Marc Bolan & T.Rex CD album 'Shadowhead' released officially in Japan on *Imperial Records* - 2001.

Above: My first modelling session for *Arena* magazine - April 2000.
(Richard Dawson)

Below: With Tony Visconti on a very hot day
at my flat in Holloway, London, 8th June 2000.

Above: Standing outside Marc's house in Weston-Under-Penyard, Herefordshire.

Left: Self-financed T.Rextasy live CD album 'The Crack Of Dawn' (sold mainly at gigs for 'fans only') - 2000.

Below: Press cutting for the BBC TV programme *Battle of the Fantasy Bands*.

Let battle commence

Marc Bolan and John Lennon may no longer be with us and Abba may have split, but there's still a chance to hear them perform — or the next best thing, a tribute band.

Battle Of The Fantasy Bands pits, among others, T Rextasy against The Fabba Girls, The Fab Beatles against the Bee Gees soundalikes Stayin' Alive. Ulrika Jonsson and Terry Wogan (above) keep the score, if not the peace, as the audience votes for the greatest pretender.

Ulrika and Terry

The Fabba Girls

The Fab Beatles

T Rextasy

MUSIC
Battle Of The Fantasy Bands
BBC1, Friday

3

11

Born To Boogie

It was time to recruit a new bass player. It had to be someone with charisma and who looked the part. I had also decided that it would be a bonus if the successful candidate could sing backing vocals too. I started to look around for the right guy. A Glam band that had supported us on various occasions in the past did have a bass player that looked cool, could sing, and was a fan of T.Rex music. His name was Paul Marks. Coincidently around the same time I was putting various feelers out through the web, a guy called Paul had got in touch looking to join a full-time professional band with Glam traits.

Unbelievably, it turned out that this was the same guy who we had been talking about. It didn't take long before Paul became a fully-fledged member of T.Rextasy. He put in a lot of hard work, day in and day out working on those difficult bass lines that Steve Currie and Herbie Flowers had recorded. When we finally got into the rehearsal stage it felt absolutely right. We heard the bass lines that were on the records actually being replicated and played live. Paul slipped into the roll instantly, and in doing so became popular with fans overnight.

To edge Paul into the band I took him with me to Portsmouth Television Studios a few weeks later for an interview I had been invited to do about our up and coming show at The Wedgewood Rooms in Southsea. We finished the interview session by playing an acoustic version of 'Telegram Sam'. As the interview was only broadcast locally, not many people actually saw the performance, and to this day neither have I!

As usual I had a few interviews organised on the radio and in the press. One in particular was a printed interview with Dino Dines and myself in the March 2003 edition of a paper called *Universe*, which was published for the

Hertfordshire University. It featured over three large broadsheets and contained an in-depth chat interspersed with various black and white photographs. Dino was on top form and very open with his comments. I gather that this is now quite a collector's piece, being very difficult to get hold of, as it was only supposedly available for the University.

Not one to shy away from a little controversy, I agreed to be photographed for a magazine article which loosely depicted Marc's final days. The magazine entitled *Bang!* was one of those cult-arty-trendy type publications. In the previous month they featured a similar article about the talented and legendary Jeff Buckley, so I guessed that I would be in good company. The publishers hired a black female model (to portray Gloria Jones) for me to be photographed with and various pictures were shot around Barnes and the tree where the fatal accident had taken place. It was photographed quite creatively and stretched over a couple of pages. The article was printed in the May 2003 edition and caused a little quake within the Bolan community as some fans thought that it was in poor taste. I saw it as not only for personal publicity, but also for getting Marc back into the glossy magazines again... for a little while at least. But like all these things, the controversy blew over as quickly as it had began. I was told later by one of those involved with the youth magazine that what it did do was transport Marc into the minds and heads of a younger generation who had never even heard of T.Rex before, so I was happy with that alone. The older generation and righteous amongst the fraternity just had to let it go.

The Marc Bolan Fan Club in Germany was always a force to be reckoned with. Their beautifully produced A5 glossy magazine called *The Slider*, even though it was written in German, was always a pleasure to browse through. In one of their publications they decided to include a whole feature dedicated to my time seeing T.Rex in concert in Germany in 1972 and 1973. I supplied them with my whole story and what I could recall from that time, which they translated verbatim. Photos in the magazine were nearly always of the highest quality and usually contained some fantastic shots of Marc that very few people had seen.

As I had taken up a good few pages in the current edition, I obtained a translation for the whole issue, which had also included an interview with Paul Fenton. I was absolutely horrified to be told that the translation read that Paul Fenton - a drummer who played mostly additional drums on later T.Rex albums, and someone who had played as secondary drummer to

Davey Lutton on a very short tour of England - had stated that he was the drummer on tracks such as '20th Century Boy'! Bill Legend was of course the original drummer on this iconic recording. Paul also failed to mention that the Bolan Anniversary Concert at the Cambridge Corn Exchange in 1997 was actually a T.Rextasy concert, conveniently forgetting to say that we had invited him as a guest to appear with us!

It was around this time that a group of fans got together a banner and phrase that stated "No Marc Bolan - No T.Rex!" Many true and genuine fans had, had enough and decided to make a stand, no matter how significant or insignificant it appeared to be. This has become a statement that still raises its head whenever a band advertises itself quite sacrilegiously, in my opinion, as 'T.Rex' - no matter if one owns the registered name or not, or even if there is an added caption of "The Music of..." It must be said that without Marc Bolan, there can be no T.Rex!

One summer morning in July 2003 the phone rang and I was surprised to hear Rick Parfitt from Status Quo on the other end. He had rung to have a chat about T.Rextasy as he had seen a video clip of us playing in Germany. Our friend Jorg Günther, had met up with them and had showed Francis and Rick some live video footage of the band. Rick and Francis had asked if it was a current band. They were very impressed with the way we had captured the feel and atmosphere of the T.Rex experience. Rick was very interested in getting T.Rextasy on a bill with them, which was also one of the reasons he had called. But like so many ideas it didn't get put into practice and went no further than that one telephone call. Even though both Francis and Rick were up for us supporting them at future gigs, their management did not take up the option. As times have rolled by, Quo have gigged time and time again, but I have never received a call from their management, so I guess it's just one of those great ideas that didn't happen. I won't pretend that I wasn't disappointed especially given that Status Quo was the very first band I had ever seen live back in Germany in 1972.

A few months prior to September 2003 T.Rextasy was asked to be filmed for various in-studio sequences for a film company who were putting together a television programme called *Who Got Bolan's Millions?* The documentary was about Marc's lost earnings, where his money had gone, and to try and get to the people involved. It was eventually shown on Channel Four on Saturday 20th September, using filmed clips of T.Rextasy in the studio and also a short live in-concert snippet too. As predicted, the

TV programme didn't uncover any secrets, nor was it able to disclose any major cloak and dagger goings on. Years later it is still a contentious issue as to where much of Marc's money actually ended up, but needless to say a few people must have got away with a fair few riches that should've gone to Marc's family.

BBC Radio Essex in Chelmsford had been good to me in the past as I have used their studios for not only doing various interviews with its DJs, but also for using their facilities to link up with BBC radio stations up and down the country to promote various projects, gigs, and concerts. One of my visits was for an interview with Eric Hall. Eric had worked for EMI in the seventies promoting many leading bands including Queen, Cockney Rebel, and other acts. While in EMI's employment he also worked for Marc Bolan as a plugger and promoter for some of his releases. He had also been a good friend of Marc's right from their early teenage days in Stamford Hill in London.

It was no surprise then that our chat turned into each of us talking about Marc as well as promoting the T.Rextasy concert that I had been asked to do. Eric talked about the time he had to dress up in a frog outfit and briefly became known as 'Eric the Frog' on the *Rollin' Bolan* TV Special when Marc performed 'New York City', which contained the hook-line, "Did you ever see a woman coming out of New York City with a frog in her hand?" Eric has since become known as a 'character DJ' to add to his roster as a promoter of professional football players.

Over the years our concerts in Glasgow had become events in themselves. We made sure that we always had time for playing this terrific city, even if we had to travel all the way up without having a show booked either side to make the long distance more practical. The Pavilion Theatre has remained one of our most attended shows, and I have consistently felt that because of the loyalty shown to us we should always pay it back to that brilliant and crazy Glasgow audience. Throughout T.Rextasy's career, we have never had a crowd at Glasgow that wasn't exactly what we expected. In terms of numbers and reaction, the Scottish audiences have never let us down. We have been fortunate in that most places we have played, we have had very responsive audiences and I have been continually grateful for that, but there has always been something quite different about those who have attended The Pavilion Theatre in that every show has had a kind of mutual-manic and crazy-warmth that is very enduring.

As things were trucking along so well there was in turn a sad start to the New Year. A few days before the end of January, I received a call from Dino's fiancé to say that he had died suddenly from heart failure on Wednesday 28th January 2004. What made this even more ironic was that just a few weeks prior to this, he had joked to me saying, "I've got a good few more years left in me yet!" He had just turned 59 a few weeks earlier in December and was full of spirit and gusto as he was excited that he was again gigging with a live band, playing songs that he'd had a hand in recording. We were getting very friendly and quite close to Dino at this time, which made it all the more shocking and saddening to have him taken away. We got in touch with a few people that still knew him well, including Miller Anderson, of course. Miller had recently moved from Brighton to a small island just off the Scottish mainland, but he still made the effort to come all the way down to Hertfordshire for the funeral, of which Caron, myself, Nigel and Paul all attended.

A host of musicians and friends who Dino had known over the years had arrived to show their respect. We noticed that a wreath had also been sent from Dr & The Medics, which I thought was extremely kind. They had been on tour with Slade and us the previous December and had got on really well with him. While standing by Miller, he remarked that, "Dino was very popular with Marc fans you know" and it was proven that day when the crematorium was filled with flowers and wreaths. The funeral wasn't a religious affair as Dino wasn't a religious man - it was a Humanitarian service with a speaker delivering a brief history of Dino's life. A light-hearted moment occurred when he read out something Dino's Mum had once said. On his request to join T.Rex, she asked, "Do you think you are good enough?" After the reading had finished, the sound of Buddy Holly's 'Rave On' blasted out from the speaker system - Buddy was always one of Dino's favourite singers.

I had got to know Clem Burke, the drummer in Blondie, since 1997 when I first met him at the Bolan Memorial Concert in New York. I hadn't spoken to him since, so it was a nice surprise when in July 2004 I received a telephone call saying that he was coming to the UK with Blondie for a short tour. The closest show to me was in Kent, an open-air affair with The Stranglers as their support. I agreed that it would be great to meet up again so Clem made sure that a couple of VIP passes would be there at the box office.

When we arrived Clem instantly made Caron and myself feel very welcome and introduced us to the whole band. Debbie Harry was friendly enough but tried to be a little aloof as we remained in their company for the next few hours. After sound checking, Clem invited us both out for a meal with him and the band. We graciously accepted and made the short walk to a nearby restaurant. While sitting at the table more and more people gathered outside looking through the window trying to get a glimpse of them all - it felt a little like being an animal in a zoo, and it was a relief when we all finished and made our way back to the concert site. As expected, Blondie were exceptionally professional and the show went as smooth as a live rock band's performance can be, and afterwards we spent time chatting to Clem and the rest of the band. It was a lovely evening and it kind of paved the way for my relationship with Clem, which put me in good stead for a few years later when another Marc Bolan Memorial Concert would take place.

Some say that things happen all at once, and literally the day after, we received two tickets from promoter John Hessenthaler to attend another outside concert. This one was for Status Quo in Ipswich. As it wasn't too far to travel we accepted the invitation and went along for the afternoon. We spent the day chilling out in the sunshine until the Quo hit the stage. As I've already mentioned, I'd been a fan of this band ever since watching them perform with T.Rex back in 1972. I must say that even without the original rhythm section of Alan Lancaster on bass and John Coghlan on drums it was still great to hear all those early hits from Rossi and Parfitt. They hadn't lost their spark, or stage presence and humour, and appeared to retain their love for playing live, which, is a very special quality to hold on to. I guess the only thing missing was that gritty and dirtiness that I loved about them in the early days.

After the show, I went backstage with the promoter who showed me around their facilities. I had hoped to catch them before they left, but as soon as they had completed their set, they had shot off as quickly as they arrived. Their stage set-up looked cool, with a stream of white Marshall 4 x 12 amps, although on a closer look it was all for show, as most were just dummy cabs!

Our summer in 2004 was quite eventful as we played shows with Carol Decker from T'Pau, and also The Manfreds. Playing with original bands always made me feel as though we were accepted not only as a tribute band, but as a decent band in our own right too, playing the songs in the way we were choosing to portray them - in the spirit of Marc Bolan.

I was also invited to Rat Scabies' home. He had known Marc in 1977 when The Damned supported T.Rex on the 'Dandy In The Underworld' Tour. Rat had kept hold of a couple of items that Marc had given to him and wanted to pass them over to me. I ended up obtaining his original 'Solid Gold Easy Action' t-shirt (a black short sleeved shirt with a gold glitter lettered logo), and an A3 black and white photograph (an unusual shot of Marc's back as he's walking away). The photo was really dog-eared, but Rat had given this to me for nothing, so I wasn't complaining. It was a great insight chatting to him about how Marc treated The Damned on tour. He said that, "I still have great admiration for Marc. I loved every minute of that tour. Marc treated us really well, not like a support band at all. He always made sure that we had a sufficient soundcheck too!" Just before I left, Rat turned to me and said, "I'm sure Marc would've wanted you to have the shirt - it's like a kind of karma." I thought that was a lovely way to say goodbye.

In December of 2004, we found ourselves yet again on our yearly Christmas tour with Slade, and Dr & The Medics as the opening band. We'd had quite a diverse year with our own headline shows, playing one of the larger beer festivals in Peterborough and then in the summer headlining another festival in Portsmouth in front of 12,000. The Portsmouth show was quite surreal as we were only told of the total attendance the next evening. It was so hard to estimate the amount of people as the crowd grew and grew until bodies disappeared over the Hampshire countryside.

Before the end of year one of the most excellent, individual and influential DJs this country has ever known suddenly died. He was John Peel. As mentioned previously, he really helped pave the way for Bolan's career to take shape. For our next few shows, and indeed, sometimes in gigs over the years, I would get the band to play John's favourite all-time track, 'Teenage Kicks' by The Undertones, directly before our encore of 'Hot Love', just as a kind of dedication to Peel and a 'thank you' for everything he did for the love of music.

Spring 2005 saw the DVD release of the *Born To Boogie* film. It was lovely to have been invited to the London film premiere for this newly restored version. Prior to the release, Caron and I had been asked by the producers to try and get a few people who had actually attended either of the two Empire Pool Wembley concerts so that they could be interviewed for a bonus section of the disc. I already knew a few people and put their names forward. This included Caron, who had attended the first concert at Wembley, Gavin Ingels, who had been a roadie for T.Rextasy, and Steve Gibbings, who would in the future be a promoter for T.Rextasy.

We all met up at a studio complex in Bayswater. It was fun to see a group of familiar faces, and some of which I hadn't met face-to-face before, such as Emperor Rosko, the famous DJ who had introduced T.Rex onto the stage for those most prestigious Wembley shows. Tony Visconti turned up, as did Bill Legend, and roadie Mick Gray. It was a shame that Elton John had supposedly refused to be involved with the DVD, especially as he had taken part in the original filming of the live studio versions of 'Children Of The Revolution' and 'Tutti-Frutti'.

As Rosko was leaving the session, we shook hands and said goodbye as he handed me a Rosko fake monetary note, based on a British Pound. He had a handful of these that he must have had printed off for this type of occasion. It was a great way to exit any proceedings and self-promote himself too.

An after-show party was also held in London which brought together a gathering of Bolan associates, family and friends that included Gloria Jones, Rolan Bolan, Tony Visconti, Harry Feld, Bill Legend, Andy Ellison, Geoffrey Bayldon, Jeff Dexter (Marc's long term friend and DJ) and a whole list of others. The party was held at The Embassy Club, which was only a short walk. We made our way there together with Boz Boorer, a long-term acquaintance and a big fan of Bolan. Boz used to be the rockabilly band The Polecats (and still does from time to time), who recorded a very worthwhile version of 'Jeepster', before hitting the big time and becoming guitarist for Morrissey's band. As we entered the party, we were greeted with a string quartet that played instrumental versions of 'Get It On', and 'Hot Love' while free miniature hamburgers were served together with cocktails throughout the evening.

I was pleased that over the years, T.Rextasy had given me the opportunity to become known outside the realms of the Bolan fraternity. This proved fruitful a few months earlier when the son of the famous talk show host, Michael Parkinson, also called Michael Parkinson, got in touch in a bid for me to "act" as Marc in a mini-docu-film he was making about Bolan's last days, loosely based on information taken from the biography '20th Century Boy' written by Mark Paytress.

At first I was pretty dubious at accepting the role, mainly because I thought it could be construed as bad taste, and also because I'm just not an actor! I was shown the script, which was extremely loose and some of it factually incorrect. I agreed to accept the job on the understanding that there would be no gratuitous scenes and also that the last scene would only imply of the accident, and that I could check any story lines that I felt were non-factual.

Michael accepted my terms and in doing so the filming began in earnest in the summer of 2004. To be honest, I didn't like doing most of it, as I just felt uncomfortable in an acting role. I only fell into my element when I had a guitar around me, so I was pleased when a club scene was arranged that involved me and a couple of punk rockers. I had to sing and play songs on an acoustic guitar while they both listened and supposedly mockingly took heed of someone from a previous generation. Caron also got a bit part, which involved sitting at the bar in the club scene. It was nice to have her around, as I would've felt quite isolated amongst all those other actors who I had never met before, and who were quite a different breed to musicians.

Ride On as it was first titled was officially released on DVD around May 2005. Most journalists slated it and the fans were split, but swayed mostly on the negative. It was to all extent a budget film, but it did the job for non-fans who enjoyed the story. It made it all the more bearable as the disc came with the approval of Gloria Jones, Rolan Bolan, Bob Harris, Eric Hall, Captain Sensible, Jeff Dexter, and Steve Harley, all of whom gave informative interviews which were included. Adding to the DVD's minor credibility was a bonus CD that contained eleven live T.Rex tracks and a very nice 32-page booklet, which I must admit gave me a sigh of relief as I felt I was within a circle of people who had at least given it their blessing. It made it all the more gratifying when it actually entered the charts at No. 26! It has never ceased to amaze me that as the years go by it has been reissued time and time again albeit with different sleeves and titles all over the world. It has also been screened dozens of times since on the UK Biography channel.

If I were to mention all of the interviews and press reviews and radio sessions over the years, it would take up most of this book, but up to this point, national press coverage for us had been mostly taken up by the likes of *The Daily Mirror* and *The News Of The World*, so it was with additional pleasure when I found out that *The Times* had decided to do a write-up from one of our shows in its August 2005 colour supplement magazine. It was superb to have received quite a substantial review, as further along the page Jethro Tull had only managed a few lines on a recent gig.

While on the road, considering the miles we have covered on the motorways, I have always found it very strange that we never seemed to meet up with many musicians. Which is why it was even more unusual when one day we stopped at a service station and met Bob Geldof and his band. They were, like us, travelling to their next gig somewhere in England. We chatted for a while and Bob said that he was saddened when he heard that Marc had died as it was only a month after The Boomtown Rats had appeared on the *MARC* show. Bob was his usual self, very self-effacing and retaining that designer scruffy look about him. I reminded him about the telephone call he had made to me a few years ago wishing me luck for the gig we were playing for Marc's anniversary concert. I'm not sure if he remembered, but he said he did, and apologised again for not being able to make it! We parted company by just wishing each other good luck for future gigs on the road.

In October, Tony Visconti was back in the country again, promoting an artist called Kristeen - an inventive and constructive writer and pop performer somewhere between Kate Bush and Björk. As she was playing in a club in London, Tony called me up and invited me down to the gig in Camden Town. The club was in a basement, cramped with around seventy or so people in attendance. Shortly before the gig began, Tony tapped me on the shoulder and said, "Danielz, this is James Dean-Bradfield from the Manic Street Preachers." We only had time for a short chat, mainly about the songs that Tony had helped produce for the band, and then we had a couple of photos taken with each other. It was one of those evenings that kind of slid by quickly. Kristeen's performance was really good and in a way, her voice that night reminded me a little of Lene Lovitch, who had a hit with 'Lucky Number' in the eighties. Kristeen, with her association with Tony, managed to earn a support on Morrissey's tour later on, while also recording backing vocals for David Bowie.

Looking back at the many gigs that we have played over the years, my memory has probably been fogged with the sheer amount of places we have been to and the people I have met. But there are always certain ones that stick in my mind. Such as when we played in Northampton around November or early December in 2005. It wasn't the gig so much, as what happened afterwards. About twenty minutes after the show, I heard a knock at my dressing room door and was introduced to two young men who I actually recognised immediately, even though I had never met them previously! They were the twin sons of Bill Legend. It was like staring at two Bills simultaneously from around the 1973 period - even their hair style reminded me of how their Dad's had looked! We had a long chat about Bill, and the T.Rex days of old. It was an interesting thirty minutes or so not only because they were Bill's sons, but also because they were two of the nicest guys one could care to meet.

Throughout most of December 2005 we toured once again with Slade, but with a change of line-up. The opening band for the tour from now on would be Mud II. The band included a couple of musicians that had played alongside original singer Les Gray. Syd Twynham, although not the original guitarist, had in fact played for many years with the reformed Mud, which then later became known as Les Gray's Mud. Their keyboard player Chris Savage had also played for some time with Les Gray's Mud. The band originally started out as New Mud but finally settled on the name of Mud II.

The three bands worked well together, although as usual, for no apparent reason, we always kept ourselves to ourselves. T.Rextasy as a band has never been that sociable. Maybe it's because I'm just not that type of person. It normally takes me ages to feel settled and comfortable with people. I'm like that even now, so I doubt if I will ever change. There were few reviews for the tour, although the Cornish news website called *This Is Cornwall* gave T.Rextasy an amazing write-up declaring that "T.Rextasy Saves The Day" as their headline prompt.

It was good to hear that just prior to the Christmas tour, *Madman Records* had decided to release a T.Rextasy compilation CD album entitled 'Solid Gold T.Rextasy', containing most of the Bolan tracks we had covered on our two previous releases. It also included two previously unreleased bonus tracks. As a further bonus, a computer enhanced version of the band's video for the song 'Baby Factory' was included, together with a lovely shrink-wrapped card slipcase.

The New Year saw us take things a step further as we made a strong step into the theatre circuit on our own merit, with the help of the agency *Sweeney Entertainments* who had seen the band at the Norwich Playhouse Theatre. *Sweeney Entertainments* was a two-person set up that were well equipped with dealing with theatre managements around the UK, and for the next few years they became our backbone for the majority of our theatre gigs. We decided that after our contractual obligated dates at holiday camps that they would be the last. They were holding us back from achieving credibility in the theatre market place and at some of the better quality rock clubs, who saw us as "a band that plays holiday camps." I have never objected or frowned upon those who wish to retain playing the *Butlin's*-type circuit, it was just my personal decision and one that thankfully helped us to branch out further.

The decision was also made easier after the bookings manager of *Butlin's* deemed to have, in my view, no quality control whatsoever. Most of the time, we would be its first port-of-call for their choice of T.Rex band. However, as we were progressing and our bookings became more and more frequent on the theatre circuit, I had to reject their offers. What became annoying was their blatant false advertising. If we couldn't accept their bookings, they would employ any other T.Rex tribute they could find, but still use the T.Rextasy photo to advertise in their brochures. They did this to us two or three times in succession. The last time was the final straw and I threatened them with legal action if they did it again and told their bookings manager not to bother to ask us back.

With the help of *Sweeney Entertainments*, we ventured on a headline tour, which I named 'T.Rextasy - The Born To Boogie Tour'. This took in a whole series of dates over a couple of months in 2006 covering much of the country. We played a two-set performance taking the whole evening without the help of a support band. We played a variation of acoustic and electric tracks and included the biggest Bolan hit songs for the casual fans, interspersed with the odd B-side and album track for the die-hards - which has since become a mainstay of the set lists for most shows.

The tour covered February and March tailing off with the odd show in April. Although it was pretty tough going doing the whole show on our own without a support to kick start the evening, it gave us a new strength and 'tightness', and also increased my stage craft. When the tour ended we carried on playing up and down the country performing in a wealth of different types of venue. It was at this juncture that I thought that a theatre tour shouldn't have to be in just one section of the year, and I questioned myself as to why it couldn't be spread out throughout the year - this would give us the opportunity to play other venues, as well as keeping the banner of 'Theatre Tour' as a separate entity. From that point on it became the way in which T.Rextasy would work.

Heading towards the tail end of the previous year, I was asked to sing and play guitar on a song for a charity located on the Isle of Wight. The track was the Ringo Starr song 'Back Off Boogaloo'. I was informed that Slade's Dave Hill had been asked to play guitar on the track but he had turned it down for reasons of his own. It didn't matter though as I was then able to sing and play some guitar myself. I spent an afternoon recording in a small London studio. I laid down two or three vocal tracks before putting down a couple of guitar tracks. When I left the session I forgot all about it for at least six months before someone emailed to tell me that they had heard the song being played on the Isle of Wight radio station. I was a little surprised as I hadn't been informed of its completion, although as it was for charity, I didn't bother making any fuss, I was just pleased that the project had been fulfilled. In the end I received a copy of the track and was quite bemused to find that it still sounded like a demo recording. It was a shame as it could've been so much better and built up into a high definition recording.

It was never pressed up into CD format and only remains as a download, although I did have to laugh when a few people who hadn't listened as closely as perhaps they should've done, thought that the recording was a demo recorded by Marc for Ringo to hear! While on the subject, I have always had my doubts about the genuine writer of this song. To this day although the writing credit is given to Ringo, it is so Bolanesque in it's construction that I still believe, and it is only my opinion, that Marc presented the skeletal idea or number to Ringo as a kind of thank you for the work he had done on *Born To Boogie*. Of course, I may be completely wrong, but would Ringo ever admit to it anyway? To date, there is nothing remotely like 'Back Off Boogaloo' throughout Ringo's entire catalogue of recorded material.

Towards the end of May 2006 *Gibson* guitars helped to launch the *Marc Bolan/T.Rex On TV* DVD. They gave up their head offices in London to show video clips of the forthcoming release and invited various Bolan family members and associates to a soirée that lasted several hours. We mixed and chatted with Gloria Jones, Harry Feld, and a few other specially invited fans. Later we were all presented with black carrier bags that contained a copy of the latest issue of *Record Collector*, some sweets, boa feathers, and plectrums. A few members of the press also showed up and we had various photos taken before leaving the premises, although to be honest, I don't recall any photos or reviews of this launch in any of the music or national press.

I felt rewarded when in June 2006 I received a letter from Brian Dunham on behalf of Marc Bolan's catalogue management *Wizard [Bahamas] Ltd.*, authorising and endorsing T.Rextasy "in their ability to help keep Marc's music alive and in the public eye in a professional and authentic manner". In doing so, I felt that I was at last able to legally call the band 'the World's ONLY official tribute to Marc Bolan and T.Rex'.

The New Year began with some cool emails. I was taken by surprise one day when I saw a message from a singer from one of my favourite bands from the eighties. Alan Savage sang and fronted a great original UK pop band called The Flaming Mussolini's. They were signed to Epic Records, but sadly never received the recognition they deserved. Their pop masterpiece was an album called 'Watching The Film'. It was an album that I played non-stop from my first hearing of their brilliant tracks such as 'My Cleopatra', and 'Masuka Dan'. A fan of T.Rextasy had known Alan for a while and had told him about us. It was then when he wrote to me saying how much Marc and David Bowie had influenced his songwriting, and how happy he was to know that I was keeping Bolan's music alive.

About a week later I received an autographed CD in the post from Alan containing all the best tracks they had recorded, together with a couple of rare songs added to the disc. It was a pleasure to have made contact with him, and I was so glad that he had bothered to write and then to compile a special CD album just for my listening pleasure. Although the band made more than one album, I would urge anyone to search out 'Watching The Film' as it is, in my view, a collection of absolute superb pop songs of the finest quality. I don't know who actually owns the *Epic Records* library, but while I'm writing this to date, the Mussolini's debut album is still unavailable on CD in the UK, which is a great shame, especially and confusingly as their follow up album was actually released on CD!

Many years ago, Tony Visconti had told me that he had been slowly and meticulously writing his autobiography, so it was with delight when he informed me that it was completed and would be published in 2007. On its publication, Tony had flown into London for various interviews and signing sessions. I said it would be great if he could come along to a gig and see us play, as his visit coincided with a show at the 100 Club in London.

A day or two later he re-arranged his schedule and said that he would love to attend the gig and if I wanted, he would enjoy playing bass guitar on a couple of songs with us. We all thought that was a great idea, so we not only confirmed and advertised his attendance, but also arranged with the venue that he could do a book signing session before the show, to make it that extra-special!

On Friday 16th February we met up for the sound check while Tony watched, making us all feel a little nervous to be honest. He said we sounded great and stepped onto the stage with Paul's spare bass. He went over to Neil's side of the stage so that the two bass frequencies wouldn't clash.

Before the gig, Tony did a signing session as the crowd lined up. Earlier on, he had given Caron and I a copy of the book and signed it with the inscription 'To Danielz + Caron, two flames of T.Rex passion! Love, Tony Visconti 16.2.07' - which was really nice and I felt, written from the heart.

I introduced Tony onto the stage towards the end of the show. While some of the audience went wild, others looked on in excitement and slight bewilderment. When I counted in 'One Inch Rock', I could see out from the corner of my eyes how much Tony loved being on stage again. It was great to see a beaming smile from him and it was a joy to see him standing on that stage with us. We followed 'One Inch Rock' with our encore of 'Hot Love'. I re-introduced Tony as he strapped on the bass for one last time while singing the backing vocals with the band on the outro.

http://www.herts-essex-news.co.uk

OBITUARY *T-Rex keyboard player 'just loved playing'*

'70s glam rocker who dedicated his life to music

● **20th CENTURY BOYS: Tribute band T-Rextasy, who were due to play with Peter 'Dino' Dines in London tomorrow;** *below,* **a recent shot of Peter**
Photo: T-Rextasy

SEVENTIES rock star and lifelong Hertfordshire resident Peter 'Dino' Dines toured the world with T-Rex, and on Tuesday his family and friends gathered to remember a life devoted to music.

Mr Dines, who lived in Tamworth Road, Hertford, died on January 28 at the age of 59. From 1974 up until Marc Bolan's death in a car crash in 1977, Mr Dines played the keyboard for the glam rock outfit T-Rex, who had No 1 hits with *Hot Love, Get It On, Telegram Sam* and *Metal Guru.*

From 1999, Mr Dines enjoyed reliving his T-Rex glory days with guest appearances in tribute band T-Rextasy. He toured the UK with them in December and was due to join the band at a gig in London tomorrow.

Lead singer and guitarist Danielz said: "Every single person in the music business used to call him Dino and that's how he was affectionately known to his friends.

"When he was on that keyboard, he just loved playing. That was his pure joy. It was like every gig was his first. Fans used to chant 'Dino, Dino' whenever he used to guest with us. He used to love going out into the audience to chat to the fans, sign

photos and have photos taken with him."

Dino was playing the Hammond organ in a 1960s progressive rock band called the Keef Hartley Band when he was spotted by Bolan's roadie.

"He was the third longest serving member to play in T-Rex with Marc Bolan, which is something people don't tend to know," said Danielz. "Marc always liked the keyboard lines Dino came up with, and he was going to be the only one left

with Marc had he lived, because the other members were going to go off and do their own things.

"Dino did have a lot of stories about them going to the States and Germany, and he was on the very last tour that T-Rex did in the UK. At the time he lived a rock 'n' roll lifestyle."

Most recently, Mr Dines taught carpentry at a school in Tottenham, north London. He is believed to have died of a heart attack, and his funeral took place at Harwood Park Crematorium, near Stevenage, on Tuesday.

Mr Dines is survived by fiancée Chris and his sons from his first marriage, Ernie, 18, and John, 15, who shared his father's love of music. His daughter Agnes, from a previous relationship, lives in Finland.

Danielz said: "I will remember him as someone who absolutely adored his music, loved his fiancée Chris, and was extremely proud of his sons. Chris and Dino were very happy together and they hoped to marry this year.

"He would have played music until he reached a ripe old age if he'd had that opportunity. He was just a great person to know and I think the lives he touched were very grateful to have known him."

Newspaper obituary for Dino Dines included an interview with me about Dino - 2004.

Above: Brochure for a T.Rextasy charity gig in Birmingham which was also turned into a 'tribute to Dino' - 2004.

Left: Flyer for Catton Park outdoor concert - 17th July 2004.

Below: Promo photo shot at The Glasgow Pavilion. From left to right: Paul Marks, Nigel Silk, Me, and Neil Cross.

170

Right: Flyer for Xmas concert tour with Slade, T.Rextasy, and Dr & The Medics - 2004.

Below: Promotional A4 photo-card.

Below: Chatting to Bill Legend at the *Born To Boogie* DVD launch party.

Below: The DJ Emperor Rosko gave me this 'Rosko £1.00' note after we had met during recording of our interviews for the *Born To Boogie* DVD in a Bayswater studio in London.

Left: With James Dean-Bradfield (Manic Street Preachers). Tony Visconti introduced him to me at a Kristeen Young gig (a Tony V protégé) that we were all attending in Camden, London.

Below, left: Front cover of the DVD biopic of Marc's final days starring me as Marc. Released by *WHE International* - 2005.

Below: In the *Mini* on the photo shoot of the controversial *Bang!* magazine article. *(Unknown)*

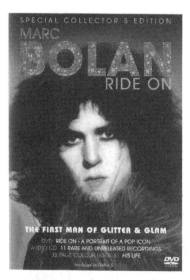

Below: Folded out sleeve for the 'Solid Gold T.Rextasy' album on *Madman Records* - 2005.

Above: At home in-between gigs with my lovely pet rabbit Jo Jo who died in January 2010.

Left: Flyer for one day festival in Germany - 20th May 2006.

Right: Caron, Gloria Jones, and yours truly at the *Marc Bolan On TV* DVD launch party - 2006.

Left: Tony Visconti signing copies of his autobiography in London's 100 Club shortly before his on stage appearance with T.Rextasy - 2007.

12

Hyde Park To Shepherd's Bush

In July 2007 the band changed personnel. This time it was primarily and sadly an acrimonious dismissal rather than a retirement. In past years there had been various occasions where I had been warned about Nigel's behaviour and told that if I did nothing about it then it would end up jeopardising the future of the band. This advice was given to me from various people such as Andy Scott and Len Tuckey who used to manage Slade at one time, but is better known as the guitarist in Suzi Quatro's band.

I must admit that I had turned a blind eye mainly because he had given me so much loyalty since the early nineties. There had been situations whereby his dismissal had come close, such as when Nigel got drunk on one of the Slade dates and for no real rationale started shouting at Dino, pushing him up against the wall and threatening him verbally as well as physically. Some of Slade saw this incident and had a word with me later on about it.

We all agreed that it was time to find a replacement, but Nigel's wife talked me out of it, so yet again, he was offered another reprieve. An earlier incident occurred when Nigel took a mask from a theatre production in Coventry but was caught on camera and had to travel all the way back to the theatre to return it. The whole band was annoyed because it affectively barred us from the theatre again under that management. There have been various other occurrences, but I think one gets the picture of just how the situation grew over the years.

The band felt unanimously that this just wasn't acceptable anymore, and was causing the band to feel uncomfortable. We even agreed to stop beer on our rider. We agreed that this time we wouldn't retract from our decision. Neil and Paul were in full agreement. Although I did feel quite sad about the situation, I knew that I couldn't back down this time as we all agreed that it would only happen again.

As we began our search for a new drummer I contacted various people who I thought could advise. I also put out various adverts, though mainly word of mouth. We did see a few guys and held a batch of auditions, but out of everyone only two came even close to our high expectations. I decided to make a call to Len Tuckey to ask if he knew of any drummers who he thought could cope with my high expectations and perfection that would be right for us. I had known Len for many years by then and he knew the way I worked. In return I knew that he wouldn't waste my time in recommending just a standard player, or someone who would be a fly-by-night.

Speaking to Len was to be one of the most important and provident telephone calls I had ever made in relation to T.Rextasy. He said, "I know exactly the guy you need in your band. He's a real pro and would be ideal. He's not only a great drummer, but a nice guy too." His name was John Skelton and I phoned him immediately. John had played in many bands, including Eddie And The Hot Rods, The Damned, Brian Connolly's Sweet, and dozens more over his long professional career. Our conversation went well and I thought that he seemed like a decent and friendly guy who had a seasoned air about him, so we arranged to meet up.

John lived in Benfleet in Essex, so it wasn't that far to travel. We ended up having a jam and rehearsed a few numbers at his home. I decided that instead of the usual endless rehearsal studio plays, we should dive in at the deep end and do a try-out at an actual gig - sometimes being thrown in like that separates the men from the boys.

We were booked to play a theatre show in Winchester. We arrived a little earlier than usual so that we could go through various numbers that John had been rehearsing himself at home, and listening to again and again on repeat all the way there in our minibus. The deep end was very deep and we were all very nervous but also excited with having a new drummer behind us. To say that John did amazingly well was an understatement. He had done so much homework that only some of the top and tails of numbers were noticeably loose. We all thought that his playing, together with his total professional attitude, was first class and he fitted in perfectly. He had a great drum kit and knew how to use it! We decided that if the feeling were mutual, then he would become a full time member of T.Rextasy. Before the end of July 2007 we had our new drummer.

From that fateful gig, we set out to rehearse properly and ran through dozens of numbers for hours at a time. John also meticulously rehearsed alone, so that when our next show was due, a large open-air concert for the *National Trust*, we quickly became a very tight knit unit again. Except now we sounded so much more powerful and sharper than before. The correspondence from fans via emails and in the post, were immediate and in favour of John. So many people wrote in with comments such as "I didn't think the band could get any better, but it is even more fantastic now!" and "He plays like a modern day Bill Legend, and what a lovely guy!" I was, to be honest, quite amazed at how the fans had accepted our new drummer so quickly. He became an instant success with everyone.

Before John joined the band, we had been using two roadies, Dave Pearcey and Colin (Bugsy), with the intention of letting Bugsy go, as he had become a little unreliable. As a new phase of the band began, I felt that it was an ideal time to let Dave take over full responsibility of all roadie duties, while Bugsy departed amicably.

I have found through the years how small the world appears to be when you are in the music business. For instance I have met so many people in the past, who have said that they have met Marc Bolan, or knew him, or know someone who says that they knew me from years ago. To add to this a short time after John had joined the band he told me that he had actually known Bill Legend since the early seventies. It seemed that they both had a mutual liking for horses and used the same stables, as both John and Bill lived in the same county.

For us as a group, it felt as if a weight had been lifted from our shoulders and suddenly, not only were we getting on together better than in the last couple of years, but it really felt like a brand new band. People who we knew outside of the T.Rextasy circle who hadn't mentioned anything previously were even now saying how happy everyone seemed to be, but it was genuinely like a new lease of life. They say that optimism brings success, but little did we know that the coming September would bring us two of the biggest events we would ever be involved in.

I received a call from a BBC official who asked if we would be interested in playing at the yearly *Proms In The Park* extravaganza at Hyde Park. It was an offer I couldn't refuse. We would perform about an hour before ex-Spandau Ballet's Tony Hadley, who would be the headline act for the early evening session. We reached Hyde Park in the afternoon of Saturday 8th September and were shown to our marquee, which acted as our dressing room for the duration of the event. After soundcheck we chilled out for a while waiting for the crowds to arrive, and slowly but surely, thousands upon thousands filled much of the greenery around the park that was only a couple of hours earlier an empty field.

Before us, a guy called Chico warmed up the crowd. He was known briefly for a couple of years for his appearance on a reality television show. He had a catch phrase that he milked well, and it was one of the first things he used on me when he came up to say hello. He greeted me with a handshake and said, "Hi, you know what time it is? It's Chico time!" If he hadn't been such a nice guy, I would've wanted to throttle him.

By the time we were due to play, Hyde Park was heaving with people of all ages. Dick and Dom, two children's TV presenters who were quite well known to the crowd, introduced us. We smashed into a blistering thirty minutes of fuel-injected cosmic rock from '20th Century Boy' to 'Hot Love'. Because it was still daylight, it was amazing to see literally thousands of fans singing, dancing, and waving Union flags along to the outro of 'Hot Love'. There were so many people in the park that the BBC had erected special large monitor screens that aired our performance simultaneously for those who couldn't see the stage from where they were.

Although we had played some great venues in our time, this had to rate as one of the best ever. We came off stage with adrenalin still running high. As we stepped backstage, Terry Wogan stood to my right looking through some typed document, which was most likely his speech for later on when the classical side of things took over the proceedings. He glanced at me and walked away without uttering a word. I did think at the time 'how rude', especially as this was the second time I had seem him, the first being at the BBC when he hosted the *Battle Of The Fantasy Bands* television show. However, I didn't let his flippancy dull what was an absolutely brilliant day.

It was estimated that there was around 30,000 - 40,000 people who watched us play, which rated as, I think, the largest crowd we had ever played to. I have never been one to think that large audiences mean that they are the best shows. On the contrary, I could play in a rock club to around 300 fans, and then play at a festival to 3,000 people, but one knows that 3,000 people didn't buy tickets just to see T.Rextasy, they bought tickets for the event, or maybe even to watch a different band entirely - so therefore it's all relative. One of the best things about playing to a large audience of this kind is knowing that we had played songs to people who may not have bothered with T.Rex before, but will hopefully go away thinking "that was great - I'm going to buy a greatest hits album tomorrow." That kind of thing has happened to us time and time again, changing non-fans into Bolan fans, something of which I am proud.

The Hyde Park concert was something that I would think about for a long time to come, but just around the corner, another milestone in T.Rextasy's canon was about to take place. From the very beginning of 2007, Caron, myself, and a conglomerate of like-minded souls, were having meetings every month or two with a view to organising a special 30th anniversary Bolan event at a major London venue. We were helped enormously by Nicky Graham and John Logan from the *PRS*, Andrew and Faye Miller from *Nordoff-Robbins*, together with Brian Dunham from *Wizard Artists*, and Bolan catalogue adviser Martin Barden, in getting together a group of performers to sing or take part in what would be the biggest Bolan anniversary event ever. A little later we were also helped by Debbie Bennett who worked on getting PR and promotion for the event.

We set our sights high and began at the top with trying to attract the calibre of artists such as David Bowie, but we received an expected negative response. It was a shame because he was a good friend of Marc's but even when word got to him that there would be people he would know and respect attending, he still wasn't interested. I wrote to Elton John and received a reply saying no because he had plans already made for that weekend! Our group of go-getters spent too much time trying to persuade Siouxsie Sioux, from Siouxsie & The Banshees, to be involved but her management became lethargic and negotiations slowed down to nothing. We also approached Holly Johnson (lead singer of Frankie Goes To Hollywood), who just couldn't and remained lukewarm throughout, but as we all knew he had been very ill over the past year, we thought that it would be unlikely that he would agree to perform in any case. I wanted to approach Adam Ant, but no one else was that keen due to his recent erratic behavioural patterns. There was also talk of pie-in-the-sky invites for stars such as Brian May and Roger Taylor from Queen, and also Noel Gallagher from Oasis, but of course nothing came of it.

It was decided that as we were still aiming relatively high we should try and obtain an established and impressive venue. The Shepherd's Bush

Empire in London was therefore booked and confirmed with the help of *Nordoff-Robbins* and the *PRS*. Our agenda and the whole point of the concert was to bring together either people who had covered Marc's songs, was an actual fan, or had known him. At least that was my personal criteria. We also managed to clinch Steve Williams, the main man behind a PA company *Viking Sound* who had been a fan of Bolan since the seventies, to organise and arrange the sound-system. Over the next few months we all spent meeting upon meeting trying to confirm the acts and tying up loose ends until finally all was set. We were happy with those who had agreed to take part but disappointed with those who wouldn't.

Linda Lewis, a star from the seventies with an amazing vocal range, had known Marc as a friend since the late sixties and remained friends with Marc and Gloria Jones right up until the end of his life. She agreed immediately to perform, 'Metal Guru', and 'Children Of The Revolution' with T.Rextasy. She put on an amazing performance even strutting on stage with a bright pink feather boa. Her voice hadn't faltered at all and she sang both songs with power and feeling in that distinctive octave range that she still possesses.

The next to confirm was Marc Almond, who really was a gem of a guy. He wanted to be involved right from the start and originally suggested around eight or nine songs that he would like to perform! He asked if he could sing some songs with T.Rextasy and perform some acoustic numbers with his guitarist. In the end due to timing restraints, we had to cut down the amount of songs he wanted to sing, so after a few emails that went back and forth between us it was agreed that he would sing a medley of Bolan songs with his guitarist Neal X (formerly of Sigue Sigue Sputnik) and perform the classics 'Teenage Dream', 'Life's A Gas', and 'Dandy In The Underworld' with T.Rextasy. It was a pleasant change to watch someone else singing the lyrics, while I played lead guitar. Marc gave an exquisite and passionate performance.

Something that I am sure will never happen again was when Gloria Jones, the original singer of 'Tainted Love' walked onto the stage to sing a few ad-lib lines of that with Marc, who of course had taken his version to the top of the charts in 1981 with Soft Cell. It was a heart-stopping moment that every fan in the building will always remember. It was the first time that Gloria had sung live in front of an audience in the UK since the seventies! If ever there was an achievement to be proud of on that day, it was getting the two of them together!

I had known Ray Dorset, from Mungo Jerry for some time. Ray is a lovely guy, but it became a little tense when we found out on the actual day of the show that he had not learnt the lyrics to either of the two songs he was going to perform. He ended up singing 'Debora' and 'I Love To Boogie' with the lyrics written on what looked like a paper napkin in his hand, which he referred to every so often. Ray's voice had helped pave the way a little for Bolan in those early days as even though he had a strong vibrato, his voice was still considered more acceptable and conventional than Marc's warble to a selection of the record buying public at the time.

Tony Visconti had flown in from the USA specifically for the concert and even took it upon himself to arrange a string quartet called Dirty Pretty Strings to perform with us on the evening. It was marvellous as well as a little surreal when I looked round and saw Tony dressed up in a dark tail suit conducting the quartet through tracks such as 'Cosmic Dancer', and 'Teenage Dream'. Tony really excelled himself and helped so much on the day and made it all just that bit more special. He even ended up playing bass guitar when we did 'Ride A White Swan'.

Someone else who had flown in especially for the event was Clem Burke. Clem had desperately wanted to be involved in the show. I first told him about it backstage at a Blondie concert at Thetford Forest. We spent quite a long time chatting to Clem and Debbie on their tour bus. I asked Debbie if she fancied appearing at the event. She said she would've liked to if she was in the country but she would be back in the USA by September. Clem however, was really up for it and confirmed that he would be there!

It was intriguing to watch John, our drummer, showing Clem the drum patterns and fills to songs like 'Jeepster' and 'Get It On' and then watching them play together on separate kits. They both got on like a house on fire and played well and tightly together. Clem seemed to want to be involved in as many songs as possible, so we hired him in a set of congas, so he could be on stage when we performed 'Cosmic Dancer' and other tracks that he couldn't learn in time on the full drum kit. Clem has amazing energy and just loves playing rock 'n' roll.

We managed to persuade a few others to come on board, one of which was Dr Robert from the Blow Monkeys. In truth I don't think he wanted to play any songs with T.Rextasy, which irritated me a little as concert wise, we were sometimes pulling more people than he does now as a solo artist. I didn't think that he had any reason to act conceited, especially as every other artist on the bill had agreed to play with us. It was a shame, because I really like Robert's voice and I think he's a great performer. He sang Marc's more obscure 1960s track 'Hippy Gumbo' and the 1973 B-side to 'Truck On (Tyke)', 'Sitting Here', on his own with an acoustic guitar and performed both songs beautifully.

As a complete contrast to personal attitude, the ever youthful and totally reliable Andy Ellison did an amazing and crazy rendition with us of the John's Children classic, 'Desdemona' and took the audience by storm, standing on top of the large speaker cabinets, ripping off his shirt, and singing as well as he had always done. He also did a couple of solo numbers with an electric guitar, which went down really well with the crowd. Andy is so well liked by Bolan fans as he always tries to make the effort attending whatever concerts or events he can. Boz Boorer, whom Andy has sometimes used as his guitarist in the modern day John's Children wanted to attend, but he was touring abroad with Morrissey at the time.

Eric Hall is a bundle of laughs and a real hoot once you get to know him. He makes me laugh each time I talk to him, even though I'm not sure at times if he knows he's being funny! Eric had agreed to host the show and introduce the acts, but seeing him with Gloria laughing and joking together gave the evening an extra touch of warmth.

Nicky Graham had been producing Shakin' Stevens for a number of years and it was a real coup when he told us that Shaky had agreed to perform a couple of songs. A few people had asked why Shaky was booked to play the event, but I remembered the fine version of 'Chrome Sitar' that he had recorded, which he had re-titled 'Come On Little Girl' on the B-side of his single 'True Love' in 1988. He had also written a very complimentary letter about Marc in *Melody Maker* some years ago when he was still in his band The Sunsets. Although the connection was there, he still had trouble choosing a second number to sing alongside 'Chrome Sitar'.

After many telephone conversations with him we both agreed that he should perform 'Laser Love'. However, as time went by, he changed the arrangement, and then the key, then the ending, then he wanted a brass section, then an additional guitarist, then an additional backing singer - in the end I got really frustrated by it all that I just said to the band "You lot play the song. I've got enough to deal with". So I left the rest of T.Rextasy to rehearse and get it together without me, and so after all my negotiations and discussions with Shaky, I ended up not even performing the two songs on stage with him. I've always had a soft spot for Shaky, but I had so many other people to rehearse with and help, that I couldn't give any more time to any one particular individual.

I really would've liked Miller Anderson to have been involved and he very nearly did but was offered a tour with soul singer Madeline Bell which, took over the whole September period. Herbie Flowers said that he would've also liked to attend but he was working on the stage version of *War Of The Worlds* which, was taking up all of his time. Bill Legend said, "yes" one minute, and then "no" the next. Bill is quite religious now and has also re-married. He does still keep his hand in and plays every so often with various musicians, and attends the odd function, but he has really left the rock 'n' roll world behind him to a great extent, I suppose it was difficult and probably nerve racking to have been plummeted back into the limelight in front of a 2,000 capacity crowd. In the end, after blowing hot and cold, his decision was negative.

One person who we searched after and managed to locate was Howie Casey, who had not only played the terrific sax solo on '20th Century Boy' and other Bolan recordings, but had also been the saxophonist for the likes of Mott The Hoople, and had also played some vital saxophone riffs on Paul McCartney's 'Band On The Run' album. In fact he married, and remains married to Shelia, one of Thunderthighs, the name that Ian Hunter gave to his backing vocalist group while recording with Mott The Hoople. Howie lives on the coast and has settled down now, but still plays the odd gig and sometimes works together, with Sheila on lead vocals.

I asked Howie if he would play on '20th Century Boy' and also on a couple of other songs. Howie really went for it and his playing was absolutely on the ball and hadn't diminished at all. When we reached the outro we gave him an extended solo, which worked exceptionally well. Howie loved it so much that afterwards he told me to call him if ever I wanted his services again.

It has always been a buzz playing the tracks together as a band, but it was thrilling to be an arranger/guitarist on the stage organising other artists just for one day. I was actually able to keep my eyes open and watch the audience, and it was great to see so many people with such beaming smiles - what a happy and enjoyable day it had been. The tiring and long rehearsals the day before had all been worth it. I had to write down a list of all those who had either performed or had helped produce the event as I didn't want to forget anyone. I read out my 'thank you's' name-by-name. When I thanked Gloria, she came out from side-stage with her arms outstretched and gave me a big hug and said "thank you so much" in my ear. It did get quite emotional at this time, and I had to stop for a few seconds to compose myself.

For the encore I asked everyone to return to the stage for 'Get It On'. It was of course chaotic with everyone dancing and jumping and singing, but the best fun ever! It was most likely the first and only chance that anyone would ever see all these people in one place performing at the same time. As I've mentioned to friends in the past, I've always liked my rock 'n' roll to be slightly anarchic and this performance ticked that box perfectly.

As those who have seen our own performances would know, I always ended our version of 'Get It On' with a bout of tambourine scratching and scraping on the guitar strings, just like Bolan did in his hey-day. Andy Ellison, always one to go that extra mile in his performance, had taken my tambourine from the top of my amp and was using it to get the audience clapping, so in the middle of the number I had to ask him to put it back on top of the amp, ready for me to use! On the eventual DVD release this looks quite humorous as you can see me saying something to Andy before he puts the tambourine back on the amp - almost like I was ticking him off!

After the first encore we left the stage before all sauntering back for the evening's finale of 'Hot Love' with the whole of the Empire audience singing and dancing, a few even shedding a tear of emotion, and so many happy faces at every turn. It was a fantastic way to end a supercharged day and evening. After the concert, the staff at the venue commented that although The Empire sells out with major stars, they could not remember a time when it was such a full and manic and crazy night all wrapped into one!

The after-show party was a great place to hang out for a while. I mixed, circulated and chatted to nearly everyone, in what was a much calmer setting as opposed to all the stress of the last two days. When I entered through the front doors, Gloria Jones and Linda Lewis, who were either side of each other, both got hold of my hands and began pulling me to each side. As I was being stretched by both of them, I didn't know which way to go. In the end they both let go and we ended up having couple of photographs taken with each other. I went up to Shaky and had a couple of photos taken with him as well. He told me that he thought the evening had gone really well and that he'd had a great time.

I also said a genuine "thank you" to Tony Visconti for what he had done for the evening. He told me that it was "one of the best times I had ever had and loved every minute of it! I then did a quick sweep to thank everyone who had turned up for the event, but I was so tired that after about an hour or so we all climbed into our minibus and made our way home. On the way out Linda and Gloria, Harry Feld and wife Sandy, and Tony Visconti were all chatting. We had another quick photo taken before saying our goodbyes. It was a night to savour and one to remember for always.

The DVD was released nearly a year after the event, via *Liberation Entertainments*, which also included bonus interviews with the artists as well as a full colour booklet. Although there was mixed reviews from various magazines and the press (aren't there always?), T.Rextasy received extremely good write-ups from them all including some lovely complimentary comments from Simon Price of *The Independent On Sunday*.

The only person unhappy with the way he was perceived and sound-mixed on the pre-release DVD was Shakin' Stevens. It seemed that he wanted to mix his own sound, which was in turn refused by *Liberation Entertainments* as they told him that if they let him re-mix his sound, then everyone else would've wanted to do the same. He was therefore, at his own request, removed from the final release.

Live at The BBC Proms Hyde Park Concert, London - September 2007.

Below: An audience of approximately 35,000 - 40,000 could watch us on the large BBC video screens. *(Pieter MacMillan)*

Above: Flyer for the 'Marc Bolan Celebration' concert at the Shepherd's Bush Empire featuring many special guests, 15th September 2007

Left: In the dressing room with Blondie drummer, Clem Burke (with Ray Dorset from Mungo Jerry in the background) prior to the concert.

Shepherd's Bush Empire,
15th September 2007.

Above: T.Rextasy with Linda Lewis and
Clem Burke.

Left: With Marc Almond.
(Michelle Robek)

Below: With Ray Dorset.
(Michelle Robek)

Shepherd's Bush Empire, 15th September 2007.

Pre-encore. From left to right: Paul Marks, Shakin' Stevens, John Skelton, Dr Robert (Blow Monkeys), Eric Hall, Ray Dorset, Andrew & Faye Miller (Nordoff-Robbins), Nicky Graham (PRS), Clem Burke, Me, Linda Lewis, Marc Almond, Dirty Pretty Strings (String Quartet), Andy Ellison (John's Children), Neil Cross, Tony Visconti, Neal X (Sigue Sigue Sputnik), and one of the Dirty Pretty Strings (seated behind). *(Kelvin Royce)*

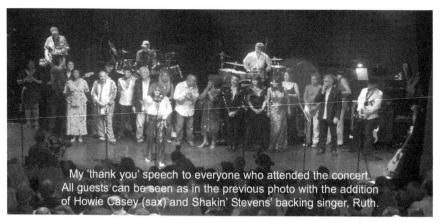

My 'thank you' speech to everyone who attended the concert. All guests can be seen as in the previous photo with the addition of Howie Casey (sax) and Shakin' Stevens' backing singer, Ruth.

Shepherd's Bush Empire, 15th September 2007.

Left: At the after-show party. From left to right: Linda Lewis, Gloria Jones, me, and Caron

Below: At the after-show party with Shakin' Stevens.

The Marc Bolan Celebration Concert at the Shepherd's Bush Empire was officially released on DVD by *Liberation Entertainments* - 2008.

Left: T.Rextasy photo session - December 2007.

Below: T.Rextasy Christmas card to fans on our mailing list. The picture featured a shot from the Shepherd's Bush Empire Marc Bolan Celebration Concert - 2007.

Right: Eric Hall (Marc's publicist, now DJ for Radio Essex) and I after a radio interview I did with him. I am wearing a mid-1970s jacket that belonged to Marc Bolan that Eric was thinking of auctioning for charity - circa 2007.

13

I Love To Boogie

The start of 2008 was a hilarious time as I had been told that the 'Official' Marc Bolan Calendar published in association with *The Daily Mirror* had made a terrible mistake on one of their photograph inclusions. They inadvertently had used a photo of me instead of Marc for the month of August. Of course, there was nothing that could be done about it, so thousands of 2008 calendars were distributed and sold containing a live in-concert black and white photo of me within its pages. I thought that it was a shame that they hadn't used my photo for the month of November, as that is when my birthday falls - now that would have been ironic!

We decided to record a few tracks for a CD single to coincide with our tour with Slade, which took place around November and December. We booked a mobile recording desk and an old barn and set up our equipment. We did a few backing track run-throughs of 'Hot Love' and 'I Love To Boogie' and put them down after only a couple of takes. We then set ourselves up for a recording of the old Bing Crosby hit 'White Christmas'. I had the idea of recording this song in the style of 'Hot Love' a few years ago, especially as we had been playing an abridged version of it at some of our past Christmas concerts. I thought it worked amazingly well, and after a few rehearsals we settled on the best take.

I decided to do the lead vocals a few days afterwards, which were recorded in a small room in Dave Dulake's house where a makeshift studio was erected. Dave was a friend of John Skelton and kindly placed a few keyboard lines for us on all three tracks. The overall sound was pretty good in the circumstances and the quality of the recordings ended up better than some tracks we had done in the past in more expensive studios! We pressed up a few hundred copies, which were sold mainly at gigs and via mail order, as well as being a good promotional tool.

A few months later I was offered a deal with *Madman Records* for the release of the three tracks as a CD single with a bonus CD-Rom video of Rolan Bolan and myself singing 'Dreamy Lady' from the Cambridge Corn Exchange gig in 1997. It was also a real coup to have the three tracks released on 7" red coloured vinyl inside a red and white replica T.Rex sleeve, something that I had always fancied. It worked well as the colours of the 7" cover didn't only replicate the original 1972 T.Rex 'Children Of The Revolution' single sleeve design, but also coincided with Christmas.

It had been a while since I had appeared on television, but in September 2007, I was invited along to the filming of the BBC's *Antiques Road Show* for an edition being filmed in Sudbury, Suffolk. I had previously told them about a few of the original Marc Bolan items that I had collected over the years. I was asked to take three items of interest, and I chose Bolan's original blue dungarees that he had worn for his 1972 *Top Of The Pops* appearance for 'Metal Guru', a famous blue tapestry-lapelled jacket that Marc had worn for many photo sessions, and the original two-inch multi-track master tape of '20th Century Boy'.

I was told that Hilary Kay, one of the antique experts from *Sotheby's* and a programme regular, would be estimating and looking over the items. As I had met Hilary on more than one occasion in the past, it made it a little more relaxing to know that she would recognise me on my arrival.

The day of filming was swelteringly hot and quite unbearable. Thankfully, I was told that I wouldn't have to wait with the hundreds of people that had queued up and could go straight to the front of the line with others that had received actual invitations. I was directed to a marquee that covered as both a make-up room and waiting room, and although I waited until I was called, I informed the officials that I wouldn't need to use a make-up artist and told them "It's okay, I'll do my own, thanks!" The dungarees and jacket were deemed valuable estimating at a few thousand pounds for both items together - even though I felt that the valuation was on the low side, especially as there are so many photos and footage of Marc wearing the items, but she was truly amazed when I brought out the multi-track tape. She couldn't even place an actual value on it as she thought that as a piece of rock memorabilia, it was so unique. Although the programme wasn't broadcast until January 2008 it was a great way to start the year with a little bit of inadvertent publicity!

Much of 2008 was taken up with gigging, promoting the 'Celebration' DVD, and the release of a special recording Bolan had made in 1964 under his birth name. This recording was in the form of a quarter-inch tape that had been paid for and recorded with his very first manager Geoffrey De La Roy Hall. Geoffrey was a guy who paid Marc's rent when he lived in Manchester Street in London. He also used to give Marc money for clothing and food and used to 'look after him' and take him to parties in his Jaguar. Geoffrey was an ex-barrister and also a pilot in WWII and had won various medals for conduct and bravery. He saw my face on a gig poster in 1994 and made contact. Touchingly, he still kept photos, various pieces of manuscripts, and poems that Marc had written all those years ago. He even retained a management contract that had been signed by Marc's parents, as Marc would've been legally too young to sign on his own.

On a visit to his home in Northallerton in North Yorkshire, Caron and I were shown some of these rare items that we didn't even knew existed. It was a great shame that other than the quarter-inch tape that we happily received I do not know what exactly happened to all of the rest of that rare collection, as sadly Geoffrey passed away in his sleep on 15th July 2002, aged 81. Caron and I both attended Geoffrey's funeral a few days later. It was grand to have known him, even though it was for just a short while.

The quarter-inch tape included takes 5 and 7 of a Cliff Richard inspired song called 'All At Once'. I doubt that it had been played for many years, but when we placed it onto our reel-to-reel we couldn't believe the quality. It was almost as if it was recorded last week! *Madman Records* agreed to release the two tracks on a special 7" vinyl single in a replica inspired sixties *Decca* type sleeve in September 2008. Only 1,000 copies were officially pressed and most were sold via websites or via *Madman Records*. It is still amazing to think that this would not have happened if I hadn't formed the band, as I would never have met Geoffrey.

In the midst of it all we began another tour that spread over various months, which I entitled 'The Greatest Hits Tour'. The name of the tour informed everyone exactly what to expect. Gone were the acoustic sessions and in came two straightforward electric performances. The nature of the show was to entice in people who liked Marc Bolan, but were perhaps dubious as to what songs they would remember. Calling it 'The Greatest Hits Tour' dangled the carrot and pulled in people that may not have come along if we hadn't included those words on the posters. It worked a treat and set us up for the next few years on the theatre circuit as we began to pull in a wide range of age groups, as parents began bringing along their children, and sometimes, their children's children.

Meanwhile the *Born To Boogie* Bolan biography originally published in 1982 by Chris Welch & Simon Napier Bell was reissued in the summer of 2008 in a coffee-table style soft back with a purple/mauve cover. A few months prior I was interviewed quite extensively for the new edition. I was pleasantly surprised when on publication, I received my complimentary copy to see that the whole of the last chapter was entitled 'T.Rextasy - a slight return' and comprised mostly of my quotes and stories about Marc Bolan, T.Rex, and T.Rextasy.

In April I received a message from a US recording company *Cleopatra Records*. They were interested in licensing our recording of 'White Christmas' for release on a Various Artists double album compilation. After the usual bout of contract negotiating, I decided that I would have the track licensed to them for a period of five years maximum, as I thought their original deal for ten years was a little too restrictive. They agreed and contracts were signed. Sure enough, the double album was released for the American Christmas market in 2009 and since then our version of 'White Christmas' has been included on other various US Christmas CD compilations via *Cleopatra*.

It was an unusual and varied compilation with artists such as Iggy Pop, James Brown, Bay City Rollers, Dweezil Zappa, and a host of others singing their own unique versions of Christmas songs. Our 'White Christmas' track was sandwiched between the rocker Gilby Clarke's version of 'Santa Claus Is Coming To Town', and Glam rockers Pretty Boy Floyd's 'Father Christmas.' It was pretty cool to have been involved in such an album, especially as we were the only tribute band that had been considered and accepted for inclusion.

Before the year was out, John Skelton was asked to take part in the BBC TV music programme *Never Mind The Buzzcocks* to be included in the 'recognise the old star' line-up with Slade's drummer, Don Powell. The panel had to pick out Don, which of course, they did without any problem. Just a few months later into 2009, John was asked back again but this time to be included in the line up with Bobby Harrison, the drummer from Procol Harum. The panel included the TV comedian/entertainer Noel Fielding, who chatted to John in the green room shortly before the filming and told him that he was a big fan of Marc Bolan and T.Rex and always thought that Marc looked great.

This wasn't the first time John had been on television outside of his comfort zone of playing the drums. He has amongst other things, played the part of the lasso cowboy in one of the TV adverts for *McDonalds*, where he lassos the 'Hamburglar' aka Ronald McDonald. Another one of John's talents is his outstanding and top-end-of-the-market leatherwork. For instance he has supplied *Madam Tussauds* with the leather holster for their waxwork model of Clint Eastwood.

To keep the ball rolling in 2009 we quickly decided, in conjunction with *Sweeney Entertainments*, to arrange a follow-up tour so by April we were already sinking our teeth into a set of dates I had named 'The Electric Boogie Tour', which ran all the way through to October that year. Once again, the title of the tour said it like it was - an upbeat, two set, and just under two hours of electric boogie. This time however, we decided to drop in a few more B-sides and album tracks to show the die-hard fans that we hadn't forgotten them either. Posters and flyers were designed by our agency using the picture that was used for the cover image of the Shepherd's Bush DVD. The end product was a striking advertising tool that many theatre managements loved and helped us gain many front-page covers on theatre brochures.

It is always an impossible situation where set lists are concerned. I think Abraham Lincoln got it right when he said, and I paraphrase, "you can please some of the people some of the time, but you can't please all the people all of the time." I think Bob Dylan once had his own version of this saying as well!* The truth is that there are many fans of Marc out there, but the majority of people still demand to hear the biggest hits. If we didn't play to the majority, then we would start getting minority audiences, which is when bookings would start to fall, and theatre managers are only interested in 'bums on seats' as they say. I have always tried to please as many fans as possible, which is why we always attempt to include a selection of songs that comprise not only the many major hits, but intersperse them with the lesser known tracks for the die-hards when we can.

I have always enjoyed playing acoustic guitar as much as I enjoy playing electric, so I was pleased when I received a call from Gary

*Dylan's paraphrasing appears in his 1963 song, Talking World War III Blues, which name checks Lincoln.

Stevenson, a record producer who had recorded bands such as the chart topping Go West and other pop acts. The various gold and silver discs hanging on the wall of his studio complex are the evidence of his success.

Earlier in 1999 I had originally been hired to play guitar for a project he had obtained with EMI for a young girl Glam band, 21st Century Girls. The album was made up of pop songs written by Gary and other session writers and was produced and recorded in his home studio in Oxfordshire. Although the girls made it onto *Top Of The Pops* and other programmes with a reasonably successful single, the album was shelved in the UK and Europe, although it was eventually released in Japan. I recorded my guitar parts for at least three tracks, 'Yesterday Morning', 'Growing Pains', and 'Record Shop.'

Gary now wanted to book John and myself to play an intimate acoustic set in celebration of his wedding anniversary, in his home garden. It was a lovely hot summer's day in June 2009 and we ended up playing a thirty-minute set in front of Gary, his wife Annette, and some of their guests that included members of Go West, Magnum, Spandau Ballet and Sting's producer. Afterwards, I had a brief chat with Tony Hadley from Spandau who told me how much he and his daughter had loved the set and that he had sung the Bolan song 'New York City' in some of his recent solo concerts!

As we had achieved obtaining our endorsement from *Wizard [Bahamas] Limited* a few years earlier, I thought it was important to obtain an endorsement from the company who had recently taken over the management of Marc's catalogue - that baton had now passed from *Wizard* to *Spirit Music Limited* in the USA. They were already made fully aware of T.Rextasy and *Wizard's* prior endorsement and therefore I referred them to our product and website in the hope that they too would authorise and endorse the band. On 28th June 2009, I received an emailed letter from *Spirit's* managing director, Mark Fried, with their full endorsement, with the added remark "I salute Danielz and T.Rextasy for helping keep the spirit and songs of Marc Bolan alive."

A few months later I received another email confirmation from *Westminster Music Limited*, who had also decided to give their endorsement to the band. This was also important, as although *Spirit Music* owned the rights to Marc's catalogue from 1972 - 1977, *Westminster Music* owned the rights from 1967 - 1971 (inclusive) so it was delightful to have received endorsements from both companies that covered Marc's complete output.

One thing I had always planned to do was to select ten or twelve Bolan compositions and record them stripped down and played acoustically, something on the lines of an 'unplugged' album. I discussed the project with John Skelton who was immediately interested, so we began arranging tracks and rehearsing them, and in the summer of 2009 John took the reigns and booked *Dog Kennel Studios* in Essex. Before long we were recording as a duo under the name of 'T.Rextasy Unplugged'. It had been a long time since I had been in a recording studio to record a full-length album, so it was pretty exciting and an absolute pleasure to do.

I was always aware that although my preference had been to record a collection of Marc's more slightly obscure B-sides and album tracks, I had to be commercially minded and make sure that I picked a few choice T.Rex singles. I chose some of the well-known titles purely because I had not recorded them previously and thought that it would be nice to record them in this way, so 'Jeepster', 'Solid Gold Easy Action', and 'Ride A White Swan' were obvious choices. I also picked out some unusual songs to record as 'Till Dawn', 'Dandy In The Underworld', and 'Organ Blues'.

In addition, and like the previous T.Rextasy albums, I included two of my own compositions. The first was a song called 'Living In Dreamland', about the harshness of the world we live in as an obnoxious and uncaring race. The second track began its life as a poem to Marc and the feelings I had for him spiritually since becoming a fan right up to the present day. The words were written very quickly on purpose. I wanted to create a feeling and a sentiment in one swoop so I didn't have to think about what I wanted to say, but what was in mind at that moment in time. All together it took just two manuscripts to level out the lyrics to make it work as a song and not just as a poem to music. My first draft used to be available to see on my personal website before I eventually terminated the site through lack of time to keep it updated. The second draft is the one I used for the final recording that eventually became known as 'A Dream That Lasts Forever.'

I always knew that recording an acoustic album would have a cult following as opposed to mass interest, but I really enjoyed the process, and I was very pleased with the results. I wanted to record it fast and furious so that it would retain much of the feeling and mood of the time. I like listening to albums with the odd bum-note and the loose endings left in. It makes an album 'real' and 'organic' and not one that feels digitally cold and superficial like so many do today. Just listen to 'Electric Warrior', and you'll know exactly what I mean. I honestly think that we achieved that too, and I'm glad to know that John felt the same way about it and was just as proud of the finished product as I was. The album, 'A Dream That Lasts Forever' eventually saw its release in late 2009 on *Madman Records*.

After around thirteen years or so of gigging on the Christmas tour with Dave Hill and Don Powell's Slade, December 2009 was to be the very last time. I wasn't at all happy with the PA or some of the organisation that was surrounding the tour. It was beginning to get a little sloppy in places and corner cutting, mainly I guess because audience attendances had been in decline. Before the end of the tour, I actually had to insist that we hired in our own soundman, as I was completely dissatisfied with the engineers that had been booked. Only after I had threatened to walk away from the remaining dates was it agreed that T.Rextasy could have its own sound engineer to regulate the rest of the tour. Jon Farnsworth travelled down from the North of England, and thankfully, after his arrival, everything began to fall into place. We were able to concentrate on what we did best and played some blinding shows right up until, and including, the very last gig.

The following year Dave Hill collapsed while on a gig abroad, and while not life-threatening it sealed the fate of another December tour around the UK. With ticket sales down, and Dave's mild stroke, it confirmed the end of what had been a yearly event. No promoter wants to throw money at three bands, pay for promotion and P.A. systems if he cannot make a decent profit, and profit for promoters is the name of the game. Even our last gig on the 2009 *Merry Xmas Tour* at the prestigious O2 in London couldn't sustain, or even contemplate another gig there the following year. It was a shame, but everything must come to an end, and this tour had run its course.

It's strange how when something substantial is coming to an end, one can get a rewind occurrence of funny stories or antics. One that sprung to mind was at a show we were playing at The Cheese & Grain in Devon, when Dr & The Medics were part of the Christmas tour in the earlier years. The Doctor (Clive) decided that even though it was in the middle of a freezing winter that it would be a good idea to take all his clothes off and walk absolutely stark naked around the backstage area no matter who was there! He just didn't care - strolling around trying to make conversation to anyone who would talk to him before darting into a nearby dressing area to get warmed up and changed into his stage clothes...

However, sometimes I guess it's the promoter that gets the last laugh, as this one instance would testify. T.Rextasy, Andy Scott's Sweet, and Les McKeown's Bay City Rollers were booked to play at a festival in Germany. It was all going along smoothly until Les started kicking up a fuss about how he wasn't happy with various aspects of how the gig was being run, and about the food and drink rider, and it kind of went on and on. The promoter had in fact treated us very well indeed and did everything by the book. After the show, we were all chauffeured to the local airport for our return flights home. The promoter told us that our tickets would be waiting at the checkout desk and waved us goodbye. Indeed all the tickets were there for us... except for the Bay City Rollers! It turned out that the German promoter hadn't bothered, or had cancelled the BCRs return tickets to the UK. They were in a terrible state and not at all pleased! To this day I still do not know what they did except for guessing that they would've had to pay for their own flights back with the money that they were paid for the show that evening!

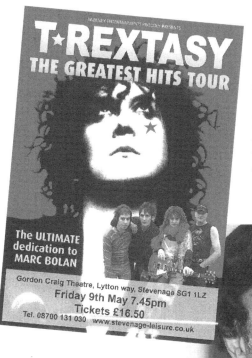

Left: T.Rextasy flyer for 'The 2008 Greatest Hits Tour'.

Below: Geoffrey De-La-Roy Hall, Mark Feld's (aka Marc Bolan) very first known manager, who paid for the 1964 recording of a track called 'All At Once'.

Below: The original August 1964 quarter-inch master tape recording of takes 5 & 7 of 'All At Once' by Mark Feld, and the 7" vinyl release on *Madman Records* - 2008.

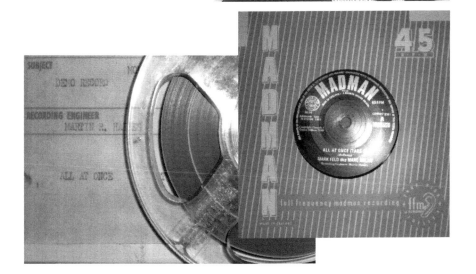

A 2008 updated re-issued version of the 1982 Bolan biography by Chris Welch & Simon Napier-Bell which included a chapter entitled 'T.Rextasy - a slight return' which incorporated a selection of my interview quotes and stories about Marc, T.Rex, and T.Rextasy.

Below: Early CD promo pressing of 'White Christmas' by T.Rextasy in 2007, and the red vinyl 7" single on *Madman Records* in November 2008.

CD single, rear cover

200

Live at Wellington Country Park, Berkshire in July 2009.

John Skelton and I at a private alfresco acoustic gig for producer Gary Stevenson - June 2009.

With Bob Harris (Old Grey Whistle Test) after his one-man-show at The Robin in Bilston, 2009.

Below: Access All Areas passes for our 'Greatest Hits' and 'Born To Boogie' tours.

Double CD Christmas album by *Cleopatra Records* in the USA, which contained T.Rextasy's 'White Christmas' - released in 2009.

Above: T.Rextasy Unplugged album: 'A Dream That Lasts Forever', released on *Madman Records* - August 2009.

14

Reborn And Bopping

It was a new year and 2010 had a nice futuristic ring to it. I had now been gigging on the T.Rextasy road for nearly eighteen years and even though I have always been pretty much of an introvert at heart and quite insecure, I have always tried at least to be a little optimistic. The outside world has always mainly seen me as an extrovert, but like many performers, deep inside is a soul that is fighting to be accepted and thought of as 'something.' In my youth, as well as my time as an adult, or a 'grown up', I have always been slightly different from those around me. On purpose I may add, as I've never been one to blend in with the crowd. Even today my hair attracts various comments, some derogatory and some not. This hasn't distracted me at all through the years, as I have always, as now, been my own person. Even in my guise as 'Danielz from T.Rextasy' I have always kept my own identity, not actually ever pretending to be Marc at any time - a hard decision considering I have been in a tribute band dedicating my musical career to Marc Bolan!

A few months prior to the New Year, Tony Visconti had told me about a woman who had worked with T.Rex in the very early 1970s that I should make contact with. Her name was Ann Ruckert. Before contacting her I did a little research and found that she was, and still is a very highly respected woman in the music industry, especially in the USA. Ann knows people in high places and there is too much to mention about her career here. She is a multi-talented songwriter, performer and public speaker and arranges a multitude of gigs and music benefits. Ann's days with Marc mainly consisted of helping the band with their various rider needs and changing the odd guitar string when required, but in time she became friends with Marc, June Bolan and the band.

I was sceptical at first because I have met so many people who have claimed to know Marc and yet, when push comes to shove, they have had nothing to show for it, or indeed no proof whatsoever. After various emails back and forth, I found Ann to be an extremely honest, and a lovely person. An achievement in itself in the music industry! After one of our corresponding emails, as a gift, she said she would send some photos of Marc and T.Rex that she had taken.

Several months passed and I didn't think anything more about it, but then in September I received a package in the post and was delightfully surprised with what was inside. Ann had sent a small photo album of colour shots that had been taken in the early 1970s of T.Rex on the road. What made these extra special was that they were non-posed photos taken from various locations such as inside a car, or just strolling around in the street. Inside a second box was a pair of green *Anello & Davide* tap shoes that Marc had once owned. Ann had kept them for all these years, but had decided to pass them onto me for, and I quote, "your years of dedication to playing Marc's music and keeping his legacy alive." I was, as one could imagine, lost for words at such generosity from someone that I had only been in touch with over the Internet, and in turn, someone that had only seen and read about me via the T.Rextasy website and from a couple of photographs that I had sent to her in emails.

In the meantime I had been conveniently backing away from any additional websites and ever more computer interaction, but Caron thought it was about time that we should set up an official T.Rextasy *Facebook* page. Especially as *Facebook* had become a much more 'instant' and popular interactive communicative tool than regular websites as it seemed easier to project information for the fans and public. I was still a little unsure, as I had never been that computer literate at the best of times. It took me completely by surprise however; just how fast it would hit the ground running. Before long it was receiving thousands of hits, with a four-figure membership within just a few months.

It was quite amazing having people from around the world, commenting on all the information that the T.Rextasy *Facebook* had to offer, be it a video, photo, or an article. Even now I still find things that astound me, and *Facebook* is yet another one of those things that I find fascinating and intriguing. To think that only twenty years ago I was still using pen and paper, or a telephone to communicate. Now I can be in touch with thousands of people all over the world with just a press of a button on a keypad... wow. I bet anyone under the age of twenty-five who reads this must be thinking "what an old duffer this guy is!"

Since forming the band I've always had people consistently asking about my formative years and interested in the songs I had written before T.Rextasy. In the age of downloading it gave me an idea to release, for one year only, from March 2010 to March 2011, a download-only album that was put together solely for *i-Tunes*, which I entitled 'Personal Touch'. The compilation consisted of twenty-one compositions that I had mainly recorded and produced in the 1980s. The reason I decided to issue it for one year only was because I was hopeful that I could get some kind of official deal in the future. At the time of writing this, I'm still waiting!

Parallel to my recent download idea I had been lucky enough to receive a distribution deal from the excellent UK independent label *Angel Air* who's managing director, Peter Purnell, had listened to a selection of songs recorded by Tarazara. Peter loved all the fifteen original and self-penned tracks I had sent to him and couldn't understand why they had not been released at the time. After a friendly and successful meeting we settled on a deal to release all fifteen songs plus two bonus live tracks that we had performed on the Channel Four show *ECT* in May 1985. The album was finally released with the title 'Behind The Mask - Danielz & Tarazara' in September 2010 coinciding with an official *Facebook* site dedicated to Tarazara and my solo career.

Every September I made a conscious effort to play a show that I would dedicate to Marc's memory, and after that grand gig for Marc's 30th Anniversary, we were back once again playing the gigs that I would call 'in-between' the key years. In the past we had invited special guests along to our yearly anniversary concerts for Marc at The Standard Music Venue in London, and in September 2010 I decided to invite back the magical Linda Lewis. Her performance at the Shepherd's Bush concert had been nothing short of brilliant, so it was lovely to have her back for another appearance.

We rehearsed 'Children Of The Revolution', 'Metal Guru' and 'Telegram Sam' at a prolonged sound-check, which all went well. Many fans came along packing out the venue and were happy to be able to see Linda at such close proximity. Although she forgot most of what we rehearsed and ad-libbed most of her performance, she still received a fabulous reception. Her voice of octaves very nearly cracked a few glasses at the back bar, and her warmth and lovely words about Marc touched the fans' hearts.

Every now and then we will play a gig at some theatre or another and something special or unexpected would happen. In September 2010 photographer Allan Ballard, who had taken all the photos for the 'Dandy In The Underworld' album session, had come along to see the show at The Pier Theatre in Cromer, Norfolk. Allan lived in Norfolk and was intrigued enough to come along having seen an advertising poster. At the merchandise table he spoke to Caron at length and said how excellent he thought the band were before asking for our contact address, as he wanted to send us something as a 'thank you' for keeping Marc's memory alive.

A few weeks later I was excited to receive a very large cardboard tube that had Allan's name and contact address on it. I was anxious to know what was inside. I opened the seal and unravelled what was a beautifully signed hand-printed unpublished photo of Marc from the 'Dandy In The Underworld' session. It was such a lovely gesture and something totally unexpected. I knew that Allan had said that he was going to send something but I didn't expect something quite so stunning. The photo was immediately framed and placed onto a wall pride of place. The next day I telephoned him to say thanks. We chatted for a while about Marc and like so many people I have met who had known him, Allan was no different and still retained a strong affection for him and said that even now, he was so missed. A sad ending to this tale is when I phoned Allan's number a year later in 2011 to invite him to another show; I was told that he had died just a few months earlier...

T.Rextasy has never been what one might call a band for corporate events, but if we were ever asked to play at one of these functions, I would always consider it if I felt that it would look good on the CV. One such gig took place in December 2010 at Koko in North London. A very large and substantial logistics company had booked us to play for just one hour at their comprehensive Christmas party. A couple of weeks beforehand I found out that popular comedian Justin Lee Collins would be the compere for the evening and since he was still quite high profile I thought it would do us no harm at all to take part in the event.

As is so typical with these occasions, we were asked to turn up early in the morning for soundchecking, only to find out that as is usual, everything was running late. After waiting around for three hours or so, we eventually soundchecked and then hung around all day until we hit the stage at about

8pm. Justin introduced us with a lovely spiel saying that "I have seen lots of tribute bands in my time and this band are the second best tribute band I have ever met, next to the Rolling Clones - ladies and gentlemen T.Rextasy!" Hmmm. I didn't know whether to consider that an impressive introduction or not. In the end I was in two minds about it. I was also confused by the word 'met' as I had never met him before in my life, although in the back of my mind I was pretty sure that he had seen us in concert somewhere before.

It all ended up as these corporate events normally do. We did our job, went down well, returned to our dressing rooms and went home. We barely had a 'thank you' from any of the organisers as they were busily getting the next act onto the stage. The only truly exciting part of the day was earlier on when we parked our car in a non-parking zone to find that on our return we had received a parking ticket - rock on! I guess that by now everyone who knows me is aware that I consider sarcasm as the highest form of wit!

The 18th December 2010 was one of those days in England when we should've all stayed at home but we were due to play a gig with Roy Wood in Market Harborough. The weather was atrocious and vehicles all over the country were having accidents or plainly not moving at all due to the dreadful road conditions. Caron and I had decided to drive in our car instead of meeting the band at South Mimms service area on the M25 where we would normally all travel up together. Caron and I arrived in good time as our part of the country had missed the dreadful snow and ice storms. We waited and waited as the rest of the band were stranded for hours in London due to the traffic and the weather conditions that lay ahead of them. As time passed by I knew that they were not going to make it so I had no choice but to tell them to turn back and go home.

Roy Wood and his band had only travelled a short way down from the Midlands, missing all the bad weather, so they were fine and relaxed, whereas I was stressed out wondering what to do. The promoter, David Allen, asked if I would do a thirty minute acoustic solo spot. As I didn't want to let the fans down I agreed, especially as I was told that some people had travelled a fair distance just to come along to see us play. It was then that I remembered that I had only brought along my electric guitars! Thankfully, a good friend by the name of John 'Wurz' Aston didn't live that far away, so he rushed home and came back with his acoustic. As I did a quick soundcheck, Roy Wood commented to a radio DJ in attendance, "I feel for that guy up there!"

When the sell-out crowd had filled the venue, the promoter stood on the stage and explained what had happened, saying that I would still perform a set on my own, to which, thankfully, I received a very warm reception. I walked onto the stage and performed a few numbers with the acoustic guitar and then with my electric, just to give the show a little lift and variation. I gave it all I had and tried to perform as if the band were behind me! The crowd sang and clapped along as my nerves slowly evaporated. As I came to the last notes of 'Hot Love' I felt relief, as the applause was truly gratifying. Afterwards, Roy commented to the DJ, "I don't feel for that guy anymore!" As I walked back to the dressing room, Roy kindly turned to me and said, "I don't know how you did it, but it was great, really great, well done mate!" I felt good. It was lovely to have received that kind of respect from someone of that stature and from someone that I had grown up being a fan of. It was one of the most stressed out performances I had ever done, especially being in front of a capacity audience, and although I do sometimes like being outside of my comfort zone, it's not something that I would want to do again in a hurry!

Towards the end of the year I received an email from a company in Australia who proposed a release of our Christmas single on their label after hearing it over the Internet. The label, *Possum Records*, had already released various albums from their roster, such as Ian Dury, so I felt that I would be in good company. They ended up changing the track listing slightly from our original, with 'White Christmas' being the leading track, followed by my own composition 'Baby Factory', and playing out with 'I Love To Boogie'. I was pleased to have the CD released down under, as it added yet another string to the T.Rextasy bow.

Unbelievably, this was the first year where we could actually all have a relaxing lead up to Christmas, which was something that we hadn't been able to do for years because of the 'Merry Xmas Everybody' yearly Slade tour. I decided that as we would no longer have the Slade dates in December, it would be quite nice to have a gig on New Year's Eve. I had told agencies in the past not to bother offering us any New Year's Eve dates because we felt that if we couldn't have many days off leading up to Christmas, then at least we should have a relaxing New Year. Now that the situation had changed, 'feelers' were put out to various agencies. The best offer came from Cardiff Council for its New Year's Eve extravaganza in the

City Square.

From when we arrived to the very end of the evening we were given more food and drink than we could put away. A hotel was booked for us, and we had a chauffeur driven vehicle on call to take us to and from the hotel whenever we needed it. Our dressing room was a beautifully lavish room with even more food and drink! Our old friends Dr & The Medics opened for us giving their usual entertaining performance with nowhere for Clive to carry out his solo nudist act. We took to the stage around 11.15pm before the obligatory fireworks display and the New Year countdown began forty-five minutes later. We then completed our show in front of thousands of Welsh revellers. It was a great way to end 2010 and to begin 2011.

The year began on a bit of a downer, as I was despondent to hear from agencies and promoters about venues closing down and marketing budgets being drastically cut. Not to mention, some of the bands I had known for years were splitting up, or dates being pulled up and down the country for various acts. I felt fortunate that we still had a stronghold of dedicated and reliable fans that were coming along to see us play. In fact, it was quite touching to notice that many of our theatre dates and rock shows were really pulling in some excellent attendances and some venues were even sell-outs too. Playing around seventy shows a year, and only having around six cancellations, was a very good average in the scheme of things in the latest economic downfall. Throughout the year I mentioned at so many shows how grateful I was to see people coming through those doors because I knew how hard it was for some fans to pay an average of £12 - £20 to see us in concert - and I really meant it too.

In December 2010 *Uncut* magazine issued an invitation to anyone who had seen T.Rex in concert to write in and they would consider including the most interesting story in a forthcoming issue. In their January edition the following month they included a small photo of me in T.Rextasy stage gear next to an article entitled 'I Was There', which told an expurgated story of my experience of going to see Marc and T.Rex in concert.

Outside my world of T.Rextasy I have always been happy to look at other projects, and I was glad to accept the job of guitar player for a futuristic poetical story that had been written by my friend and artist Paul Thomas. In February 2011, I made my way down to the West Country and set up my guitar and effects and recorded a selection of guitar phrases that would later be set to short story pieces of prose read by Fran Isherwood - a poet who tours the clubs of London with her own brand of poetry.

I recorded small snippets of acoustic guitar, electric guitar, feedback, and various short lead solos. When mixed down, Paul released it via an *i-Tunes* download later in the year as an eight-track mini-album by Zinc Harlequin, entitled 'Exploder'.

Although T.Rextasy has very rarely accepted supports or opening bands it was a joy and a breath of fresh air to have a David Bowie band opening up some of the shows for us in 2011. *Sweeney Entertainments* had originally asked me to check out a band that were performing in a small pub near Peterborough to see if they would cut it as a group that could grow and upgrade to theatre level. That band was called Aladdinsane. I thought that they were great and before long they began opening up for us at selected theatres. As many people are aware, I am very fussy and astute as to whom I think cut it as musicians and especially bands on the tribute circuit. Aladdinsane really did and what made it extra-special was that Paul Henderson, the lead singer, was truly a dedicated Bowie and Bolan fan. All in all, throughout the year, the two bands got together for around a dozen dates or so. On the last date of the tour, at the Felixstowe Pavilion Theatre, I decided to go on stage with them and play guitar on 'Diamond Dogs' - one of my favourite Bowie numbers, which was great fun. Afterwards, Paul returned the compliment and joined us for the finale of 'Hot Love.'

In all the years I had been playing an original replica of Bolan's *Gibson Les Paul Standard*, *Gibson Guitars* finally decided to issue a signature model. It had taken decades for them to arrive at this decision, but at long last they recognised that Marc was a force to be considered. I was pleased that in April 2011 I was commissioned by the highly respected *Guitar & Bass* magazine to write an article about Marc's famous and unique *Gibson*. The deal with *Guitar & Bass* was contract exclusive, however, I didn't mind and they published my four-page feature in the June 2011 edition.

I was very pleased with the way they had laid out the article, which included some very unusual shots of Marc, some of which were quite rare. I made sure that although the signature guitar that *Gibson* had produced was mentioned, I also commented that it was a little dubious that they had decided to issue it as a *Custom* model, whereas it is a well known fact that Marc's guitar began as a *Les Paul Standard*, and only had a *Custom* neck fitted some years later. I'm not even sure that *Gibson* is even aware that this is the case. Nevertheless it is still gratifying to know that *Gibson* has finally deemed Marc worthy of a signature guitar, alongside such luminaries as Jimmy Page and Slash.

One of the best 'Unplugged' gigs to date was when I appeared with John Skelton at the Acoustic Festival of Britain in Uttoxeter in Staffordshire on 22nd May 2011. We were asked to play as 'T.Rextasy Unplugged' in the Songwriters Marquee as the penultimate act to the headline band on that stage. We were due to play in the giant beer tent initially in front of a thousand or so people, but the wind and weather had been so bad that the pegs had loosened and had been deemed dangerous, so by the early afternoon the tent was dismantled.

Earlier in the day, we chatted to other artists from The Sea Horses, Quill, and Fairport Convention. It had a totally alternative feel to what we have been used to at rock 'n' roll festival events. When we reached the green room for drinks and food, we were shown to white clothed tables with cheeses and wine, amongst the teas and coffees and side biscuits and crisps and snacks. At rock festivals we are normally greeted with beer so it did make a nice change.

I was also quite pleased to later find out that we were the only tribute act that had been booked over the three-day event, and with around sixty or so original artists, I felt quite privileged to have been asked. The only person who seemed a little distant and tried to remain aloof was eighties star, Nick Kershaw. He walked into the green room and didn't even acknowledge or say hello to any of us, so along with members of Fairport Convention and Quill we ignored him and carried on chatting amongst ourselves.

At 9pm we took to the stage and played for an hour to an audience that seemed to be all Bolan fans or at least interested in Marc's music. The marquee was so packed out that the organisers had to remove all the chairs and tables to make additional room. As we played our way through the set, more and more people gathered around the perimeter of the marquee, so that by the time we were halfway through the gig we had attracted more people than the venue could hold. The audience appeared to know every single song and sang along so loudly that it was sometimes a little difficult to hear the monitors from the PA system.

I don't think anyone, John and I included, expected such a rapturous response or applause for just the two of us. By around 10pm the crowd had built up so much and were singing so loudly, that when we hit into our encore of 'Hot Love' the guys on the main stage must have wondered what the hell was going on! John and I have performed at some truly brilliant unplugged evenings, but I must be honest and say that to date, performing at the Acoustic Festival of Britain was one of the most amazing experiences.

A few months previously I had been asked to contribute my lead vocals to a track called 'Circles' that would go towards inclusion on an album entitled 'Doctor Doctor'. I was told that all the proceeds would go to a charity organisation awareness known as *Grey Children* that helps people who suffer from OCD (Obsessive Compulsive Disorder).

The main-man behind it was a guy in Oxfordshire called David Griffiths. On Sunday 29th May 2011 he booked a small studio for a few hours just a few miles from where I lived in Sudbury, Suffolk so that I could record my vocals for the song that he had written. The track was a ballad in the key of 'C', and even though Bolan songs such as 'Dreamy Lady', and 'Light Of Love' were written in that key, the tone for the song was a little high for the Bolanesque sound he wanted. However, after I had re-arranged a couple of the vocal lines and inflections we got it down in just four or five takes and were finished within the three hour session.

I told David that I thought the song was really good and that the tune had played around my mind over the past few days, which was always a good sign. The album was eventually made available via download and those who felt the need could use their own discretion to donate any amount or sum that they felt was worthy. Dave had put a lot of work into the recording and it became a labour of love for him. It was a very worthwhile project and I felt really happy to have been involved in such a good cause.

On 2nd June a 'Marc Bolan Music Workshop' had been organised to take place by *The Witney School of Rock* in Oxfordshire. Something which, had been originally initiated and helped along by ex-*Wizard [Bahamas]* employee Brian Dunham. John Skelton and I were invited along to set up and play a few Marc Bolan songs, to take part in a 'Questions & Answers' session about Marc's musicianship and his writing, and involve ourselves with some of the young students and bands who would come on the stage to play alongside us for a few numbers.

We were picked up from my home in Halstead and chauffeur driven to a small venue in Witney in Oxfordshire called Fat Lil's. Because of a bad accident on the M25, there had been a massive hold up. The tailback was so long that we didn't think we would arrive in time and that the whole event might have to be cancelled! We finally arrived very late and stressed out after a journey, which ended up taking well over three and a half hours! There was no time to stop for coffee or a bite to eat, as we had to set up our equipment immediately. We were still setting up and soundchecking while the students and their families were coming in, and as the PA equipment was not all that great in the venue, it took a lot longer than usual to get things underway.

As the proceedings eventually started at around 1pm, I introduced ourselves as Danielz & John Skelton from T.Rextasy before kicking in with '20th Century Boy'. We then played 'guest' to nearly all of the musicians and bands that had been instructed to rehearse and to learn one or two Marc Bolan songs in their curriculum. Some of the students were as young as eight or nine years old and it was pretty incredible to see a full-sized guitar swamping some of the children who were only around four foot tall.

The musicianship was surprising as most of the kids had done their homework well and their original interpretations of Bolan songs were sometimes inspiring. I chatted to a few of them afterwards and gave away some of my embossed T.Rextasy plectrums. A couple of hours later we were asked outside for a photo session in front and inside what was being called the 'Bolan Bus' - an old style London double-decker, which was flagged and draped with large banners of Marc Bolan and T.Rex images. A local press photographer snapped a few shots, which later appeared in the Oxfordshire papers.

Before the evening closed, Brian Dunham, Bolan expert and friend Martin Barden, and myself all took to the stage for a twenty minute Q&A session with the students. Questions about Marc came quick and fast, asking such things as "What was Marc's real name?" "What was his first official record?"*, and "Which were his favourite or most well known guitars?"** I wasn't sure whether or not it was the volume we played at, or just a coincidence, but one out of the two stage monitors blew out. For the remainder of the afternoon, we had to adapt to just one front of house monitor for everyone, which made hearing what we were doing individually a little difficult. Thankfully, the students took it all in their stride and we all had an enjoyable time ending the day with songs such as 'Buick Mackane', 'Ride A White Swan', 'Get It On', 'Telegram Sam', 'I Love To Boogie', and 'Children Of The Revolution'.

---

*'The Wizard', released on *Decca Records*, 1965.

**The 1950s *Gibson Les Paul Standard*, white *Fender Stratocaster*, and *Gibson Flying Arrow*.

It was a pleasurable experience being involved in such an unusual event, and made me happy to think that such young people, some who were more than forty years younger than me, were getting involved and excited playing Marc's music in such an enthusiastic way.

Anyone who is in a live rock band will agree I am sure, that private bookings along with corporate can be a hit or miss to say the least. As many is the time the person who thinks it would a great idea to book a specific band or group is the only fan of the band that works for the company! However, every now and then a private booking can be great fun, and one of the most welcome turned out to be a booking for the *North Kesteven School* re-union in Lincolnshire in July 2011. From our arrival we were treated admirably with lots of food and drink, but then not content with that, they, together with the help of the local *Poachers Brewery*, had decided to have special bottled *T.Rextasy Ale* for the evening! The bottles arrived in crates with the professionally printed labelled slogan, "Celebrate twenty years of the fabulous T.Rextasy with this specially brewed limited edition bitter." Underneath it stated, "Best enjoyed slightly chilled while grooving to your favourite Bolan track." The 500ml bottles looked great with a photo of the Bolan image that we had been using to advertise our own shows. Although the 'twenty years' caption was only a few months off as I wouldn't be celebrating twenty years of T.Rextasy until September 2012, the sentiment was there, and I guess it rang better than 'nineteen years'!

The bottles were sold at the bar throughout the evening, while on tap; there was T.Rextasy bitter for the punters who were not so concerned in having a collector's edition bottle. Dare I say it but the actual gig almost took second place for us, as we were all pretty excited about getting a few bottles for ourselves as souvenirs! I wonder if one day I'll see one or two of them being auctioned off on *Ebay*!

Our '2011 Anniversary Concert for Marc' was held on Saturday 17th September at the prestigious 02 Academy in Islington, North London. We made it extra special by inviting my old friend Andy Ellison, from John's Children to sing 'Desdemona'. Andy pulled out all the stops and went a little wild, throwing water over the audience and then climbing over the safety barriers into the crowd. The security had to rush over to help balance him while he sang precariously on top of the barriers before jumping back onto the stage, still holding onto the microphone while the lead wrapped around my effects pedals and stage monitors, causing slight mayhem. Andy's such a wild performer and I wouldn't want it any other way!

I also called up Alvin Stardust, the one-gloved Glam Rock performer from the 1970s who hit the big time in 1973 with 'My Coo Ca Choo'. Alvin was a good friend of Marc's so I felt that it was fitting for him to come along and sing a few songs with us. He wasn't very keen on learning any Marc songs, so it was agreed that we would perform the old Chuck Berry number 'Sweet Little Rock 'n' Roller' as Marc and Alvin had sung this together on *Supersonic*, and 'I Love Rock 'n Roll' (the old Arrows' song, made popular by Joan Jett) as Alvin wanted to link the introduction with saying something like "Marc just loved rock 'n' roll music". We ended the triplet with Alvin's blockbuster hit 'My Coo Ca Choo' and although this track had nothing to do with Marc, Alvin did say that the backing track was written with T.Rex in mind.

Every song went down well with Alvin performing in his well-known black leather attire, even though I was initially a little dubious about playing non-Marc songs in the set. However, it all fitted together perfectly as Alvin told little short stories about him and Marc in-between numbers. Alvin came across as a very warm and sincere guy. It was nice of him to actually comment on stage that "although I have always been a little doubtful of tribute bands, this band are a 'cut above the rest' and it's a pleasure to be on the same stage working together." I know that Alvin does have to play on the bill with tribute bands in some cases, so it was good of him to say what he did. In the dressing room after the gig he said that he had had a really good time and that he hoped that we would work together again.

As no 'new' Bolan material had been released officially for a while, I thought it would be a bonus to coincide the Anniversary gig with the launch of a CD of previously unreleased tracks from the quarter-inch tapes we now owned. *Spirit Music*, kindly agreed permission to let us issue the CD officially, so a merchandise stall was set up and CDs entitled 'Marc Bolan & T.Rex - Rock 'n' Roll Ensemble' were made available before and after the show. The official release date wasn't until 30th September, so it made the evening even more special for fans to take a copy away two weeks prior to release.

We played a double-set that night to a most receptive and energetic crowd of die-hard and casual fans that had arrived, not just from the UK, but also from Denmark, Sweden, Germany, USA, Canada, Japan, and other countries from around the globe. It was one of the most enjoyable anniversary concerts I had played at since the special 2007 Shepherd's Bush event. We kick-started the gig with a T.Rex B-side 'Raw Ramp' before linking it with its sister track 'Electric Boogie'. As the venue was filled with like-minded fans, we also included a few non-singles such as 'Beltane Walk', and 'Jitterbug Love.'

We closed the evening with Andy Ellison and Alvin Stardust joining us for the grand finale of the expected 'Hot Love'. It was great to see to my right both Andy and Alvin together on one microphone singing the coda 'la la's' while looking out to a sea of fans with their arms stretched above their heads singing along too. It was one of those nights that I didn't want to end, but of course after 'Hot Love' there is nowhere to take it, so we all bid farewell to the fans and left the stage to the roar of an exceptional crowd on the day after Marc's 34th commemorative year.

Between 8th September and 1st October 2011, a Marc Bolan musical took place at The Wolsey Theatre in Ipswich. Brian Dunham (who had been trying to get this off the ground with partner Nicky Graham from the *PRS* for the past seven to eight years) had invited Caron, John Skelton, his partner Trina, and myself to the show's opening night. It was difficult, as I knew that I would have to try and be non-critical, as I would be watching every detail. I tried to pull myself away from being an ardent Bolan fan, and in doing so I enjoyed it for what it was. I found it hard to understand why the 'Marc Bolan' didn't play any lead guitar and also his singing voice needed a lot of work, although his speaking voice was very good. The storyline was, I was informed, written with 'artistic license', so obviously I knew to expect that certain years would be out of place, some of the outfits were sometimes incorrect, and story lines concerning T.Rex would be out of place or not in context, which is where I sometimes found it difficult to comprehend. The bottom line I guess is that the musical was aimed at music fans and not necessarily fans of Marc. In which case it would appeal greatly to non-fans, and to those who can perhaps step back and see it as a story but not necessarily about the actual facts or his biographical life.

One venue that had meant a lot to me in particular that finally had to close its doors after more than four decades of celebrating live music was The Standard Music Venue in Walthamstow.* This was one of the first clubs that gave T.Rextasy a break back in the very early nineties and I had always

*' Previously known as The Royal Standard.

told the management that even if we grew to playing the larger venues, we would always have time to play there. I kept my word, and it was always a pleasure to return there at least twice a year.

I was extremely flattered when I was told that T.Rextasy would be the last ever band to play The Standard. The management, Paul and Amanda had actually asked for an extension of their license so that our date would fall on the very last day of trading. Tickets sold out weeks before the gig so I knew it was going to be a belter! I asked Andy Ellison to join us and he came on stage for the encore numbers 'Desdemona' and 'Hot Love'. On the last song, while the audience were singing along to the final coda of 'la la's', I could feel a sad tension in the air and I wasn't wrong. Fans, as well as Paul and Amanda began shedding a tear or two knowing that such an iconic rock club would be no more after our gig (Saturday, 3rd December 2011). It was also an added sadness for Paul and Amanda as they were losing their home as well as the venue and were moving to Colchester to start a new life. It is times like these that being in a band makes it all the more poignant. Sometimes it's not just getting up on that stage and playing your heart out, but knowing how much work and passion is required to make the whole evening into an event, and then what it can mean, if after years of working in that environment it is suddenly ripped away from you.

Thankfully the year ended on a complete high, with gigs leading up to Christmas at The Komedia in Bath, The Arts Centre in Banbury, The Brook in Southampton, and the Exeter Corn Exchange. Our final gig of 2011 took place at The Picturedrome in Holmfirth, Yorkshire, the town where they used to film the BBC comedy, *Last Of The Summer Wine*. I looked around expecting Compo, the raggedy gentleman from the show to slide on a sledge down one of the many steep roads (it was cold enough!) that surround the town. It was a freezing day as I took a wander around the small but picturesque setting before the organisers treated us to a lovely meal prior to soundcheck to get us warmed up for later. With the added attraction of snow machines and a sell-out crowd, it put us all in a great mood to end the year with our rendition of 'White Christmas'.

Yes indeed, being in a rock 'n' roll band can certainly mess with your mind at times if you let it. One minute playing in London at a venue closing, with tears all around, and the next, having a great time in the Yorkshire countryside with indoor snow filling the air against the live raucous sound of 'Hot Love'...

Left: With Perri from the futuristic dance troupe Diversity backstage at a UK summer festival in 2010. On that day, T.Rextasy also appeared alongside acts such as Jason Donovan, and Levi Roots.

Right: Cover of the 'Barmstedt Boogie' DVD recorded live in Barmstedt, Germany' on 13th June 1997. Released in Germany with my approval by Jorg Günther.

At The Americana Festival, Leicestershire - July 2010. *(Neil Sidz)*

Below: T-shirt design for T.Rextasy merchandise!

With John Skelton at The Americana Festival, Leicestershire - July 2010. *(Neil Sidz)*

Below: Flyer advertising Roy Wood, T.Rextasy and Mud II at The Derngate Theatre, Northampton - 1st December 2010.

With Paul Marks at The Americana Festival, Leicestershire - July 2010. *(Neil Sidz)*

Right: A box of presents sent to me in 2010 from successful music mogul Ann Ruckert who worked for T.Rex in the early seventies. A pair of Marc's original *Anello and Davide* shoes and a photo album of her travels with T.Rex.

Above: 'Personal Touch', my download album of original material,
and the Tarazara album 'Behind The Mask' (originally recorded in the eighties) and
issued on *Angel Air Records*. Both released in 2010.

At The Brook, Southampton - 2010.
(Jonathan Rawlinson)

Above: With Captain Sensible of
The Damned shortly before our
T.Rextasy / Damned gig in
Ipswich in 2010.

Left: Banner advertising Cardiff's New Year Celebrations in 2010. *(Katrina Divine)*

Below: T.Rextasy performing at the event. *(Des McLeish)*

Left: Flyer for the 2011 'Get It On' Tour.

Above: In front of the 'Bolan Bus' organised by the WSOR. Photo includes from left to right: Brian Dunham (2nd along), Martin Barden (4th along), John Skelton and me (6th and 7th along) with the organisers of the WSOR - June 2011.

Below: Performing at the invitation of the 'Witchwood School of Rock (WSOR) - Marc Bolan Day' at Fat Lil's in Oxford, with tomorrow's generation of musicians - June 2011.

Left: With Tony Visconti posing on a 'Bolan' scooter that was lovingly transformed by a fan with images of all things associated with Marc Bolan - July 2011.
(Brian Cheeseman)

Below: Caron and I obtained official permission from Spirit Music NY to release this CD of a previously unreleased Marc Bolan Rock 'n' Roll session on *Madman Records* - September 2011.

Above: T.Rextasy 20th Anniversary Bitter specially bottled and labelled by *Poachers Brewery* in Lincolnshire in 2011 for a private gig for the North Kesteven School.

Left: Mr & Mrs O'Halloran in 2011. Mick, who was Marc's personal roadie, is a great supporter of T.Rextasy, and always comes to see the band when we play on the Isle of Wight.
(Neil Cross)

34th Marc Bolan Commemorative Concert
O2 Academy in London, 17th September 2011

Above: Alvin Stardust performing with T.Rextasy at the Bolan Commemorative Concert, and flyer for the gig.

Right: Andy Ellison performing at the gig.

Below: T.Rextasy in John O'Groats on the day after a private gig in Wick in Scotland in October 2011. From left to right: Neil, Me, John and Paul.

15

Moving Forward

It's been quite a journey all in all and I must admit that I am quite proud of what I have achieved along the road in T.Rextasy. It remains one of the most pleasurable musical experiences I have ever been involved with. My tiny sizeable amount of fame gave me a life in music, something that I had always wanted to do for a living. Although it arrived later in life, I have always appreciated it more than if I had had any success when I was, say, in my late teens or early twenties. I don't think I would've had the maturity to savour the trips to Japan, the Far East, or any of the other countries around the world if I had gone there as a younger man.

Over the many years within the history of T.Rextasy I have met and made good friends and acquaintances, I have received so many wonderful gifts including tapestries, presentation discs, photos, pendants, sweets, posters, books, magazines, charms, watches, rings, cakes, CDs, records, sculptures, ornaments, artwork, clocks, toys, clothing, and so many other things and I have always been grateful to receive from fans all over the world.

I know that many musicians get into the music business for different reasons, including girls, fortune, drugs, and all the rest of it - me, I just always wanted to get on that stage and entertain people who wanted to listen to me sing and play. In my time as a musician, I have also met many fickle people. We all have come across them haven't we, but for some reason many appear to have been involved in the music industry! However, there are still those like me who are genuinely interested in purely getting up on that stage to perform, turning up the amp, and letting rip into that strange cosmic unexplainable feeling that is rock 'n' roll!

In October 2011 I received a call from an old friend, Paul Sinclair (who was now going under the name of Paul Roland), who interviewed me for a Marc Bolan biography that he was writing, entitled *Cosmic Dancer*. He questioned me about Marc's guitar style, his ability for writing poetry, songs and lyrics, his lifestyle, and what I thought made Marc appear so contemporary decades after he was taken from us. It was pleasing to see on it's publication in March 2012 that Paul had used and utilised plenty of what I had told him and had given me a name-check credit throughout.

Towards the very end of 2011 *Madman Records* licensed the rights of a selection of recordings made by T.Rextasy in the 1990s to an independent record company called *Eastworld*. They released the tracks on a CD, entitled 'Total Rextasy' just before the year was out. The album consisted of both of our two earlier albums 'Trip & Glide' and 'Savage Beethoven' put together as one. Like many artists who have talked about their earlier recordings, I consider these recordings to be from my formative years and as such, although unrepresentative of the band as it entered a new decade, I am still happy for the product to be out there and satisfied of what I achieved at such an early stage in the band's formation and career.

As I get older many rock and pop fans from my era will follow suit, and rock 'n' roll as we know it will surely, slowly fade into the midst. The age of *i-Pods*, downloads, and computer games, have all contributed to killing off so many CD music shops, including some *HMV* stores, *Virgin*, and *Zavvi*, which is so sad. Thank goodness that there are Indie stores that can still hold their heads above water! I am sure that there will always be a large following for rock and popular music in its own spectrum, but it can never return to that golden age when bands and musicians were held in such high esteem, and almost looked upon as 'other worldly'. Some of that accolade now appears to have been handed over to footballers and sport stars, and also those in the celebrity field who have no talent whatsoever other than getting their face in the papers or on a TV reality show.

I have always considered myself fortunate to grow up through an age where rock music was all and everything to most teenagers. When rock stars were untouchable and had almost a sense of being beamed down, as far as we were concerned, from another planet - I know that Marc always appeared to me like that when I was growing up and I loved that feeling.

Whether your liking was for T.Rex, Slade, Sweet, Mott The Hoople, Pink Floyd, Bob Dylan, Alice Cooper, The Beatles, The Rolling Stones, Led Zeppelin, Deep Purple, Sex Pistols, or any of the other bands that I loved and admired, if you spent your life growing up through the sixties and seventies, then you have a right to be just a little smug knowing that you and I grew up in the best of times, and I wouldn't change it for the world.

Of course, I would like to think that I will still have time to write and record my own material even now. I still have it in me to do so and I have plenty of songs and back catalogue to dip into. But as I trundle on my merry way, I am just so happy to continue on my journey down my current road for as long as I am possibly able to do so.

The T.Rextasy backdrop.
This was made by the Scottish company *Rock 'n' Roll Backdrops* in the 1990s.

16

A Brief Guide To 'Tribute'

Many people have asked me in the past how to get started as a tribute act, what the advantages are, and is it actually easier than being an original? The answers are really down to the individual and how much passion and interest one has in the music one has chosen to play for a profession. I can only say here what my personal feelings and preferences are to all of this, and how it worked for me...

After toiling away for years at trying to find a record company interested in releasing my own original music and getting rejection after rejection, I eventually decided I would play music that I had loved all my life. This is a great starting point - if you begin a tribute band just because you look a little like one of the original band but do not necessarily adore the music, then I can almost guarantee that you will most likely get bored of playing the same songs week in, week out. For a tribute to last, I would suggest that you form a band that you find absolutely enthralling and adore the majority of aspects of what that band entails. Rehearse well, but not to the extent of becoming either a caricature or a mimic as this tends to place you in the bracket of a 'cabaret' or 'holiday camp' performer. It is important to capture the actual spirit and essence and feel of the band's performance as in this way it shows you as a musician in your own right as well as capturing all the best parts of the original band.

In T.Rextasy it was of course inevitable that I became the focal point of the band, which is why it was imperative that I obtained the correct amplification, guitars, and dress-sense that Marc had. It was also important to nail those guitar solos and inflections - if indeed, like in my case, it was the main man who originally played those solos.

It has always been important, not to pretend to be Marc Bolan, but to put across the essence and spirit together with the guitar sound and voice, and movement. Otherwise that terrible curse of the caricature can easily raise its head, as one can see from a few of the other tribute bands on the scene.

I've always said that in some ways, if done right, being a good tribute act can be more difficult than being an original. An original artist or band can play a solo badly and say that it was 'artistic licence.' Or forget lyrics and say that you'd decided to change them, wear whatever you fancy and say that you are developing an image. I've been there, and it's so much easier because as an original you can do whatever you want without question. With a tribute there will always be certain guidelines to follow and fans of that band will find it unacceptable if some of those guidelines such as I've mentioned above, are broken. Therefore to an extent one really has to 'keep to the rules' if your tribute act is to be a success of any kind.

Start as you mean to go on and follow your heart. You will have to most likely begin by playing in pubs and small clubs, but this is a good grounding and learning curve and will make you into a tighter unit. You will also learn how to judge and treat an audience. Make sure you have a definite direction and goal, as it is so easy to stay bogged down month after month and not progressing in your field. Check up on agencies and promoters and invite them to gigs - if you are good enough they will want to include you on their books, which should in turn start to get you better quality venues. If you go down the holiday camp route though, you may find that some promoters and venues will view you as a 'holiday camp' band and that may prevent you from branching out to some of the more established bookings.

Try and change at least two or three songs around in your set list every so often, as in that way it not only keeps the band fresh, but it also gives the audience a little bit of a nice surprise too. It is so important to play to the 'majority' and not the 'minority'. Therefore always play the biggest hits, as they will always go down the best. There will always be the die-hard followers of any band who will want obscure songs played for them, and although it is always interesting to play one or two lesser-known songs, you may find it harder to get return bookings if these start to outweigh the hits.

I never thought about actually 'making money' as such and perhaps sometimes that is the best way to think about it. Love the music you are playing first and see what happens. On the whole, agencies and promoters are astute and will know if an act can make them money or not. Realistically, there are more popular artists than Marc Bolan and so a tribute band dedicated to acts such as The Beatles, The Rolling Stones, Michael Jackson, or Abba will more than likely pull in more revenue. This is where the heart ruled my head and I could never portray any other artist in a tribute situation other than Marc Bolan. However, I feel the reason why it worked out so well professionally is purely because I have been so persistent in my tunnel vision and blinkered outlook. I just carried on regardless, knowing in my mind that I was playing some of the best popular rock music that had been written in the 20th century... and it worked... and if it worked for me, it can work for others too.

I was lucky enough to become one of those people who were able to give up a 'normal' job and earn enough to live a decent life out of playing music that I loved and still love today. I will always say to anyone that if you have enough passion in your efforts to pursue a career or a dream, then you should go for it otherwise you'll only regret it in later life. In some respects, my minor success later in life probably enabled me to gain a little more respect from professionals knowing that I know nearly as much about the business as they do!

If you're fortunate you may even obtain a recording contract which may, in turn, be a chance to finally record a few of those original songs you've had stashed away (if you are lucky enough to have been blessed with being able to write in a similar style as your chosen tribute act). Being in a decent tribute act may also give you the opportunity to travel to different countries and play the game there too. Because that's what it is - a game, but a serious game in which one strives to be the best one can be in a musical arena that is at the same time both fake and real. It depends on how you see yourself. I've survived by knowing exactly who I am - a musician in my own right who takes the music and the business seriously, and at the same time portraying the spirit, the essence, and performance of a guy who I've admired all my life... I've also learnt to know when to have a laugh and have a great time in the process!

If you do decide to take up the mantle - then don't forget to keep it live, keep it real, and enjoy yourself when you're up on that stage - and good luck!

Left: My special *USA Gibson Les Paul Standard* which I had stripped down to a semi-opaque orange and transformed to replicate Marc's 1950s *Gibson Les Paul Standard*, together with my unique Marc Bolan/T.Rex Japanese album covers guitar strap.

Right: My white USA *Fender Stratocaster* 1960s re-issue, complete with a replica of Marc's hard-resin 'teardrop.'

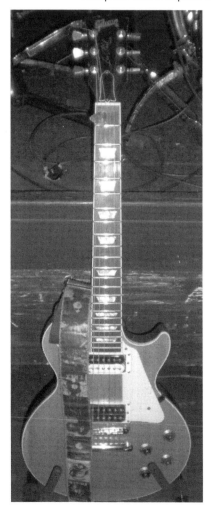

Left: My original USA Epiphone Hummingbird acoustic guitar, fitted with an anti-feedback centre and internal pickups.

Right: Playing my favourite guitar!

Left: Playing my second
favourite guitar!

Below: Playing my third
favourite guitar!

Discography

PRE-T.REXTASY RELEASES

Weird Strings - Ancient & Square* / Oscar Automobile**
Double A-sided 7" vinyl single, Velvet Moon Records, 1979
*written by John Willans, **written by Paul Roland.
Recorded in Ace Studios, Kent. Produced by Willans/Roland.

Weird Strings II - Criminal Cage / Millionaire
Double A-sided 7" vinyl single, Ace Records, 1980
Both tracks written & produced and credited to Daniels (sic).
Recorded in Ace Studios, Kent. Produced by Danielz.

Midnight Rags - The Werewolf Of London
12" vinyl album, Ace Records - 1980 and Armageddon Records 1981
Featuring Danielz on guitar. Reissued on CD on the PRAS label with various outtakes.
Featuring guest appearance by Danielz on guitars.

Beau Brummel - Hot George* / Oscar
7" vinyl single, Moonlight Records, 1982
Featuring Danielz on guitar although un-credited. *Produced by Andy Ellison.

Various Artists - An Exalted Companion... to T.Rex Nights
12" vinyl album, Barracuda Blue Records, 1988
Includes Danielz recording of the Bolan song 'Cadilac'.
Features songs by artists such as Boz Boorer, and Andy Ellison.

Various Artists - The Point & The Rays
Barracuda Blue Records, 1991
Includes the original Danielz recording of 'Baby Factory', and the Tarazara song 'Fantasy'

This was issued as a double-LP length cassette tape only release featuring twenty artists including Andy Ellison, Nikki Sudden, and Miller Anderson.

Danielz - Personal Touch
Download album, private release, March 2010
Tracks: Gunshots At Midnight / Some Romantic Night* / Master Plan* / Looking Through Your Mind** / Baby Factory (pre-T.Rextasy version)**** / Voice From The Silent Heart (pre-T.Rextasy version)*** / Personal Touch* / Tail Lights Flashing* / I Wouldn't Lie (pre-T.Rextasy version)***** / Cadilac*****# / Woman In The Gallery** / Crying In Your Sleep* / Observation*** / I Don't Need A Reason** / Where Were You?* //
*All songs written by Danielz, except # by Marc Bolan. All tracks are studio demos recorded with various sessions musicians including: *Martin Dobson (Eurythmics) - saxophone, **Steve Mann (Michael Schenker Group) - keyboards and guitar, ***Ced Sharpley (Gary Numan Band) - drums, ****Tom & Tim Farmer (Blackfoot Sue) - guitar, bass, backing vocals, *****Knox (The Vibrators, and Colvin Mayers (The Sound) - keyboards.*

Danielz & Tarazara - Behind The Mask
CD album, Angel Air Records, September 2010
Tracks: Fantasy / The Time Is Right / All Too Late* / Behind The Mask** / Master Of The Deadly Kiss** / Hold Me Tonight / Wake Up*** / Shout It Out / Send Me Your Love Tonight / Shoot Away The Memory (studio demo)**** / Turning Away From You (studio demo) / Sweet Suicide (studio demo) / 17 (studio demo) / Love Comes Easy (studio demo) / Sweet Suicide (studio demo mix 2) //
Bonus Tracks: Behind The Mask** / Fantasy (both live on C4 ECT May 1995) //
*All songs by Danielz/Henderson/Williams except: *Danielz/Street/Henderson/Williams, **Danielz, ***Danielz/Henderson/Williams/Lever/Street, *****Danielz/Lever.*

T.REXTASY RELEASES
(All songs written by Marc Bolan unless otherwise stated)

Baby Factory* / Planet Queen / Girl** / Baby Factory***
CD single, Madman Records, March 1994
*Written by Danielz, *single edit, **acoustic radio session, ***extended version.
Recorded at Fortress Studios, London. Produced by Danielz.*

Baby Factory* / Planet Queen
7" vinyl single, Madman Records, March 1994
Released in a mock-styled replica 1970s blue/red 'T.Rex' company sleeve
*Written by Danielz. Recorded at Fortress Studios, London. Produced by Danielz.
Baby Factory* / Planet Queen / 20th Century Boy (live)*
12" vinyl single, Madman Records, March 1994
written by Danielz. Recorded at Fortress Studios, London. Produced by Danielz.

Trip & Glide In The Ballrooms Of T.Rextasy
CD album, Madman Records, April 1995
Tracks: 20th Century Boy / Rapids / Cadilac / Baby Factory* / Zip Gun Boogie / Village* / Laser Love / Over The Flats** / Ballrooms of Mars / Chrome Sitar / Solid Gold Easy Action / 20th Century Baby***
*Written by Danielz. **Arranged by Danielz & Neil Cross. ***Arranged by Danielz.*
Laser Love and 20th Century Baby feature Dino Dines on keyboards
Recorded at Fortress Studios, London, 1994. Produced by Danielz.
Engineered by Shaun Harvey. Cover sleeve photos by Caron Thomas.

Trip & Glide In The Ballrooms Of T.Rextasy
CD album, Quattro Records, Japan, May 1995
See Madman Records entry for track listing. Contains two bonus tracks: Girl / Planet Queen. Sleeve design as the UK version but includes a lavish 24-page lyric & photo booklet & OBI.

Baby Factory* / 20th Century Baby
Special 3" promotional CD single, Quattro Records, Japan, June 1995
Written by Danielz. Recorded at Fortress Studios, London.
Produced by Danielz. Released in black and white card sleeve.

Wind Of Illusion
VHS video release, Solid Baby Records, April 1996
Tracks: 20th Century Boy (BBC1 Punt & Dennis Show - August 1995) / Danielz and fans outside Tower Records in Tokyo after acoustic show (May 1995) / Interview and acoustic version of Solid Gold Easy Action (MTV Japan - July 1995) / Cadilac (Danielz at Glam Rock Easter, Tokyo - September 1995) / 5 Minutes with T.Rextasy (Interview with Danielz on TVK TV Japan - July 1995) / Baby Factory (Official promotional video - 1995) / Zip Gun Boogie (live in Tokyo - September 1995) / T.Rextasy meeting fans outside Club Quattro, Tokyo - September 1995) / T.Rextasy arriving in Osaka (September 1995) / 20th Century Boy (live at Club Quattro, Osaka (September 1995) / 20th Century Baby (live) and interview on Bubblegods TV, Japan (September 1995) //

Savage Beethoven
CD album, Madman Records, September 1997
Tracks: Cigarettes & Alcohol* / Magical Moon / Children Of The Revolution / I Wouldn't Lie** / Sanctified / Metal Guru / Savage Beethoven / Hang Ups / Classic Rap*** / Buick Mackane / Voice From A Silent Heart** //
*Written by Noel Gallagher, **written by Danielz, ***arranged by Danielz with additional lyrics. Guest musicians: Jim Berry (keyboards) and Simeon Jones (saxophone).*
Recorded at Fortress Studios, London, 1997. Produced by Danielz.
Engineered by Shaun Harvey. Cover sleeve photos by Detlev Flohr and Jorg Günther. Released in a mock-cover design of the T.Rex album 'Electric Warrior', with a triple fold-out sleeve. The cover photo was taken in a TV studio while in Germany for an acoustic solo performance and interview on the Kuno's music television show.

Savage Beethoven
CD album, Columbia Records, Japan, September 1997
See Madman Records entry for track listing. Contains two bonus tracks for Japanese release only: Dreamy Lady (acoustic) and Children Of The Revolution (single-edit version). Sleeve design as the UK version but includes a 4-page booklet with lyrics and photo fold-out and OBI.

The Crack Of Dawn (Live In Germany & UK)
CD album, Solid Baby Records, January 2000
Tracks: Cadilac / Jeepster / 20th Century Boy / Hot Love / Interview with Danielz on Talk Radio / Tutti Fruitti / Get It On / Hang Ups / Sailors Of The Highway / Dreamy Lady* / Children Of The Revolution / Danielz & Neil Cross interviewed on the Johnnie Walker Radio Show including a live version of Life's A Gas.
With Rolan Bolan on vocals (Cambridge Corn Exchange, 30 September 1997).
The album contains a mixture of tracks recorded in the 1990s in Germany and the UK. Includes a 4-page detailed booklet.

Solid Gold T.Rextasy
CD album, Madman Records, November 2005
Tracks: 20th Century Boy / Solid Gold Easy Action / Planet Queen / Metal Guru / Savage Beethoven / Children Of The Revolution / Magical Moon / Buick Mackane / Laser Love / Classic Rap / Zip Gun Boogie / Over The Flats / Chrome Sitar / Baby Factory / 20th Century Baby / Cigarettes & Alcohol / Spaceball Ricochet* (Danielz & Mickey Finn) / Dreamy Lady** (Danielz & Rolan Bolan) / Baby Factory** //
*Compilation of previously released tracks from the albums Trip & Glide and Savage Beethoven. Includes bonus tracks *live at The Cambridge Corn Exchange, 30th September 1997, and **computer play version of the official promotional video. Released in a card slip-case and contains a glossy 8 page booklet with quotes about the band from Marc's contemporaries, sleeve notes by Danielz, and track listing.*

White Christmas* / Hot Love / I Love To Boogie
CD preview single, November 2007
Issued in a slim-line plastic case with a glossy 4 page fold-out sleeve containing photos and track details. Recorded at Dog Kennel Studios, Essex.
*Features Dave Dulake (keyboards) *written by Irving Berlin, arranged by Danielz.*
Produced by Danielz & John Skelton.

The Marc Bolan Celebration Concert - 30 September 2007
DVD, Liberation Entertainments, September 2008
Featuring T.Rextasy and Special Guests At The Shepherd's Bush Empire, London.
Concert footage from the Marc Bolan Anniversary Concert celebrating Marc Bolan's 60th Birthday. Tracks include: A wide and varied selection of Bolan's hits, album tracks, and B-sides from 1967 - 1977. Featuring special guests Gloria Jones, Tony Visconti, Andy Ellison,

Eric Hall, Clem Burke (Blondie), Marc Almond (Soft Cell), Neal X (Sigue Sigue Sputnik), Dr Robert (Blow Monkeys), Linda Lewis, Ray Dorset (Mungo Jerry), Howie Casey, and The Dirty Pretty Strings, who play alongside T.Rextasy in this one-off extravaganza. The DVD also features a full colour brochure containing performer biographies, bonus backstage interviews, and fans prior to the concert.

White Christmas* / I Love To Boogie / Hot Love / Dreamy Lady**
CD EP Single, Madman Records, November 2008
*Written by Irving Berlin, arranged by Danielz.
 **DVD enhanced CD track with Danielz & Rolan Bolan from the Marc Bolan Birthday gig at the Cambridge Corn Exchange, 30th September 1997.

White Christmas* / I Love To Boogie / Hot Love
Special 7" red vinyl, Madman Records, November 2008
Issued in a mock-company T.Rex 'Children Of The Revolution' record sleeve.
*Written by Irving Berlin, arranged by Danielz.

A Dream That Lasts Forever - T.Rextasy Unplugged
CD album, Madman Records, 2009
Tracks: Prelude / Solid Gold Easy Action / Dreamy Lady / Living In Dreamland* / Organ Blues / Ride A White Swan / Cosmic Dancer / Dandy In The Underworld / Jeepster / Till Dawn / 20th Century Boy / A Dream That Lasts Forever* //
*Written by Danielz. Recorded at Dog Kennel Studios, Essex.
Project produced by Danielz & John Skelton in which all vocals and instrumentation were undertaken by the duo. The package also contains an 8-page glossy booklet including photos, track listing, and short biographies of Danielz and John Skelton.
Cover design by Jorg Günther and Duncan Muir.

Barmstedt Boogie
DVD, Rexpert, Germany 2010
Tracks: Raw Ramp / Electric Boogie / Telegram Sam / Jupiter Liar / Solid Gold Easy Action / Metal Guru / Teenage Dream / Zip Gun Boogie / Jeepster / Ride A White Swan / One Inch Rock / Children Of The Revolution / Born To Boogie / New York City / The Groover / I Love To Boogie / Get It On / Baby Strange / 20th Century Boy / Tutti-Frutti* / Hot Love* / Bonus tracks: Sailors Of The Highway** / Baby Factory*** / 'Aftershow' //
*Written by Penniman, **recorded at sound-check, ***promotional video.
*guest vocalist Ray Dorset (Mungo Jerry). Filmed and recorded by Jorg Günther.
Cover photo by Graham Willans with additional foldout booklet photos by Dedi and Jorg.

White Christmas* / Baby Factory** / I Love To Boogie
CD single, Possum Records, Australia, November 2010.
*Written by Irving Berlin. **Written by Danielz. Issued in a replicated sleeve design of the 2008 T.Rextasy UK release of the White Christmas CD single.

Total Rextasy
Double CD album, Eastworld Records, November 2011
A combination of the 'Trip & Glide' and 'Savage Beethoven' albums previously issued in the UK.

VARIOUS ARTIST COMPILATIONS INCLUDING T.REXTASY

Party Megamix
CD albums released on Prism Leisure/Crimson Records, 1996 & 1997
Contains short segments and edits from various artists such as Gidea Park, The Sweet, Abba Medley, etc. T.Rextasy extracts include very early rehearsal-type recorded demos such as The Groover / Telegram Sam / Hot Love / Get It On / 20th Century Boy / Metal Guru / Hot Love //

Legacy - The Music Of Marc Bolan & T.Rex
CD album, Anagram Records, 2001
Tracks: Hot Love & I Love To Boogie (Ray Dorset) / Telegram Sam & Metal Guru (John Matthews, Undercover) / Raw Ramp & The Motivator (Steve Overland, FM) / The Groover (Chris Farlowe) / Get It On (Danielz) / 20th Century Boy & Jeepster (Doogie White, Rainbow) / Children Of The Revolution (Jill Saward, Shakatak) / Ride A White Swan (Dave Paton, Pilot)
This project brought together various artists to perform the songs of Marc Bolan. T.Rextasy recorded all the backing tracks, while only one track could be deemed a fully blown T.Rextasy recording with Danielz taking lead the vocals on Get It On.
Recorded at Hatch Farm Studios, London. Produced by John Burns.

Legacy - A Tribute To T.Rex & Marc Bolan
CD picture disc album, Arena Music, Russia, 2001
See Anagram Records entry for track listing. Cover design was copied from the original cover of the Tyrannosaurus Rex album My People Were Fair..., while the inner sleeve design was extracted from the T.Rex album Tanx.

Universal Love - A Tribute To Marc Bolan & T.Rex
CD album, Eggtoss Records, Japan, September 2002
A collection of various songs by Marc Bolan including performances by Akima and Neos, Johan Asherton, and Nikki Sudden. The T.Rextasy tracks included are Children Of The Revolution, Get It On, Jeepster, and 20th Century Baby and were extracted from previously released product except for 'Jeepster' which was recorded by Jorg Günther at the Vestlandhalle, Recklinghausen, Germany on 1st November 1997. The CD has an oversized jewel case so it could include a beautiful 24-page black and white booklet of early Marc Bolan and T.Rex photos taken by photographer Pete Sanders. It also includes an excellent foldout booklet that depicts various mock-up photos and posters behind an image of Marc and Mickey Finn.

The All Star Salute To Christmas
Double CD album on Cleopatra Records USA - November 2009
Includes one T.Rextasy track, White Christmas. This was a 30 track Christmas compilation album that featured recordings by various artists such as Iggy Pop, Judy Collins, Bay City Rollers, Pretty Boy Floyd, Glenn Hughes, L.A. Guns, George Lynch, James Brown, and many others.

SESSIONS

Hotei - King & Queen
CD album, Toshiba EMI, Japan, 1998
Features Danielz on guest backing vocals on the track Captain Rock* - a 13 track album by the Japanese superstar Tomoyasu Hotei. Recorded in Abbey Road Studios, London. *Written & produced by Hotei.

21st Century Girls - 21st Century Girls
CD album, EMI Japan, 1999
This 11 track album by this all-girl UK rock group features Danielz on guitar on the tracks Record Shop*, and Yesterday Morning*. Recorded at The Creative Recording Studios, Oxfordshire. Produced by Gary Stevenson. *Written by Todd/Allen.

*Back Off Boogaloo - Isle of Wight Radio Charity Recording
Officially unreleased, 2005
Recorded in an unknown studio in London, instigated by Alex Dyke (Isle of Wight Radio). Never completed, although it can be found on various websites and audio players. Danielz sang lead, backing vocals, and played guitar. *Written by Starkey.

Various Artists: Doctor, Doctor - Grey Children
Digital album, 2011
Danielz recorded a track entitled Circles. It was included on the above album whereby all proceeds went to the charity 'Grey Children' to help those who suffer from Obsessive Compulsive Disorder. Recorded in Fat Nelly Studios, Sudbury, Suffolk.
Written & produced by David Griffiths.

Zinc Harlequin - Exploder* & Triad*
CD and Digital Release mini-albums, unlabelled, 2011
Exploder included 8 tracks and an A5 lyric brochure. Triad included a 5 track extended play and a set of A5 lyric cards. Danielz recorded all guitars, effects, and additional vocals together with Fran Isherwood on vocals/word-speak recitals for this unusual futuristic poetical dreamscape. *Written Paul Thomas, produced by Zinc Harlequin.

Two of my favourite shots showing the excitement
and enjoyment I get out playing in T.Rextasy.

Left: Another of my favourite shots that portrays the excitement and enjoyment I get from playing in T.Rextasy.

Below: Pictured amongst the many boats I now own on the quay… (the only untruth I've written in this whole book!)

A Dream That Lasts Forever
©Danielz

I heard you on the radio when I was just 13
A captivating, hypnotizing, rock 'n' roll machine
I never heard a voice before that meant so much to me
In later years that sound remains a loving memory

A hippy child, then warrior, you never let me down
A future mind, one of a kind made words that captured sound
I never met you face to face, my one and true regret
But I would like to say my friend, I never will forget

You will remain forevermore a legendary man
While poets dream, you rock supreme, a diamond in the sand
An inspiration to us all and when your records play
I can't believe how quickly time has washed the years away

Now every time I hear you sing, I just can't help remembering
A time that was so magical, at least that's how it felt
And every time I hear you sing, I just can't help imagining
A dream that lasts forever, where you never say goodbye...

Acknowledgements

I must mention everyone who has directly worked within the band's infrastructure throughout this slightly crazy lifestyle I have lead over the past twenty years.

Therefore I would like to thank Caron Thomas/Willans, Mike Bezzi, Vince Lyte, Nigel Silk, Boo, Tiger Tim, Neil Cross, Paul Rogers, Lisa DaVinci, Michelle De Pass, Dino Dines, Paul Marks, John Skelton, Jim Berry, Miam Davidson, Will Crewdson, Carl Axon (Big Bopper), Dave Dulake, Glen Sissons, Brian Kennard, Gavin Ingels, Gordon Willans, Ian Potter, Bugsy, Dave Pearcey, Sweeney Entertainments, Jon Farnsworth, Pieter MacMillan, Geoff Beadman, Andy Linklater, Jorg Günther, Martin Barden, Brian Dunham, Paul Thomas, Ady Hart, Duncan Muir (Sunshine Designs), Graham Willans, Helen Bennett, Gary Smith, Steve Gibbings, & Mandy Bennett.

I would also like to say 'thanks' to all the record companies, promoters, agencies, photographers, radio/tv stations, newspapers, magazines & fanzines who have helped over the years, plus all of the worldwide fan clubs, not forgetting the PA companies and sound/lighting engineers, and the hundreds of venues where the band have played throughout the years.

A big thank you also to:
Marc Bolan - for everything!
Spirit Music and Westminster Music Ltd - for endorsements.
Picato Strings Ernie Ball, Arbiter, Orange, Two Tribes, & Robert Gardiner - for instrument, equipment, and string sponsorships.
Tony Visconti, Rolan Bolan & Marc Almond - for the forewords.
Jerry Bloom at Wymer Publishing.

...And of course the longevity of T.Rextasy wouldn't have happened at all without you, the fans, so a gigantic 'THANK YOU' for all your support and please don't forget to "Keep a little Marc in your heart!"

For anyone who would like to see the band or would just like to keep up-to-date in the world of T.Rextasy, then please don't forget to log onto www.trextasy.com, www.facebook.com/t.rextasy, or www.twitter.com@TRextasyBand

steve emberton
music photography

Marc Bolan Studio CS-2-Edit-1

Marc Bolan Lyceum BWS-14-Edit-1

Marc Bolan edit

85-Edit

T Rex 02

Marc Bolan Studio BWS-25-Edit-1

Mark Bolan Recp 19tif-Edit

Marc Bolan Interview BWS-10-Edit

Mark Bolan Recp 09-Edit

Limited edition signed fine art prints available of Marc Bolan
and many other artist from www.steveemberton.com

Also available from Wymer Publishing

BOOKS

The More Black than Purple Interviews (compiled and edited by Jerry Bloom)
For over ten years the Ritchie Blackmore magazine, More Black than Purple has featured many interviews within its pages. Wymer Publishing has collected the best and most riveting of these in to one book. There are also previously unpublished interviews, and additional, previously unpublished parts to some of the others.
Each interview also includes background information and some amusing tales surrounding the stories behind them. The book is bolstered further by a selection of b/w photos, many of which have never been published before.
• Includes interviews with: Don Airey° • Ritchie Blackmore (x3) • Graham Bonnet • Tony Carey* • Mark Clarke • Bob Daisley* • Glenn Hughes* • John McCoy° • Steve Morse • Cozy Powell.
° Part, previously unpublished * Previously unpublished
ISBN 978-0-9557542-0-3
Paperback 149x210mm, 180pp, 33 b/w images. **£14.99**

Rock Landmark's: Rainbow's Long Live Rock 'n' Roll (Jerry Bloom)
This book, the first in a series on landmark albums is an in-depth look at the classic Rainbow album 'Long Live Rock 'n' Roll'. The full story behind the making of the album; track by track analysis, recollections by the band and crew, all combined in a full colour CD size book designed to sit on your CD shelf alongside the album as its perfect companion.
ISBN 978-0-9557542-2-7
Paperback 125x140mm, 64pp (8 x colour). **£7.99**

Sketches Of Hackett - The authorised Steve Hackett biography (Alan Hewitt)
The first full and authorised biography of former Genesis *guitarist Steve Hackett. Written by Alan Hewitt, a recognised authority on* Genesis, *whose previous writings include the critically acclaimed* Genesis Revisited. *Hewitt is also editor of the* Genesis *web fanzine* The Waiting Room. *First edition hardback plus 90 min DVD.*
ISBN: 978-0-9557542-3-4
Hardback, 234 x 156 mm, 320pp (16 b/w, 43 colour images). **£24.95**

Rock Landmark's: Judas Priest's British Steel (Neil Daniels)
The second in our series of landmark albums looks at the sixth album by the British heavy metal band Judas Priest, recorded at Tittenhurst Park, home of former Beatle John Lennon. It is arguably the album that really defined heavy metal and is regarded as the band's seminal recording.
Written and researched by respected Judas Priest authority Neil Daniels, author of the first full Judas Priest biography, Defenders Of The Faith.
Foreword by Ron "Bumblefoot" Thal
ISBN 978-0-9557542-6-5
Paperback, 125x140mm, 72pp, including 17 b/w images. **£4.99**

A Hart Life- Deep Purple & Rainbow's tour manager's Life Story (Colin Hart)
Hart devoted over thirty years of his life to these great rock musicians. This is his story and indeed theirs. A tale of excess in terms of greed, petulance, anger and devotion. It is counter balanced by extremes of pure talent, showmanship and, of course musicianship. He was the constant 'man in the middle' through all of the break ups, make-ups and revolving door line-up changes. A story of two of the most innovative, often copied, rock bands; seen through the eyes, ears and emotions of their 'mother hen' as Jon Lord described him. He was their minder, chauffeur, carer, provider, protector, father confessor & confidant. In truth he is the only one who can tell this tale of both bands as he was the only one there on the road throughout the life of, not one, but both gigantic bands.
ISBN: 978-0-9557542-7-2
Hardback, 234 x 156 mm, 288pp (15 b/w, 73 colour images). **£19.95**

Hart's Life- 1971-2001 (Colin Hart)
Limited edition, deluxe slipcase version of 'A Hart Life' with bonus book, 'Hart's Life 1971-2001'; 80 pages of photos and memorabilia from Colin's collection including reproductions of tour itineraries, faxes and letters. Also includes a facsimile of the 'Burn' 1974 tour programme.
ISBN: 978-0-9557542-8-9 (plus ISBN: 978-0-9557542-7-2)
Paperback, 240 x 160 mm, 80pp (plus A Hart Life, 288pp). **£35.00**

Zermattitis: A Musician's Guide To Going Downhill Fast (Tony Ashton)
Written in 1991, Tony Ashton's incredible tales of his career with Ashton Gardner & Dyke, Paice Ashton & Lord, bankruptcy, skiing in Zermatt, Switzerland and many other adventures within the heady world of the music business are documented in this hilarious roller coaster of a ride. His writings have laid unpublished for twenty years, but in conjunction with Tony's wife this wonderful and unbelievably amusing story will now finally see the light of day. With a delightful and moving foreword from his dear friend Jon Lord, this is truly the last word from a man who sadly died in 2001, but whose life enriched so many. Although Tony wasn't a household name, within the entertainment world his numerous friends read like a who's who, including Dave Gilmour, John Entwistle, Eric Clapton and George Harrison.
Foreword by Jon Lord (endorsed by Billy Connolly and Ewan McGregor)
ISBN: 978-0-9557542-9-6
Hardback, 234 x 156 mm, 192pp (Limited edition with DVD)* **£24.95**
*The DVD contains previously unreleased Ashton Gardner & Dyke material including a live performance from the Gala Rose of Montreux in 1970; a rare promo film, and a performance of their biggest hit 'Resurrection Shuffle'. The DVD also includes Tony's song 'Big Freedom Dance' written about John Lennon and filmed at Air Studios by TV presenter Chris Evans.

Zappa The Hard Way (Andrew Greenaway)
With a foreword by Zappa's sister Candy, this book documents Zappa's last tour, which was full of bitterness, skulduggery and band mutiny on a scale that no one could imagine. Greenaway has interviewed the surviving band members and others associated with the tour to unravel the goings on behind the scenes that drove Zappa to call a halt to proceedings, despite the huge personal financial losses.
ISBN: 978-1-908724-00-7
Paperback, 234 x 156 mm, 250pp (37 b/w images). **£14.95**

Sketches Of Hackett - The authorised Steve Hackett biography (Alan Hewitt)
Revised and expanded 2012 edition of the first full and authorised biography of former Genesis *guitarist Steve Hackett. With additional chapters and expanded appendices that takes us along the journey of Hackett's rich, diverse and exceptional musical career right up to the Beyond The Shrouded Horizon and Fire & Ice releases.*
ISBN: 978-1-908724-01-4
Paperback, 234 x 156 mm, 356pp (16 b/w photo pages). **£14.95**

Fire In The Veins: Norfolk Rebels (Joanna Lehmann-Hackett)
Stories of Norfolk's rebels, from Boudicca to the modern day. Many of them linked and weaved into the vibrant tapestry of rebellion that is our inheritance. With a foreword by one of Norfolk's most well-known modern day rebels Keith Skipper, and an introduction, beautifully written by Joanna's husband, former Genesis *guitarist Steve Hackett, this book depicts the many fine men and women of Norfolk who through the centuries have defended their ways, as only Norfolk people can.*
ISBN: 978-1-908724-02-1
Paperback, 275 x 191 mm, 120pp (97 b/w images) **£9.99**

All titles can be ordered online at our webstore- www.wymeruk.co.uk/Store
or from any decent retailer by quoting the relevant ISBN.

MAGAZINES

More Black than Purple
Established in 1996 this is the leading Ritchie Blackmore magazine, documenting the Man In Black's exploits with Rainbow, Deep Purple & Blackmore's Night.
ISSN 1478-2499
More info at: www.moreblackthanpurple.co.uk

Autumn Leaves
The official magazine of Mostly Autumn, established in 2000. This A4 magazine published twice a year is the official spokespiece for York's finest band, and arguably one of the greatest British bands to have emerged over the past decade.
ISSN: 1473-7817
More info at: www.autumn-leaves.co.uk

Available from Wymer Records

Wymer Records

The Good Old Boys - Live At The Deep Purple Convention
Catalogue No: TSA1001. Released 13th July 2009
The Good Old Boys is: Nick Simper (Deep Purple); Richard Hudson (The Strawbs); Pete Parks (Warhorse); Simon Bishop (Renaissance) & Alan Barratt (Jo Jo Gunne).
Recorded live 3rd May 2008 at the Deep Purple Convention to celebrate the 40th Anniversary of the formation of Deep Purple. A unique performance that showcases their rock 'n' roll roots and musicianship. This 13-track CD includes a blistering version of Hush, the song that launched Deep Purple all those years ago. It also comes with a 12-page booklet with full band history, behind the scenes stories and previously unpublished photos from the actual performance and soundcheck.
Tracks: I'm Ready / A Fool For Your Stockings / My Way / Shakey Ground / Sleepwalk / Twenty Flight Rock / Somebody To Love / Don't Worry Baby / C'mon Everybody / Shakin' All Over / Oh Well / Hush / All My Rowdy Friends Are Comin' Over Tonight //

Nick Simper & Nasty Habits - The Deep Purple MKI Songbook
Catalogue No: TSA1002. Released: 16th August 2010*
The Deep Purple MKI Songbook is up to date re-workings of Deep Purple songs from the first three albums performed by original Purple bassist Nick Simper with Austrian band, Nasty Habits. Powerful and hard-hitting arrangements of Deep Purple songs that have largely been over-looked since Deep Purple first had success in America with these songs. This initial release is a special limited edition (1,000 copies only) enhanced CD with bonus video footage including a Nick Simper interview.
*Reissued as standard CD without video, 19th September 2011 (TSA1004)
Tracks: And The Address / The Painter / Mandrake Root / Emmaretta / Chasing Shadows / Lalena / Wring That Neck / The Bird Has Flown / Why Didn't Rosemary / Kentucky Woman / Hush //

Nick Simper & Nasty Habits - Roadhouse Blues
Catalogue No: NOR500. Released: 16th August 2010
Three track single with storming version of the Doors' Roadhouse Blues, plus The Painter and alternative version of Hush (unavailable elsewhere).

Liam Davison - A Treasure Of Well-Set Jewels
Catalogue No: TSA1003. Released: 21st March 2011*
The debut solo album by Mostly Autumn guitarist Liam Davison is a cornucopia of aural delights. Guests include fellow Mostly Autumn band mates, Heather Findlay, Anne-Marie Helder, Iain Jennings and Gavin Griffiths plus Paul Teasdale (Breathing Space) and Simon Waggott. The first edition strictly limited to 1,000 copies, is an enhanced CD with bonus tracks and video footage. *Reissued as standard CD, 2012 (TSA1006)
Tracks: Ride The Seventh Wave / The Way We Were / Emerald Eternity / Eternally Yours / In To The Setting Sun / Once In A Lifetime / Heading Home / Picture Postcard / Bonus tracks: A Moment Of Silence / Immortalized // Bonus video: Liam's Treasure //

Amy Leeder - Fisticuffs With Cupid
Catalogue No: TSA1005. To be released: Late 2011
With this album we have broken with our own policy of only releasing works by established artists. Just 18, Amy has been writing songs since she was 14 and we believe she is destined for stardom. The maturity in her songs belie her age. Songs such as Chavs Of 2023 and Rough Around The Edges will resonate with people of all ages.

All titles can be ordered online at our webstore- www.wymeruk.co.uk/Store
or from any decent retailer. Also visit Wymer Records at http://records.wymeruk.co.uk